BRENDA LEE-WHITING

.R4L44

Harvest of Stones

*The German settlement
in Renfrew County*

UNIVERSITY OF TORONTO PRESS

Toronto   Buffalo   London

© University of Toronto Press 1985
Toronto   Buffalo   London
Printed in Canada

ISBN 0-8020-2562-5 (cloth)
ISBN 0-8020-6580-5 (paper)

Canadian Cataloguing in Publication Data

Lee-Whiting, Brenda, 1929-
  Harvest of stones:
  the German settlement in Renfrew County

  Includes index.
  ISBN 0-8020-2562-5 (bound)   0-8020-6580-5 (pbk.)

  1. Germans – Ontario – Renfrew (County) – History.
  I. Title.

  FC3095.R4Z7 1985   971.3'8100431   C85-098393-2
  F1059.R4L44 1985

This book has been published with the help of a grant from the Social
Science Federation of Canada, using funds provided by the Social Sciences
and Humanities Research Council of Canada. Major funding also was
provided by the Ontario Heritage Foundation, Ontario Ministry of
Citizenship and Culture. Further financial assistance came from
Multiculturalism Canada.

CONTENTS

ILLUSTRATIONS

Photographs

Photographs appear in groups at the end of each chapter, the epilogue, and Appendix A.

Maps

Figures

Tables

PREFACE

My interest in documenting the material evidence of German settlement in eastern Ontario began when someone asked me, in 1977, why the German people had left their homeland in the nineteenth century in order to emigrate to this part of Canada. I realized that I had no answer, even though I had been researching the social history and old buildings in the Upper Ottawa Valley since 1962. English-speaking immigrants, whether born in Britain, Canada, or the United States, provoked no such curiosity for they were widely dispersed and assimilated. The small and compact Polish settlement in the Ottawa Valley had received much attention from the media; it is centred on three parishes of the Roman Catholic church at the end of the Opeongo Road. In contrast, the German settlement scattered through thirteen townships of Renfrew County and just across its borders was not so well defined and had not been studied.

Soon after I began to visit German homes with my cameras, my notebooks, and my curiosity, one elderly man remarked that I was about twenty years too late. Many old people had died, he said, and many old buildings had been demolished. This was a grandson of an immigrant who had left Germany in 1859 and pioneered in the rough wooded land of Renfrew County. In retirement, he and his wife lived in a small and modern house near Pembroke, the largest urban centre (population 16,500) in the county; they had no tangible objects to show me that illustrated the struggles of their grandparents, no old buildings, no hand-made furniture or tools or textiles, not even photographs of the past – only memories. In order to find the material evidence of the German presence in eastern Ontario, I had to travel into the countryside, where descendants of the immigrants still live on the land. On a farm there is plenty of storage space, and even if the old furnishings in the house have been replaced and the hand-made tools become obsolete they have seldom been thrown away.

Census records of Renfrew County show that from 1861 to 1961 the number of German people steadily increased. The census of 1971, however, revealed that for the first time in more than a century the population of German descent had dropped in numbers, from 14,041 in 1961 to 12,865 in 1971. There was a further decline by 1981, to 11,005. So my informant was correct when he said that I was about twenty years late in beginning to study this German settlement, for its peak had passed. The evidence was beginning to disappear.

Arriving in eastern Ontario later than the British settlers, the Germans moved into the less desirable swampy lowlands and stony hills of the hinterland. By the end of the nineteenth century they had become the dominant ethnic group in the townships of Alice, Petawawa, Wilberforce, North Algona, South Algona, Raglan, and Radcliffe. In the township of Sebastopol, they had become as numerous as the Irish whom they were replacing; they constituted a distinctive and visible minority (with churches that held services only in the German language) in the townships of Admaston, Grattan, Hagarty, Brudenell, and Lyndoch. By the time of the 1901 census, the German people in Renfrew County totalled 9,014, and the pattern of their settlement in the rural townships remained unchanged for decades. This county is one of only two areas in Canada where residents of German origin have increased in numbers in the first half of the twentieth century, the other area being Waterloo County in southern Ontario.

In 1941, when the question of language was first posed by the federal census, the number of people in Renfrew County who claimed German as their mother tongue was more than half of those that were German in descent (6,122 out of 11,125). The children and grandchildren of the immigrants had grown up in an environment where German was the language that was commonly spoken in the home and church. It helped to maintain their identity and encouraged marriage within their own ethnic group. But by 1981 scarcely one person in six (of those descended from German immigrants) could claim that German was the first language they had learned to speak. The barriers to assimilation had been eroded. (See Figure 1.)

Those German families who lived in the townships farthest from the Ottawa River, distant from the urban influence of towns and federal institutions, would change more slowly. The isolation of this area, and the adjacent townships in the counties of Hastings and Lennox and Addington, was not ended until 1933–5, when the construction of roads was financed by the province in order to relieve unemployment. While the roads made it possible for rural dwellers to travel more easily, they did not significantly improve the economy of small farms that had experienced modest prosperity

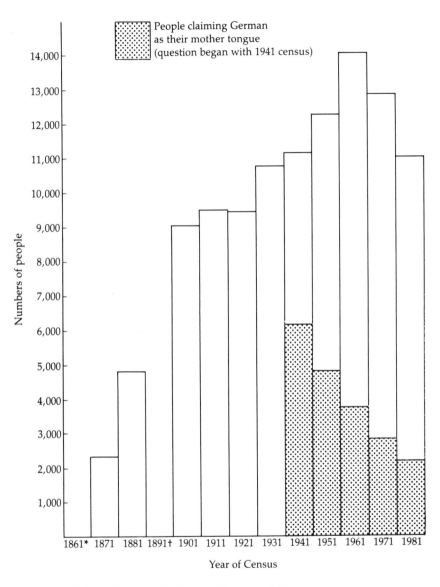

*No individual count for those of German origin

†No question on ethnic origin in 1891 census

Figure 1 Population of German descent in Renfrew County

with the advent of the railroad spurs in the 1890s. It was marginal land for agriculture in any case, and it is questionable whether its cultivation should ever have been attempted. The decline in the population of German people in Renfrew County that began in the years following the 1961 census is evidence that attempts are being abandoned.

When a farm that had been occupied by a German family for several generations was sold, the contents were usually dispersed. Relatives often claimed the more personal effects, such as the portraits and the spinning-wheel, but the obsolete farm machinery, the tools, and most of the old furnishings used by earlier members of the family would be available to the highest bidder at an auction sale. Inevitably, collectors of Canadiana became attracted to the area and the hunt drew pickers and dealers; it also prompted me to take a camera to auction sales on German farms, in order to photograph hand-made articles before they disappeared into the possession of new owners. This unsatisfactory method was another reason that nudged me into a study of this German settlement. Taking such pictures in a barnyard failed to show the item in its normal surroundings, and so I began to visit the homes of German families on a quest to find and photograph the old tools, textiles, and furniture in a more natural setting. If there was a calendar on the wall or a pair of slippers on the floor, I did not remove them, for it was my intention to show that my records were being made inside homes and not in museums. (An exception had to be made for looms, for these large and bulky pieces of equipment could be found assembled only in museums.) Obsolete tools such as wool-winders and bobbin-winders were often up in the attic, while the cradle might be out in the barn. Even when items had been discarded as far as the woodshed, I could still be certain that I was recording furnishings that had been used by German families. The identity of the person who had fashioned the article from local materials was often known; in some cases it was a grandparent or another relative, while in others it might be a skilled village artisan.

Pictorial records compiled in eastern Ontario reveal the similarities of the styles of people who had come from various German-speaking states that eventually became part of the German Empire. The changes in boundaries and political units in central Europe during the period of exodus of these immigrants to eastern Ontario, 1858–90, are confusing to any historian, whether researching a family tree or attempting a more general study such as this one. Records of birthplaces in church archives or family Bibles frequently list a village or town that cannot be found on any map. Many descendants of the German pioneers refer to their grandparents' place of origin as 'Pommern' (German for 'Pomerania'), a region in western Poland conquered and colonized by the German-speaking armies of Prussia in the nineteenth century and later reclaimed by Poland. In this work the term *German* is to be taken in its widest sense, that is, as a linguistic, cultural, or ethnic affinity.

Admittedly the camera was used as a recording device, and no claims are made for artistic merit. I had to rely on my own photography to capture the material evidence of German settlement which was dwindling fast. Even though they were collected over years of travelling across the townships of Renfrew County and visiting German families, such records are necessarily scanty and can be considered only as a sample.

One criticism levelled against any historian who relies mainly on local sources is that the location of the evidence is not made available to future writers. I have therefore listed every newspaper source that I used, though many are not yet preserved on microfilm, and every published pamphlet, though some are long out of print. The publications of historical societies were also consulted. Similarly, I have recorded the source of any letter or conversation. At the very least, this should give my account an air of veri- similitude; persistent researchers should find it helpful. Distance did not prevent me from using the various archives in North America. The mails were used to track down information from distant places, from West Vir- ginia to Kirkland Lake. Living in Renfrew County all year round meant that I was able to be on the scene of events when they happened, whether it was the demolition of an old building in October or a farm auction sale in March.

Many of the people whose knowledge, memories, and possessions contri- buted information to this book admitted me willingly into their homes, even though they were puzzled by my interest. To all those who answered questions and gave me their time, to all those who provided opportunities for photography and lent me documents and old pictures, I owe a debt of gratitude. Some residents of German descent whom I consulted repeatedly year after year deserve special mention: Adolph Gust of Petawawa, Barney Ristau and Misses Teresa and Sarah Luloff of Golden Lake, Mr and Mrs William Lemke of Rankin, Mrs Ethel Michel of Ottawa, Norman Antler, Rob Gorr, and Mrs Erna Hein of Pembroke, Miss Beatrice Verch of Augs- burg, Oscar Boehme of Palmer Rapids, Mrs Geraldine Keuhl of Lake Clear, and Mrs Elsie Zadow of Eganville. I am also indebted to two local represen- tatives of government, Len Hopkins, MP for Renfrew North–Nipissing East, and Sean Conway, MPP for Renfrew North, who were of great assistance in enabling me to proceed with this study.

My occasional articles on local history in the *Eganville Leader*, dating back to 1965, had made my name familiar to the thousands of its readers scattered across sixteen western townships in Renfrew County. This proved to be an excellent introduction to sources, and through the pages of this weekly newspaper I was able to appeal for help in locating rare items. The publishers, Ron and Gerald Tracey, allowed me generous access to the back issues of the paper, a privilege that provided me with contemporary information and for which I am most appreciative. (The *Eganville Leader* was microfilmed in the spring of 1985.)

The head of the German-Canadian Archives Branch of the National Ethnic Archives in Ottawa, Dr Art Grenke, responded promptly to requests for information regarding the early years of immigration from Germany, unearthing the letters written by the Canadian government's immigration agent there; he gave me encouragement from the beginning and was always willing to translate any information that I had discovered written in the German language. (I have no proficiency in this language.) I have sought to present German names and words as they were rendered by the German settlers and by the English-speaking officials with whom they came in contact. Inconsistencies and variation from standard usage in Germany were not uncommon. Antique dealers within the county of Renfrew, especially Lorna and Dennis Peterson of Homestead Galleries, were willing to share with me their knowledge and the origins of hand-made articles that came into their stock from German homes. Mrs Evelyn Moore Price, the busy curator of the Champlain Trail Museum until 1983, always found time to help me look for material.

For use of the interloan service of the Eastern Ontario Library Region, through which I was able to borrow so many articles and books, I must thank Deep River's head librarian, Irene Cox, and her cheerful staff. Professional photographer Larry LeSage, formerly of Deep River, deserves credit for telling me, in 1965, what type of camera to buy, what type of film to use, and a number of useful maxims that aided me in taking photographs. Photos not otherwise attributed are ones that I took. George P. Puttenham of Lowe's Studio in Pembroke had the unenviable task of interpreting my instructions for cropping negatives in order to highlight the significant features of my pictures.

Major assistance in the expenses of this study was provided by grants from the Ontario Arts Council; a grant from the Secretary of State's Department of Multiculturalism program also made it possible for me to travel around the German farms and homes of eastern Ontario for five and a half years in order to prepare this book. Without these grants it would have been difficult to prepare a pictorial record of this German settlement before it was too late.

Finally, I wish to acknowledge the editorial help of Gerald Hallowell of the University of Toronto Press, whose guidance was invaluable in helping me to reduce an unwieldy mass of material.

Harvest of Stones

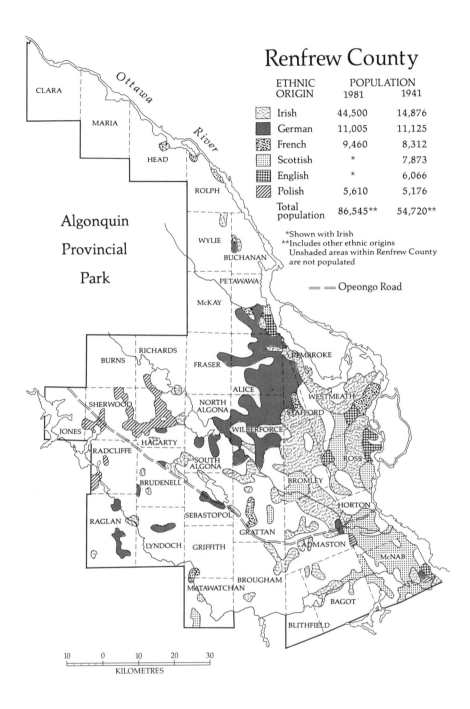

Renfrew County

ETHNIC ORIGIN	POPULATION 1981	1941
Irish	44,500	14,876
German	11,005	11,125
French	9,460	8,312
Scottish	*	7,873
English	*	6,066
Polish	5,610	5,176
Total population	86,545**	54,720**

*Shown with Irish
**Includes other ethnic origins
Unshaded areas within Renfrew County
are not populated

= = Opeongo Road

Algonquin

Provincial

Park

Ottawa

River

CLARA

MARIA

HEAD

ROLPH

WYLIE

BUCHANAN

PETAWAWA

McKAY

RICHARDS

BURNS

FRASER

PEMBROKE

ALICE

WESTMEATH

NORTH ALGONA

STAFFORD

SHERWOOD

WILBERFORCE

JONES

HAGARTY

RADCLIFFE

SOUTH ALGONA

ROSS

BRUDENELL

BROMLEY

HORTON

RAGLAN

SEBASTOPOL

GRATTAN

ADMASTON

LYNDOCH

GRIFFITH

McNAB

BROUGHAM

MATAWATCHAN

BAGOT

BLITHFIELD

| 10 | 0 | 10 | 20 | 30 |

KILOMETRES

CHAPTER ONE

Opening up Renfrew County

Eastern Upper Canada was still only sparsely settled in the first half of the nineteenth century. By the time of the census of the 1860–1 the population of Renfrew County was 20,325,[1] in an area that encompassed 3,000 square miles. Part of the watershed of the Ottawa River, this land was being systematically denuded of its pine forests by the lumbering companies who came and went with the seasons.[2] The river, 780 miles long, was a watery passage for timber that travelled from the woods to the waiting ships at Quebec. Throughout the nineteenth century, settlement in the Ottawa Valley had been closely related to the activities of these lumbermen who cleared the land and provided a ready market for farm produce. On the river grew up communities such as Arnprior and Pembroke, and, on some of the Ottawa's tributaries, places such as Renfrew, Douglas, and Eganville. The hinterland was largely uninhabited, except for a few settlers such as the Davidson family who farmed on unsurveyed land in Grattan Township before a colonization road was blazed through the bush.[3] The townships that lay close to the Ottawa River had a stable farming population of British origin by the time Pembroke was incorporated as a village in 1858. Records show that as the year that German immigrants began to arrive in eastern Upper Canada, attracted by the prospect of access to readily available land.

The possibility of settling immigrants in the wild lands of the province had been scouted by Alexander Sherriff in 1829 and by Lieutenant F.H. Baddeley, Royal Engineers, in 1836.[4] Though the latter stated that the greater portion of the land was poor, both men favoured the idea of a colonization road through this area.

A later report, prepared by Alexander Murray in 1853, described the potential of the land adjoining the Bonnechere River from Golden Lake, through four chutes, to its entry into the Ottawa River: 'There are many parts of the Bonnechere country highly capable of cultivation, a great portion of which is already respectably settled, and settlements extend, more or less, the whole way up to a short distance of Round Lake. Wherever the calcareous rocks occur, either of Laurentian or Silurian age, the country exhibits a superior quality of soil; on these, many good farms are already established, more particularly on those parts underlaid by Silurian formations, which, being in a nearly horizontal attitude, offer a more regular and level surface for the application of agricultural labour than the country occupied by the highly disturbed series of rocks on which they rest.'[5] This observer had visited a farm at Eganville that displayed every sign of success. The English tenant on Egan's property had grown wheat, oats, hay, potatoes, and other root crops; he had also raised a large stock of horses and cattle from which he had made a handsome profit. Nevertheless Murray concluded that the countryside was essentially a lumbering district rather than a new agricultural frontier.

Despite the negative reports, the policy of colonization roads was enthusiastically supported by the politicians in the province; it was seen as a means to halt the flow of farmers to the United States resulting from the scarcity of agricultural lands in Upper Canada.[6] Eager to see this area populated, the government failed to appreciate that the natural environment of this region was very different to that of the earlier-settled parts of Ontario bordering on the Great Lakes: the frost-free season is shorter and geological factors presented obstacles to agriculture which, in hindsight, seem insuperable.

Conflicting reports on the potential of this countryside for agriculture did not owe their contradictions entirely to hypocrisy, though politicians' motives are suspect. Although the German immigrants did indeed settle on the fringe of the Canadian Shield, the lands they chose were not uniformly poor. The Shield has been described as a warped and very ancient land surface (the oldest, Archean rocks formed more than 2.5 billion years ago), 80 per cent of it granite,[7] though other factors have created variety. Where there are two parallel faults and the crust between them drops to form a graben, the resulting pattern of the landform, with minor faults and erosions contained within the valley, may include some pockets of good soil.

A profile of the topography of Renfrew County[8] shows a rift valley that extends about thirty-five miles wide between the Coulonge fault-line scarp on the Quebec side of the Ottawa and the 1,750-foot scarp that rises steeply at Foymount (see Figure 2). Within this structurally depressed belt, known as the Ottawa-Bonnechere Graben, there are deposits of sedimentary soils

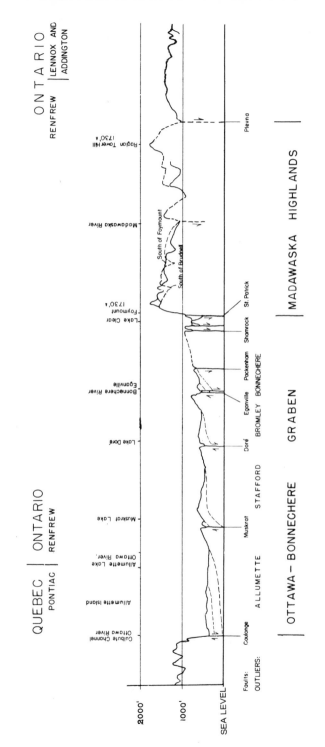

Figure 2 Topography of Renfrew County
From *Bulletin of the Geological Society of America* 53 (1942) 610

in dips alternating with rocky outcrops of less than 1,000 feet, and at low elevations the mantles of clay have not been disturbed by glaciation. This rift valley, which is well watered by tributaries of the Ottawa River, the Muskrat, the Snake, and the Bonnechere, was the area into which the German immigrants had penetrated by October 1860, when a record of their presence was made by William Sinn, an immigration agent.[9] The majority had established themselves in Alice and Wilberforce townships, some in North and South Algona, all townships that had not been densely occupied by the earlier, English-speaking settlers. Sinn commented in his report to A.C. Buchanan, chief emigration agent in Quebec, that the German pioneers might find some scattered good lots of land in the 'old settlements' of Horton, Admaston, Bromley, and Stafford if they took the trouble and time to search. But few later arrivals chose to venture into those townships. Instead, with the exception of those who cleared the sandy plains of Petawawa Township, they moved westward from the initial beginnings. The immigrants from Germany began to settle in the hillier region – the Madawaska Highlands – in the townships of Hagarty, Sebastopol, Brudenell, Lyndoch, Raglan, and Radcliffe, where the soils are not good for agriculture.

Classes of land according to capability are determined by considering the physical factors affecting land use. These include soil conditions – physical, chemical, and biological – slope, stoniness, degree of erosion, and other environmental features such as climate and drainage. In this classification the mineral soils are grouped into seven classes based on the capacity or potentiality of the land to produce. Such sophisticated analysis was not within the capacity of the early explorers or the colonization road agents, but the agricultural expertise of later experts underlines the differences between the different parts of the county.

Appendix C classifies township by township the agricultural capability of the land in Renfrew County. Renfrew County does not have any class 1 soil, that is, soil highly suitable for cultivation with no physical characteristics that would interfere with tillage implements. Classes 1, 2, and 3 are considered suitable for sustained production of field crops if specified management practices are observed. The townships settled by English-speaking farmers before the Germans began to arrive in 1858 have substantial areas of class 2 and 3 soils, for example, Admaston, Bromley, Horton, McNab, Ross, and Westmeath. In contrast, there are townships in the western part of Renfrew County, such as Brudenell, Lyndoch, Radcliffe and Raglan, where virtually all the soils belong to classes 4–7. Class 4 is physically marginal for sustained agriculture, class 5 is capable of use only for permanent pasture and hay, class 6 is capable of use only for grazing, and class 7 is considered unsuitable for agriculture altogether. In Raglan Township class 7 soil covers 53,240 acres out of the total 67,760, and 2,880 acres are classified organic (probably bog).

It was to this unpromising countryside that the Ottawa and Opeongo Road was begun in 1854. Starting at Farrell's Landing, from the head of steamboat navigation on the Ottawa River, near Renfrew, the road was laid out westward through Renfrew County for ninety-nine miles, as far as Bark Lake. The location of the road had been suggested at a meeting of the Councils of United Counties of Lanark and Renfrew, in Perth, in 1851. It was hoped that the thoroughfare would become a land route to the mouth of the Magnetawan River on Georgian Bay.[10] It was never completed. By 1856 there were 132 families comprising 515 individuals on the fifty-two miles of the surveyed portion of the road,[11] which was supervised by Crown Lands Agent T.P. French, who had opened an office close to the colonization road, at Mount St Patrick, twenty-one miles west of Renfrew.

Heavy immigration had exhausted the supply of crown lands in the fertile southwestern peninsula of Upper Canada, and the price of real estate had advanced beyond the reach of the ordinary person.[12] The only crown land left was north and east of Lake Huron, between the Ottawa River and Georgian Bay. A government committee held hearings in 1855 regarding the opening to settlement of this last area, nearly all of which was on the Canadian Shield. Despite its obvious limitations, already reported by surveyors, this land of forested wilderness was committed to a policy of settlement. Pressure from lumbering interests for good roads was certainly a factor; the presence of nearby farms would provide seasonal labour and provisions for the shanty market.

The government built a grid of five roads running north and south and four running east and west, but free grants of land were made available along only three at first – the Ottawa and Opeongo in 1855 and the Addington and the Hastings in 1856. A road agent was appointed to supervise settlement on the surveyed lots and to report on the progress on these roads to the Bureau of Agriculture and Statistics.

On each road the first season attracted farmers of British origin or French Canadians. Philip VanKoughnet, minister of agriculture 1856–8 and later commissioner of crown lands, realized that these free grant settlers were almost wholly the descendants of families who had been resident in the country for some years.[13] By July 1856 he could report that the number of location tickets on these three roads amounted to 332, comprising 1,218 individuals, but he was not satisfied. He wanted to attract immigrants from Europe with the aid of advertisements declaring the advantages of the roads that had opened up new country for settlement. His campaign began in the summer of 1856, under the authority of the bureau.

Full and comprehensive advertisements had been circulated throughout Great Britain, including 12,000 copies of an anonymous pamphlet that purported to impart full and truthful information about Canada to all classes. This twenty-four-page document covered the condition and location of the land offered, climate, soil, products, capabilities, and municipal and educational institutions. It was translated into German (6,000 copies), Norwegian (5,000), and French (4,000), and most copies were sent by the bureau to the continent of Europe for circulation.

By 1857 Crown Lands Agent T.P. French had acquired a lot himself and had tackled the duties of settlement, as outlined by the government: 'One hundred acres will be given FREE to any settler, 18 years of age, who shall take possession of the Lot within one month from the date of his application, erect on it a house, 18 by 20 feet, put in a state of cultivation at least 12 acres in the course of four years, and live on the Lot during that period. Should he fulfil these conditions he will obtain an indisputable title to the land, but failing to do so, it will be sold or given to another.'[14]

Having gained 'practical personal experience' of bush life in all its roughest phases, French felt well qualified to write in 1857 a thirty-six-page pamphlet conveying detailed information for prospective settlers. Since French stressed that he had not exaggerated his description of life on the land in eastern Upper Canada, some of his roseate claims must be held responsible for attracting immigrants to this road and its vicinity, at least initially: 'The soil in this part of the province is a sandy loam, in some places light but in others deep and rich. The country presents rather a hilly aspect, but by far the larger portion is composed of gently undulating and flat lands. Few of the highest hills are incapable of cultivation, and it is strange that the best soil is not infrequently found on their summits. A good deal of rock and surface stone is also to be met with, and while it must be denied that such often proves a source of much annoyance to the farmer, yet they do not prevent the proper cultivation of the land, nor form any great obstacles to the raising of excellent crops.'

The Bureau of Agriculture and Statistics also distributed this pamphlet;[15] its wide circulation may explain why the Ottawa and Opeongo Road received more attention than the other roads from the immigration agent later sent to Germany, and thus why the area attracted most of the Germans who went there. Another reason was its accessibility. As the government pamphlet proclaimed, the Ottawa and Opeongo Road could be reached from the Ottawa River. The Addington and the Hastings roads were approached by routes over land.

But whichever road was chosen, the newcomer was offered a most promising future by VanKoughnet, the minister of agriculture: 'The Lands thus opened up and offered for settlement, are in sections of Canada West, capable both as to Soil and Climate, of producing abundant crops of winter wheat of excellent quality and full weight, and also crops of every other description of farm produce, grown in the best and longest cultivated districts of that portion of the Province, and fully as good.' VanKoughnet admitted that there was considerable variety in the character and quality of the soil, some being much superior, but he believed that there was an abundance of excellent land for farming purposes. Though he concentrated on providing details of the three colonization roads – where they were located and how to reach them – he did not neglect to mention that the land in their vicinity was very similar in quality. He remarked that this land was covered with every variety of timber – some with hardwood and some with heavy pine.

Making no mention of the labour that would be needed to clear the forest, the minister expressed the opinion that heavily timbered land is almost always the best for farming. He mentioned that water for domestic use was abundant, while omitting the fact that patches of swamp, unfit for agriculture, were numerous. He considered that the expense of clearing and enclosing the land would be repaid by the initial crop of potash derived from burning the trees and by the first wheat crop.

The log house required by the regulations of a free grant could be constructed in four days by five men, according to VanKoughnet. He believed that neighbours generally helped to build the cabin for newly arrived settlers, without charge, and that therefore the cost of a new home would be small. He suggested that the spaces between the logs should be plastered with clay and whitewashed, while the roof should be covered with bark.

VanKoughnet's report echoes French's claims so closely that it suggests that the minister was using evidence gathered by the crown lands agent. When VanKoughnet claims that a settler possessing capital of from £25 to £50 could make himself comfortable on these lands, he may have based this statement on estimates that French had collected in answer to a query from the bishop of Bytown (later Ottawa). The quantity and cost of provisions necessary to support a family of five for twelve months were calculated, and there was appended a list of useful articles that could be purchased in Renfrew County (see Table 1). French assured the bishop that the calculations were intended only to show what amount of capital was sufficient to place a man entirely beyond all danger of difficulty and distress, and declared that an energetic and self-reliant family man could venture to Canada with less.

The physical features of the Canadian Shield were extolled by French and

VanKoughnet, and the latter speculated that landownership might even prove to be a wise investment. In his opinion the climate throughout the district was uniformly good, and winter was not to be considered a handicap. 'The snow does not fall so deep as to obstruct communication; and it affords good material for good roads during the winter, enabling the farmer to haul in his Firewood for the ensuing year from the woods, to take his produce to market, and to lay in his supplies for the future – and this covering to the earth, not only facilitates communication with the more settled parts of the District, but is highly beneficial and fertilizing to the soil.'

Settlers were assured that there would be good markets for their surplus, farm produce of all kinds being in demand by the lumbering companies who carried on extensive operations in this part of the country. More promises followed.

Judging by the progress that Upper Canada had made during the previous ten years, the minister believed that the value of a property had doubled within that period, even if no improvements had been made by the settlers. This he considered to be merely an average increase, one that he expected to continue. It was his opinion that in some countries the value of the land had increased by 400 per cent within ten years.

The sections of country opened by the three colonization roads (Ottawa and Opeongo, Addington, and Hastings) were claimed to be in the southern part of the 'Great Ottawa Region.' This was described to immigrants as an immense extent of country stretching between Lakes Huron and Nipissing and the Ottawa River, ripe for development, rich in resources, and obviously well watered. VanKoughnet declared that this land offered for settlement was capable of sustaining a population of 8 million people, a forecast that he felt was all the more likely because the western portions of Canada were being rapidly filled up. Some of the government's plans – for railways and improving navigation on the Ottawa – were also responsible for his enthusiasm.

By 1859 the bureau had intensified its activities, encouraged by reports of the superintendents on the three colonization roads. Extensive distribution of pamphlets in English, German, and Norwegian was planned, together with a map showing particulars of the free grant roads.

Many of these maps were sent to Germany and Norway under the care of people allegedly well acquainted with Canada and able to give the most reliable information on the province and the prospects of settlers. Special instructions had been given as to the classes of persons to be encouraged and those who should be positively discouraged.[16] In 1859 an emigration agent, a Mr Hawke, had been sent to Great Britain to encourage immi-

TABLE 1
Provisions necessary for one year for a family of five (1859)

	£	s	d
Provisions			
8 barrels of Flour at 2. 10s per barrel	20	0	0
2 barrels of Pork at 3. 15s per barrel	7	10	0
80 bushels of Potatoes at 2s per bushel	8	0	0
30 lbs of Tea at 2s 6d per lb	3	15	0
1 barrel of Herrings	2	0	0
½ barrel of Salt		7	6
Cost of Provisions	41	12	6
Seed			
20 bushels of Potatoes at 2s per bushel	2	0	0
3 bushels of Wheat at 7s 6d per bushel	1	2	6
10 bushels of Oats at 2s per bushel	1	0	0
Cost of Seed	4	2	6
Other Necessaries			
1 Axe	0	8	9
1 Grindstone	0	7	6
1 Shovel	0	1	10
2 Hoes at 3s 6d each	0	7	0
3 Reaping-hooks, at 1s 6d each	0	4	6
1 Scythe	0	5	0
1 Inch Auger	0	5	0
1 Inch and a half Auger	0	7	6
1 Hand-Saw	0	7	6
2 Water Pales, at 1s 6d each	0	3	0
1 Window Sash, and Glazing	0	5	0
1 Bake-Oven	0	5	0
2 Pots, at 5s each	0	10	0
1 Kettle	0	5	0
1 Frying pan	0	3	0
1 Teapot	0	2	6
6 Small Tin Vessels, at 4d each	0	2	0
3 Large Tin Dishes, at 2s 6d each	0	7	6
6 Spoons, at 2d each	0	1	0
6 Knives and Forks	0	5	0

Table 1 — *Continued*
Provisions necessary for one year for a family of five (1859)

	£	s	d
3 Pairs of Blankets, at 1. 5s per pair	3	15	0
2 Rugs for Quilts, at 2s 6d each	0	5	0
2 Pairs of Sheets, at 3s per pair	0	6	0
1 Smoothing Iron	0	2	6
1 Pig	0	15	0
	10	7	1
Total capital needed	56	2	1

gration to Canada. The following year, similar agents were placed on the
continent: Helge Hangan in Norway and William Wagner in Germany.[17] 'In
February, 1860, Mr. Wagner, a Prussian by birth, and intimately acquainted with the Province of Canada, from several years residence as a
Provincial Surveyor in the Ottawa country, was sent to Prussia and Germany, and fully supplied with many hundreds of pamphlets, translated into
the German language, and accompanied with large and accurate maps of
the Province, lately compiled and published by the Crown Lands Department.'

For the more educated class of immigrants a pamphlet by A.T. Galt,
Canada from 1849 to 1859, was translated into German and furnished to
Wagner and to many other groups in that part of the continent and very
widely circulated.

A document showing the rapid progress of the free grants and the settlements adjoining, and describing the large crop of cereals and vegetables
grown in 1860, was translated into German and forwarded to Wagner for
extensive circulation. It revealed that the new settlers were growing wheat,
potatoes, barley, oats, peas, rye, and flax.[18]

Similar attention was paid to secure the immigration of Norwegians with
advertisements, maps, and books distributed by Helge Hangan from his office in Christiania (now Oslo) and on trips throughout the country. However, only 53 Scandinavians were listed in the 1881 census of Renfrew
County, compared with 4,831 settlers of German origin.[19]

One of many boulders, a souvenir of glaciation, on the Noack farm, Hagarty Township

Terrain in South Algona Township, typical of the county's western townships

Concession road dividing Alice and Wilberforce townships, in the days of horse-drawn vehicles and before snow ploughing (courtesy Locksley-Rankin Women's Institute)

CHAPTER TWO

Bismarck's legacy

'Those emigrants chiefly fit for our climate and for clearing the Canadian woods are those who are living in the eastern part of Germany, that is to say in quarters which have only been cleared during the last century, or to name them more particularly, the Provinces of West Prussia, Pomerania, Posen, Silesia, and the eastern part of Brandenburg. Here lives a people used to tearing out the stumps of the trees from the soil, for which work they received the use of the land for a few years, and now mostly are turned off from it or [have] to pay a very high rent.'[1]

So wrote William Wagner, immigrant agent for Canada in Berlin, in 1862. In his reports he expressed eagerness to visit 'the settlement on the Ottawa' in order to gather information at first hand. He had received a letter that year from a German emigrant who was satisfied with his move to Canada but scornful of the free land offered as an inducement.[2] It was an attitude that must have been shared by many of his countrymen who had moved to a country that had land in abundance. For the next thirty years difficulties at home and the prospect of free land in Canada led many people to leave Germany and settle in Canada, particularly in Renfrew County.

Throughout the first half of the nineteenth century the agrarian population of Germany had been declining, and the development of commerce and industry could not provide enough jobs for the increasing numbers who moved to urban centres. The major cause of emigration at this time was therefore economic. The majority of those who left Germany were farmers and artisans bound for countries where land was available and industries could absorb them. In 1816–17, for example, 20,000 had gone to the United States and probably a similar number to Russia and to Austria-Hungary. In later years overseas migration assumed paramount importance, with Australia, New Zealand, South Africa, South America, and eventually Canada competing with the United States for the landless agricultural workers who had earned a reputation as hard-working and stable farmers.[3]

There had been earlier German migrations to Canada. Of the 2,444 settlers who arrived in Nova Scotia 1750–2 in ships from Hamburg, 1,327 were from southwest Germany and 233 from northern Germany. The British government, which had decided to recruit foreign Protestants as colonists, had realized that the offer of unsettled land was an inducement that did not require the expenditure of public funds.[4]

Substantial numbers of Germans moved from the northeastern United States overland to Canada, beginning in 1783 and continuing until 1820, but their movements and motives were not homogeneous. After the American War of Independence the United Empire Loyalists had to flee the country, leaving behind them all their possessions. With assistance from the governments of British North America, 45,000 Loyalists resettled in Canada and the Maritimes. German people composed the largest ethnic group in this migration, and it is believed that many of them came from the state of New York.[5] Some 2,400 soldiers from Germany, who had served the British government during the War of Independence, accepted discharge and resettlement in the remaining British colonies for which they had battled. Beginning in 1786, a trek began from Pennsylvania, which had been founded as a haven for persecuted religious groups; many areas in this state were completely German-speaking, consisting of Mennonites, Amish, Dunkers, Baptists, and Moravians.[6] These pioneers were farmers, and after several generations had absorbed the available land the need for expansion forced them to move. In the empty lands of what became Upper Canada four new districts had been established by the British and called Luneberg, Mecklenburg, Nassau, and Hesse; these were united in 1791 to form the province of Upper Canada. While the earliest Pennsylvania Germans took up land in the Niagara peninsula, later groups spread to Waterloo County and several adjacent counties.

Direct immigration from Germany to Canada began in the late 1820s, with Waterloo County serving as a focus for the newcomers; there they could find neighbours who spoke the same language. Assimilation was easy in the counties that bordered on Lake Ontario and Lake Erie. Later arrivals are credited with pioneering the Ontario counties of Bruce, Grey, Perth, and Huron. The German-speaking immigrants were still coming primarily from the southern and western German states, from Württemberg, Baden, and the Palatinate. The number from northwestern Germany was increasing, for in states such as Hanover, Oldenburg, Schleswig-Holstein, and Mecklenburg over-population had become a serious problem.

When the Canadian government decided in the 1850s to open up the unsettled lands of the Shield in eastern Upper Canada, its recruiting campaign was concentrated on the northern and eastern states in Germany. Just how hard emigration agent William Wagner worked to encourage German immigrants may be gauged by his surviving letters. Written 1860–2 from Germany to the Bureau of Agriculture or the commissioner of crown lands, they portray a man underpaid, over-worked, and sorely tried.[7] His letter of 27 October 1860 to William Hutton, secretary of Agriculture and Statistics, Quebec, underscores the major obstacle in his efforts to promote Canada: 'You complained in your last letter, that not enough German settlers reached Canada, and it appears to me you think it is my fault. A century has passed away, and the German emigrant has never heard anything but New York, or of the western states; they have their relatives there, who send them money to follow them, and on whom others hang on, and at this present moment, agents of the western states, as Michigan, Wisconsin, etc., have established sub-agencies here.'

Wagner felt that he started with a disadvantage. Even though he learned that six families from the county of Bromberg had left 1 October 1860 for Canada via New York, he doubted whether they would actually reach the country for which he was working. (It would be impossible for anyone to forecast their destination, for many German immigrants who settled in eastern Upper Canada travelled via New York, especially in the winter, when the St Lawrence ports were icebound.)

In a letter of 21 January 1861, Wagner thanked Hutton for specimens of wheat which he intended to show to the Geographical Society of Berlin and leading grain dealers. He hoped that it would offer convincing proof that wheat was a standard grain in Canada, but the sample had been collected from the Gaspé. He hoped for a good emigration the following spring: 'Mostly every day I have visitors, in consequence of my advertisements, and of late from people who have money, say from 1600 to 6000 thalers. They probably will all go to the German settlement on the Ottawa.' In January he received twenty-one written applications.

On 2 February 1861, Wagner delivered a lecture on Canada, especially the Ottawa country, before the Geographical Society of Berlin. He wrote the next day that he had been invited to return the following month to address this society on the subject of the Ottawa canal.

The commissioners of the Berlin-Hamburg railroad had given Wagner permission to exhibit a map of Canada, which he believed had produced some beneficial results. He had arranged for a view of the Ottawa River to be reproduced from one that he owned. He had noticed that views of American cities had been exhibited in the windows of stores in Germany, and he suggested that views of the principal places in Canada should be sent to him for the same purpose.

From Hirschberg in Silesia, Wagner wrote on 31 January 1862 to Philip VanKoughnet, commissioner of crown lands, that he had been travelling all that month, the first half near Frankfurt-on-the-Main, the second half in Saxony and Silesia; he planned to continue on to Berlin, where he expected Canada to be the subject of a debate in the Prussian parliament.

Wagner was aware that the prospects for emigration were most promising in the northeastern German states, where he had been most active, and in March 1862 he estimated that as many as 2,000 people might leave West Prussia, Pomerania, Posen, Silesia, and Brandenburg. From other parts, such as central Germany and Westphalia, he hoped for another 2,500, but admitted that only the summer would show whether his forecasts would prove to be correct. He was pessimistic about attracting immigrants from southern Germany, because in almost every village or hamlet someone had a relative in the United States.

Wagner's exertions had been extensive. During his year and a half in office, he had advertised in papers totalling more than 400,000 copies. He had distributed more than 3,500 pamphlets and had caused to be hung on railway stations and other public places 172 small plans and about 50 large maps of Canada, with instructions about where more detailed information could be obtained. He had lectured in Berlin, Breslau, Hirschberg, Erfurt, and Frankfurt-on-the-Main. He had answered 178 letters of inquiry, some from Hungary, Sweden, and Denmark, and was planning to mount an exhibition of Canadian grains and woods, made up into furniture, in May at Berlin. He had come to the conclusion that distribution of pamphlets on Canada could best be performed by people well known in their communities. For this purpose, he had recruited schoolmasters, ministers, hotelkeepers, druggists, and merchants.

Wagner's reports make it clear that some emigrants would be able to purchase land on arrival in Canada. His letters give little hint of the economic distress in Germany. Only in his communication of 29 May 1862 does he mention that in West Prussia "most of the people were starving for want of a good crop last year." The superintendent of that state's bureau of agriculture had told him how much was spent every year by societies and government to assist the poor.

In 1862 the emigration agents were recalled from western Europe, for their Canadian employers judged that these efforts were not meeting with success, but other forces encouraged German immigration to continue.

Some German-speaking settlers in eastern Upper Canada had been writing to relatives and friends in the Old Country, urging them to emigrate. The ambitions of Otto von Bismarck, appointed prime minister of Prussia in September 1862,[8] provided further inducement to leave Germany. Bismarck was convinced that only by forceful measures could Germany be welded into a national state. In 1863 he joined with Austria in attacking Denmark; after the Treaty of Vienna in 1864 he prepared for war with Austria, and this conflict of 1866 left Prussia supreme in Germany. In 1870 Bismarck played a prominent role in events leading up to the Franco-Prussian War. Having united the country, he remained chancellor until 1890, and during his years in power the wave of emigration continued, almost without a break.

In the interval between the war with Denmark and the war with Austria, there was at least one other attempt to recruit settlers for Upper Canada. The Canadian Land and Emigration Company, based in London, England, had purchased ten townships in the Ottawa-Huron tract of unsettled land, for the purpose of selling lots to immigrants at a profit.[9] Sales began to lag after the initial land rush of 1864, for the countryside proved more rocky than the English board of directors had expected. In order to co-ordinate development, a board was established in Toronto with C.J. Blomfield as secretary.

The company placed advertisements in German and Norwegian newspapers and in 1866 sent an immigration agent, a Mr Bechel, to the German states of Hanover, Hesse-Cassel, Brunswick, and part of Prussia, where he found that even well-educated men were ignorant of conditions in Canada. Bechel also found that news of the Fenian raids into Canada had reached Germany and discouraged migration, but he obtained promises from no less than thirty families with capital of from $3,000 to $15,000 that they would, if circumstances permitted, leave Germany for Canada the following spring. The outbreak of the Prussian-Austrian war ended his efforts.

Nevertheless, Blomfield was confident that the expedition had been successful and noted in a letter to D'Arcy McGee, minister of agriculture: 'Even under existing circumstances Mr. Bechel could have brought with him a considerable number of poor Emigrants, but you will probably coincide in the view of Mr. Bechel and myself that a small Immigration of men of means and position is worth far more than a much larger Immigration of men who leave their own country chiefly on account of want of the necessities of life.'[10]

In 1868 passage of Ontario's Free Grant and Homestead Act considerably undermined the efforts of the Canadian Land and Emigration Company by opening up forty-one more townships in northern and eastern Ontario for settlement without fee. In Renfrew County locations were made in eleven townships: Admaston, Bromley, Brougham, Burns, Grattan, Hagarty, North Algona, Richards, Sherwood, South Algona, and Wilberforce. The effect on land values was predictable.[11]

In South Algona Township Thomas McCabe had paid $70 for 100 acres in 1860, acquiring Lot 4, Concession 2. After the 1868 Homestead Act was passed, Hermann William Pop from Germany was able to locate as a free grant settler on the adjoining two lots, #5 and #6, Concession 2, without any payment. McCabe's widow eventually sold Lot 4 to Pop on 16 August 1882, for $15, by which time it had probably been cleared and improved.[12]

Where settlers in free grant townships in occupation of their lands by 2 March 1872 owed the crown, the money could be remitted and the settlers placed in the same position as those who had located under the free grant regulations.[13] Settlement duties had to be performed in order to qualify for a patent after five years' residence; this may explain, for example, why Frederick Schutt preferred to purchase from the crown his 111 acres in Wilberforce Township (for $88, on 10 June 1872).[14]

Following the Franco-Prussian War of 1870–1 there was renewed immigration. Three wars in seven years had disrupted life, obliged men to participate and possibly die in military service, destroyed property in the path of battle, and produced a climate of uncertainty. Military service continued to be compulsory. Those who left Germany in the 1870s and 1880s included skilled artisans, such as tailors, blacksmiths, and gunsmiths, who, according to their obituaries in the 1920s and 1930s, had learned their trades during their military service. There were also wagon-makers, carpenters, weavers, and shoe-makers listed in the 1881 census records of the western townships of Renfrew County, where the German immigrants settled in the largest numbers. In the maturing industrial society of Germany, the rural craftsman was being displaced by factories.

The Franco-Prussian War had established an empire that would remain peaceful for decades, but the Germans could not be sure of a serene future. In any case, economic distress remained. In the period 1870–95, emigration continued steadily, with 2,375,000 people leaving the country, most of them from rural districts in northern Germany, particularly Pomerania, Brandenburg, Schleswig-Holstein, and Hanover.[15] The majority settled in the United States, but there was still a steady trickle to Canada, some arriving in New York and some in Canadian ports.

Although many of the German immigrants had received an elementary education and a few were fluent in English, written records of their journeys to North America are rare. Paul Stein, a member of a family from Silesia who pioneered in the Denbigh area on the Addington Road, has left an account of the journey and some of the travails endured:

Crossing the Atlantic in the 50s in the steerage of an immigrant sailing vessel, in which they had to furnish their own provisions, bedding, etc., for a trip lasting from seven to ten weeks, and in one case with small-pox, and no physician on board ship thirteen weeks, was no trifle, but they landed safely in Quebec, reached Napanee, where they with the assistance of a countryman, who acted as their interpreter, purchased the necessary supplies and engaged a couple of teams which brought them to their destination in Denbigh Township in the summer of 1858. They took possession of and located on adjoining lots on the Addington Road, built, with the help of a few neighbours, a log shanty large enough to hold both families and all their possessions, and went to work with a will to clear yet a little land for a late crop of turnips and some other roots. They were the first pioneers of what was for years afterwards known as the German or 'Dutch' Settlement.[16]

In 1863 the proportion of immigrants who crossed to Canada in steam-ships was 46 per cent, in 1869 it was 95 per cent, and by 1875 all newcomers came by steam vessels.[17] The transition from sailing vessels to steamships was slow in the German mercantile navy; as late as 1870, it owned a steam tonnage of only 82,000 out of a total of 982,000 tons.[18] But many German immigrants crossed the Atlantic in British steamships.

It was from Liverpool that T.P. French expected immigrants to begin their voyage, and some of his advice might have deterred the faint-hearted.[19] He cautioned them to choose a ship that had bulwarks at least six feet high, at the side of the outside deck, to prevent passengers from being drenched every time they went up for fresh air. A ship that supplied cooked provisions daily was to be preferred, since this would diminish the chances of diarrhoea, dysentery, typhus fever, and cholera. The berths on these ships were about six feet long and eighteen inches wide, ranged one over the other in double shelves along the side of the vessel. Passengers were urged to be as hygienic as possible, to sprinkle vinegar on the floor to sweeten the air, and to include in their luggage a slop pail, a broom, and a small shovel. 'Almost any sort of clothes will do for the voyage, dirt, grease, tar and salt water will spoil anything good.'

Steamships were more expensive but quicker, thereby reducing the likeli-hood of epidemics and health problems. The change from sail to steam was encouraged by Canadian government subsidies, which reduced the rates for

immigrants arriving by steamship and also provided the cost of railway
fares to the point of destination. From 1885, when construction of the Canadian Pacific Railway (CPR) reached Manitoba and Saskatchewan, and from
1886, when the line was laid through to British Columbia, the west became
accessible to land-hungry Europeans. Although many new arrivals were
heading for the prairies, some were still drawn to eastern Canada, which
had established settlements[20] and to which Canadian immigration officers in
Europe had been directing people for years.

Official maps, guidance, and publications did not delve into as much
detail as those of private enterprise, such as the Allan Line Steamship Company which had a fleet of ships travelling between Liverpool and North
America and dominated the Canadian Atlantic route for nearly a century.
Its advertisements were published in newspapers from Scandinavia
throughout Europe to the remotest parts of the United Kingdom. The company described its best and cheapest routes to all parts of Canada and the
United States, commencing with special rates for the first railway journey to
the ship at Glasgow or Liverpool, and ending with arrangements for travel
by 'colonist cars' from the port of disembarkation in North America to the
Pacific coast if need be. In 1872 its booklet, *Practical Hints and Directions
to Intending Emigrants to Canada and the United States*,[21] promised that
any emigrant who was sober, industrious, and persevering would be assured
of a happy and comfortable home in Canada. The physical advantages of
Canada were not omitted. 'The climate of this vast country is hotter in the
summer and colder in the winter than Western Europe; but it is healthy and
favorable to the growth of a hardy and industrious population, which,
although at present under four millions, has laid the foundation, under
shelter of the British flag, of another great North American Confederation,
where people, lightly taxed, live happily and contented on land which they
could call their own.'

The Allan line in 1872 consisted of twenty-two steamers, some with
names that hinted at the origin of their passengers, such as the SS *Germany*,
the SS *Austrian*, the SS *Prussian*, as well as ships named after the patron
saints of Scotland, Ireland, and Wales. Those that sailed from Liverpool on
Tuesdays and Thursdays called at Londonderry; those that left Glasgow on
Tuesdays called at Dublin. Their average length of voyage westward in
1872 was 11 days and 17 hours.

Steamship service had been in operation for nearly twenty years on the
New York route before it was inaugurated to Quebec and Montreal.[22] In
1856 the Allan line's fortnightly Atlantic mail service commenced, and two
years later four new vessels were added and the mails carried weekly. During the gradual transfer of the emigrant trade from sailing-ships to steam-

and-sail, the employment of sails to supplement the power generated by steam continued long after their use was essential to maintain good speed. By the mid-1870s, the line had enough ships to cope with the Canadian trade at the height of the summer season. There were rival shipping firms, and the line was kept solvent only by subsidies from the Canadian government. With improvements in design and navigation, this company lost only one vessel between 1870 and 1900, but it did not have a monopoly. Rival firms brought immigrants to Canada and returned to the British Isles with cargoes that included livestock.

Transatlantic shipping companies such as the Allan line operated feeder services for their ocean routes, bringing European immigrants to Hull by sea before they crossed England by train to join their ship at Liverpool. The steamship *Sweden* was put into service about 1870 to collect Scandinavian immigrants; German immigrants usually travelled from Hamburg to Hull.

Few descendants of German families are aware that the steamships that brought their ancestors to Quebec or Montreal took on passengers at Liverpool.[23] One who knows this is Bernard Rosien of Ottawa. In shipping lists at the Public Archives of Canada, he found that Albert Drefke and his wife, Ottilie (née Rosien), boarded the ss *Sarmatian* at Liverpool 29 May 1881; Ferdinand and Charlotte Rosien embarked on the ss *Circassian* 4 May 1882, at the same port. Both ships were of the Allan Line.

German immigrants who boarded a ship at a British port would not travel exclusively with those of their own language. The crews of the British ships would be English-speaking. Foreigners who could not speak English were sometimes subjected to exceptional brutality. Details are on record of a voyage toward the close of the sailing-ship period in which Germans, Swedes, and Dutch formed a large proportion of the passengers, the remainder being Irish. The passage from Liverpool to Quebec occupied nine weeks and was a time of unmitigated terror. The Irish were let alone, but the others were treated like slaves.

Though sketches made on these voyages show dome-shaped trunks as luggage of the immigrants, flat-topped containers were more practical, and travellers were advised to nail strips of wood to the base, in order to lift the trunks off a damp floor.

Large travelling chests must have been cumbersome to transport, first by sea and later by train or wagon, but the immigrants from Germany were well prepared for their life in a new country. The women took domestic tools, especially spinning-wheels and related equipment for the production of yarn. Ernestine Luloff packed a pestle and mortar for grinding spices. William Gutzman is said to have arrived in Petawawa Township in the 1860s with a sewing machine that he needed to continue his trade as a tailor.

Frederick Reiche, who reached the township of Wilberforce in 1863, had
with him a fine pigskin saddle which his descendants still possess. Several
furniture-makers who had trained in Germany took with them a fitted box
of tools, and many an immigrant who expected to make a home in the
wilderness took an axe or scorp to use in making implements from wood. In
the Champlain Trail Museum at Pembroke is a delicately woven egg basket,
with a lid and handle, which was carried to Canada by the Schroeder family, who settled in Rosenthal. At a farm in South Algona Township, established by German people in the nineteenth century, the new owners found a
double-barrelled rifle hidden in the wall of one old barn. The gunstock was
carved with the image of a hunting dog in relief, and the ebony was studded
with silver decorations, including a plate bearing the word 'VON' between
two initials. It was a reminder that the European immigrants who came to
eastern Ontario were expecting to kill wild game for their larder and cope
with the dangers of bears. They may not have believed French's assertion
that such animals would flee at the sight of a human being.

Immigration from Germany had virtually ceased by 1895,[24] by which time
Canada's economy had improved. In 1901 there were 9,014 people in Renfrew County described as of German origin.[25] Only 1,317 were living in the
three towns of Pembroke (794), Arnprior (440), and Renfrew (49), or the
village of Eganville (34). The remaining 7,697 were living on the land,
apparently by choice.

    A study of the migration of German-speaking people to North America in
the nineteenth and twentieth centuries has categorized the motivations for
and the goals of such a move.[26] In the third and last phase in the nineteenth
century, ending in the 1880s, the bulk of immigrants came from the agricultural regions of northeastern Germany. It has been concluded that their primary motive was not to seek employment in industrialized urban centres of
the United States but to continue as farmers and live in rural surroundings.
Those among this migration who journeyed to Canada were able to achieve
a life similar to their old way of life, in eastern Ontario at least. The temptation of abundant land had been well advertised, and those that survived the
wretched voyages were tough enough to tackle the uncleared wilderness of
Renfrew County. It was their dream to achieve independence in this way,
but the reality of life on this new agricultural frontier was harder than the
immigration agents had forecast.

Though it is too late to question the pioneers who came from Germany in
the nineteenth century, some children and grandchildren were told why
members of their family had left their native land. Theirs was not the press-

ing spur of poverty, like the Irish fleeing from the hardship that resulted from a potato famine; it was not the persecution of a religious sect that produced closely knit communities of Amish or Mennonites in other parts of North America.

When queried, descendants have answers that usually fall into three categories, which substantiate information from books and immigration agents and colour events with more detail. They have heard that the immigrants came to obtain land, or to get away from the wars, or because they were persuaded by letters from a relative already settled in eastern Upper Canada.

Some will reply with all three reasons, and some stories fit into no categories. Ludwig Raglin, a 40-year-old horn player, was one of the earliest immigrants in 1858. He was advised by his doctor to give up horn-playing for health reasons and to take up an outdoor occupation such as farming.[27] When he immigrated to Canada he settled in Wilberforce Township, and later his grandson, his great-grandson, and his great-great-grandson made homes on the land that he cleared. Not all the families have stayed in the same location.

Aloysius Schmitt, the scion of a department store family in Germany, was one of the later immigrants, migrating to Renfrew County in 1890. Schmitt's exit from his native land was suggested by his family who were affronted by his marriage to a scullery maid and offered him a sum of money to move to a distant country.[28] When he purchased a farm from an Irish family in Sebastopol Township, the community of Vanbrugh on the Opeongo Road included German Lutherans and German Baptists. Schmitt's family was Roman Catholic. According to his grandson, Jim Schruder, Catholic Germans were disliked by Protestant Germans even more than by the Catholic Irish. In this lonely place of exile, Schmitt was occasionally visited by relatives from Germany, lending credence to the belief that he was from a moneyed family.

Religious discord is seldom mentioned as a reason for immigration, though descendants of Johann Lipke believe that this is the reason he left Neu Collatz in 1863.[29] A grandson of Franz Witt, who also came from Pomerania, expressed it succinctly.[30] Said Ferdinand Witt, born 1900, 'It was because the church and state were not separate.' The German-speaking settlers were as varied in their religious affiliations as in everything else – they were Lutheran, Baptist, Evangelical, Methodist, and Roman Catholic.

The overwhelming attraction of Canada was the availability of land, whether free or not, and the tales told by descendants feature this theme prominently. The newcomers ranged from landless peasants to men of capital, from artisans to multilingual university graduates, and from 18-year-olds to mature parents with families.

When August Mohns left Nuremberg in 1862, with his wife, Louisa, and his one-year-old son, Frederick, he settled in Petawawa Township, where some of his descendants remain today. His grandson, Henry Mohns, born 1895, knew that it was the promise of free land that attracted his 28-year-old grandfather. 'It was hard times in Germany,' he said, 'and they thought that if they had free land they would have it made.'[31]

To the same township travelled Gustave Michel, a stonemason, who immigrated with his family from Schleswig-Holstein in 1866. His grandson, Oscar, born 1905, spent his entire life in the farm-house that his grandfather built and furnished with his own hands, and he knew why his ancestors had immigrated: 'Because they were under Lords in Germany – they had no chance to better themselves – they all came out for freedom and better living – and to own their own land.'[32]

Another senior citizen, Henry Grahl of Wilberforce Township, had graphic memories of the stories told by his father, Daniel Grahl, who left Germany in 1875 at the age of 21 years. 'He was like all these other people here from Germany, who were more or less like slaves, working for landlords – a class of people that were held down. For example, for firewood, if they went into the forest and took the dead limbs that had fallen off the trees, they were punished. My father came out from Germany because of conditions like this. His father had the job of looking after the smoked sausage, but he was not allowed to get a bite of the sausage, so he used to untie the sausage to take a bit of it and retie it the same way.' This young man had worked on an estate for the equivalent of $11 a year, and when his father remarried he decided to leave home.[33]

Bismarck's wars had a devastating effect on the lives of many Germans. Most young men who ventured abroad on their own had completed their military service of three years. August Behm was one of these. With his brother he travelled to Renfrew County and worked for years to earn the money to buy a farm in Bromley Township in the years before Confederation. This century farm is now in the hands of the third and fourth generation of the family, and Henry Behm knew why his grandfather immigrated. 'He left Germany as a very young man to get away from the army,' said he.[34]

Eduard Julius Ziebarth, born near Stettin in 1863, also crossed the ocean when he was 21 years old and discharged from the army, in 1884. Said his son, Clem, born 1908, 'He was of peasant stock and worked for the landlord. His father had died young and he was the only boy in the family.

When he left school at 14 years, his uncle had him apprenticed to a black-smith; there was little or no pay for the four years of apprenticeship. When he was 18 years old, he was conscripted into the German Army. He had to serve three years and by the time he came out at the age of 21 he was fed up. He heard of an immigration scheme to Canada and the idea of owning his own land appealed to him.' He settled on the Opeongo Road in Sebastopol Township, where he earned his living as a blacksmith.

Wilhelm Kuhnke left Germany with his wife shortly after 1871. They travelled on a sailing vessel to New York and made their way to Renfrew, settling on land in nearby Admaston Township, where there was a small community of German people at Northcote. Carson Kuhnke, his grandson, born 1898, grew up in that vanished Lutheran congregation and remem-bered the tales of his grandfather. 'He used to tell me there was nothing in Germany for him. Two wars he was in. The last one was the Franco-Prus-sian War, 1870, so he left.'[36]

'My grandparents left Germany because they did not want their sons to be taken by the army,'[37] explained Teresa Luloff. Johann Friedrich Luloff, his wife, Ernestina, their four young sons, and a widowed grandfather arrived in Golden Lake, North Algona Township, in the spring of 1867. Johann Luloff had been a drover operating between Berlin and Stettin, and Ernestina was a midwife; they met fully the requirements of Mr Bechel who visited Germany in 1866 to recruit immigrants with capital. The Luloffs purchased a 180-acre property cleared by the son of a Hudson's Bay Com-pany factor and were generous in hospitality to German immigrants who arrived later.

Before her marriage in 1873 to William Druve, Louisa Panke, who had crossed the Atlantic at the age of 16 in the charge of Mr and Mrs Nicholas Kranz from Breitenbach, Herzberg, Hesse, in 1859,[38] worked for this family.

The Luloffs immigrated after the second war that resulted from Bismarck's ambition; there was a fresh surge of arrivals in their district following the third war. When Julius Popkey died in 1928, aged 93, the *Eganville Leader* commented: 'The late Mr. Popke bore arms for the Father-land, being a soldier in service in the war of 1870–71 between Germany and France. He is the last of the soldier comrades who settled hereabouts. For years the old gentleman had his home close by the Golden Lake Road. There he cultivated his garden and there as a blacksmith and gunsmith he achieved a widespread reputation as a very skilled workman.'[39] His Chris-tian name was a surprise to neighbours who had known him only as 'Schlüssel' Popke, a nickname meaning keys. His grandson, Wilfred Popke, still has some of those keys and a patent for a wrench that his grandfather designed after he came to Canada, in 1881.[40]

One who left Germany after the Franco-Prussian war more promptly, in 1871, was William John Michaelis, a tailor, the first settler of German origin to establish a business in Eganville.[41]

Political dissent was given as the reason why Carl Walther left Germany in 1862, at the age of 30 years. By all accounts he was well educated. According to his grandson, William Walther, born 1901 in Sebastopol Township: 'He had completed his army service which they all had to do in those days and he disagreed with the government's policy. ... He felt that he might get into trouble if he stayed. My grandfather was a landlord's son, who could speak six languages. When he arrived in Canada, they wanted him to stay where the immigrants were coming in, so he could help. With all his education, I don't know why he wanted to come up here where all the stones are!'[42] Carl Walther was one of a number of progressive and well-educated German settlers who formed a community on the Ottawa and Opeongo Road, in Sebastopol Township, where farms were purchased from earlier free grant settlers, most of them Irish.

Another member of this group was Albert Kosmack, who left Germany at the age of 20 and travelled to Canada in 1862, settling first in Lyndoch Township. He had completed his education at a trade school by the age of 17. His progress and achievements were judged good in mathematics and accounting, fairly good in German grammar and style, literary history, English language, geography, history, business style, and banking and commerce, and rather good in religion, French, science, arithmetic, and penmanship. Some of his talents proved useful when he became postmaster of the German community on the colonization road, which he named Vanbrugh.[43] His obligations of military service may have included duty in the merchant navy, for he served on the ship *Flora*, which voyaged from Stettin to British ports in 1860; his discharge paper records that he was dependable and had a strong bodily constitution, an asset to any pioneer farmer. His travel pass, issued in Prussia 3 January 1862, allowed him to move without restriction and requested all civil and military authorities to provide him with protection and support in case he required it.

The obligation to serve three years in the military forces continued long after the wars that had united the German States and was a source of much discontent. 'They felt that they were used like pieces in a chess game,' said Mrs Eleanor Tiegs, a granddaughter of Louis Frederick Verch, who left Prussia in the late 1870s. 'Wars were started and they would be involved. It was like a ball game between two teams, with someone else telling them what to do.' Verch was an educated man, but there was little opportunity for him to use his university degree when he arrived in Renfrew County. Like many other German immigrants he worked on railroad construction for a few years before he began to farm, in Grattan Township.[44]

One of the earliest German families in this township was the family of John Martin Tiegs, who left Pomerania in 1866, with his wife and seven children.[45] They were allowed to emigrate because there was a surplus of carpenters on the estate where Tiegs worked and lived as a tenant. The family docked in the United States and made its way by boat and open wagon to the township of Grattan. The large house that they subsequently built served as a stopping-place, providing food and accommodation for new arrivals from Germany.

Arnold Bartscher travelled to the New World in 1878 as a stowaway at the age of 18, in order to escape military service. He escaped detection by hiding among a cargo of wool until the ship had left the German port, bound for New York.[46] Bartscher sampled life in the United States and later the west of British North America before settling to farm in Renfrew County.

When the sons of the kaiser's coachman decided to try their luck in the New World in 1884 they landed in New York: all the brothers stayed in the United States except for Henrich Duchrow, who travelled to Pembroke, where his girl-friend, Ernestina Kohls, was working and waiting for him.[47] She had crossed the ocean earlier with her family and was employed by the first postmaster in Pembroke, Alexander Moffat.

Ironically, one opportunity offered by the United States in the early 1860s for young men to earn money was by volunteering to serve in the American Civil War. Fredrich Gorr, with his third wife and the children of three marriages, arrived in New York from Answalde-Soldin, Marienwerder, in 1863. The two oldest sons enlisted in a regiment of the infantry of the New York State Volunteers, while the parents and younger children continued their journey to Canada. The oldest son, Johann, stayed in the United States, but when William Gorr was honourably discharged in 1865 he travelled to eastern Upper Canada and purchased land in Alice Township, beside the Indian River, about five miles from Pembroke. This century farm is still worked by his descendants.[48]

Evidence that relatives in Germany planned to follow earlier arrivals is provided by two letters preserved by a descendant of Mr and Mrs Friedrich Witt.[49] They were written by Michael Biesenthal to his sister, Johanna Louise, and to her husband, Friedrich Witt, who had left the village of Sammenthin, near Stargard, with their three children and had arrived in Alice Township in the spring of 1859.

The faded writing on the tattered remains of the letter to Witt sounds an optimistic note: 'We got your letter and saw from it that you are all in good health, that all was well with you. We rejoice in that and we hope that we will be sooner or later your guest; not just us, but the whole group of friends, our people and your people. Whoever is not able at his own means will be helped, so that he can come along too ... My brother-in-law from Wardien won't leave me alone, he is anxious to buy his permit and is coming too. I have a sinking feeling when I think how we'll get settled there. But then I feel comforted since, after all, you got settled.'

The letter to his sister tackled more practical details: 'My wife and your sister want me to ask your advice on household matters. Let us know what is necessary to bring. From the last letter I see that you are in need of a spinning wheel. Father will bring it for you. He has sent two, one for Sonia and one for Christian's wife, by Wilhelm Fischer, who also wanted to go there. I am in doubt whether he has delivered them or not; let us know. Now my dear brother-in-law and dear sister and dear sister-in-law, I would really like to know how things are with you.' After inquiring about sundry relatives such as the Maus and the Fredericks and grumbling about the lack of replies to his letters, Biesenthal returned to specific requests. 'I should like to know how far it is from your place to where they sell the tracts of land, or whether in your vicinity there is something available. Or where is the road and what is the name of the community where you live, so that when we come we can find you. The best would be for you to choose a hotel in Pembroke where we could stay and you could find us there. Dear brother-in-law, let us know what equipment to bring, whether a gun or a trap for fishing. I notice there are so many rivers there, they must have salmon and golden trout in them. I have a feeling that a trap could be useful if you can't get one there.'

When Friedrich Witt's family had first migrated to Canada in 1857, together with that of Christian Biesenthal, the two men had examined land in the area around Berlin (later Kitchener) but had found it too expensive. After hearing that land in the eastern part of the province was being offered without fee, they travelled to Pembroke and in nearby Alice Township found a sandy loam similar to soil they had known in Germany. They returned to southern Upper Canada to collect their families and made their way back to Pembroke. A teamster was hired to transport the two families with their possessions from Pembroke to the land that the men had chosen. A wheel on the wagon proved faulty, and the travellers had to halt while the wagon was unloaded, so that a repair could be attempted. The teamster decided that he would have to go back to Pembroke for a repair to be made to the wheel. The two families huddled under some trees for two days in cool spring weather and eventually realized that the teamster was unlikely to come back. (The teamsters were paid by the load.) The Witts and the Biesenthals, unwilling to wait any longer, chose land on either side of the Indian River and paced it out. There they stayed, and there they were when they were visited by William Sinn in 1860.

The *Sarmatian*, a passenger ship that travelled between Liverpool and Quebec ports, pictured in the *Canadian Illustrated News* of 27 May 1871 Public Archives Canada C-54411

In Liverpool en route to Canada (*Canadian Illustrated News* 4 April 1874, Public Archives Canada C-61174)

German immigrant William Gorr, who served in the Union Army before purchasing land in Alice Township

OPPOSITE

Albert Zadow in Prussian uniform (courtesy Mrs Elsie Getz, Pembroke)

Susana Warnke (in the bonnet), pictured here with her third husband and her children, arrived in Admaston Township from Germany in 1884. Her descendants now number at least 1,400. (Courtesy Robert Corrigan, Barry's Bay)

Mr and Mrs John Albert Drefke (far right), who travelled to Canada in
1881 on the *Sarmatian*, in front of their home in Sebastopol Township in
1913, with Mr Drefke's brothers (seated), the couple's sons (standing
left), and their daughter, her husband (standing centre), and their
children (courtesy Mrs Geraldine Keuhl, Lake Clear)

Dome-shaped chest brought from Germany by Johann Krohn in the 1860s

Flat-topped chest brought from Silesia by Gustave Michel in 1867

CHAPTER THREE

Taming
the land

One of the first observers to comprehend the extent of German settlement in the Ottawa Valley was Reverend Ludwig Herman Gerndt, a missionary sent to the area in 1861. Appointed by the president of the Canada Synod of the Lutheran church at its first meeting of that year, this forty-year-old minister was serving parishes in southern Ontario when he was asked to explore the Upper Ottawa Settlements. He found that the land on which the German immigrants had settled extended 100 miles from north to south and was 40 miles in breadth.[1] There was no Lutheran pastor at that time, but the Canadian government had made a grant of fifteen acres on which to build a church, school, and burial ground at Locksley in Alice Township. Gerndt, with his wife and three children, settled into a parsonage there in 1862, and he continued to make journeys around the countryside, which was receiving more German immigrants. By 1865, the Canada Synod's account of his activities in eastern Ontario commented, 'The region through which Mr. Gerndt peregrinates and preaches the word and administers the Holy Sacraments is 150 miles long by 60 wide.'[2]

Of the four colonization roads advertised in Germany and recommended for settlers with limited means, three led north from the settled 'front' of Upper Canada into the unsettled lands of the Canadian Shield. These were the Addington, the Hastings, and the Frontenac, and, as VanKoughnet had suspected, the farmers taking up free grants on these roads were not immigrants. Families who farmed in the southern counties of the province may have viewed the colonization roads as an opportunity for some of their sons to acquire land, when the scheme was first started. Along the Addington Road the first settlers in the township of Abinger were from Leeds County in 1856–57, and the first homes in Denbigh Township were established by newcomers from the county of Prince Edward.[3] By the end of 1859 the population on the Addington Road was numbered at 699, and only four families were described as having come from Prussia.[4]

The crown lands agent for the Hastings Road, M.P. Hayes, reported that he had located 144 new settlers in 1858, of whom 31 were natives of Germany.[5] In 1863 only 22 new lots were taken up, and the following year not even one.[6] The immigrants from Germany who travelled along the Hastings Road had journeyed to an intersection with the Peterson Road and formed a small settlement at Maynooth. Those who had investigated the Addington Road had a choice of land at its farthest extremities, where villages named Denbigh and Letterkenny by earlier settlers eventually became totally German in character. The few German immigrants who ventured to the end of the Frontenac Road established the hamlet of Plevna. Settlement along these three roads did not result in a spread of agriculture in their vicinity, as had been anticipated.

The main purpose of the colonization roads was to raise the value of crown lands through which the roads were run. They were intended as channels to lead the stream of population to the land for sale in a new agricultural frontier.[7] Only the Ottawa and Opeongo Road, which ran from east to west, fulfilled this purpose. In the earliest years the German immigrants who landed at ports on the St Lawrence could continue their journey to this colonization road by water, until they reached Farrell's Landing on the Ottawa River. After 1872, they could travel by train as far as Renfrew.[8] As immigration agents Wagner and Sinn had noted, many would arrive with some money; they had been made aware, before they left Germany, that there was land for sale, in addition to the free grants that had been widely advertised. The immigration pamphlet of 1857 by T.P. French included a description of the vicinity of the Ottawa and Opeongo Road: 'There are three new Townships now being surveyed along the Opeongo Road, and the Surveyors state that the lands are excellent for agricultural purposes. When the surveys are completed the lands will be sold by the Crown, in lots of 100 or 200 acres, at a price yet to be fixed, but which will not exceed some four or five shillings per acre. Such lands are usually sold subject to the obligations of actual residence, and the cultivation of a few acres annually; and the payments for them are generally made in four annual instalments. Settlers are never prevented from making farms on the wild lands of the Crown wherever they find them best adapted to their wants, and all who may have gone to live on them previous to their being sold, will be permitted a preemptive right to purchase.'[9]

Most German immigrants who arrived in eastern Upper Canada in the mid-nineteenth century journeyed to the Ottawa and Opeongo Road, or its vicinity. This road may have been more popular than the other three colonization roads because it was more easy to reach or possibly because it had received more publicity as a result of the translation of T.P. French's pamphlet of 1857. In his report for 1859, French listed the 234 settlers located on the road, according to their place of birth, and expressed his pleasure at the blend of nationalities: 'The presence of the Poles (14) and Germans (2) forms a new and pleasing feature of the Settlement. In the summer of 1858 these people were attracted to Canada by the report of the Free Grants and they came direct to Renfrew. When they arrived here however, they found they had yet much to learn before they could venture with but little means upon uncleared lands, and consequently they and their children hired out as Servants wherever they could find employers. By this means they have succeeded in acquiring a partial knowledge of the English language, also the experience necessary to use the axe with some effect and to become permanent and in time, prosperous Settlers themselves.'[10]

A number of German immigrants settled in Pembroke, the county seat from 1866, and the most obvious centre for employment. The parents of Ernst Daber met there. His father, Henrich, had travelled to Renfrew County in 1884, at the age of 25, because his brother, lonely in Canada, offered him return fare if he would make the trip to see him. The visitor decided to stay, and although he purchased a farm in Petawawa Township he worked for twenty years as a lathe operator with the firm of Thomas Pink, where logging tools were made. The future Mrs Henrich Daber, who had grown up in the same province of Pyritz, met her husband for the first time at a dance in Pembroke. She had immigrated to join a sister who was so lonesome in her new country that she repeatedly said, 'If only a stone would take me.' Before her marriage she worked as a domestic servant for Thomas Mackie, twice MP for North Renfrew and a prominent lumberman.[11]

Pembroke was a bustling centre in the second half of the nineteenth century. Many fine brick mansions were built for residents who had prospered on the lumbering trade that used the Ottawa River as its artery.[12] Construction of the large houses afforded temporary employment for carpenters and unskilled labour in the season when the logging camps were not operating. The farm-house built in 1865 for Richard White, mayor of Pembroke 1862–4,[13] has apical ornaments at the gables that suggest carpenters from West Prussia worked on this colonnaded frame structure, one mile east of the town.

The huge Victorian houses, with their extravagant turrets and towers, required a staff of servants to maintain them. Young women of various nationalities were employed in domestic service in Pembroke at the time of the 1881 census; they included French, Scots, Irish, and German girls, most

in their twenties, but some as young as 14-year-old Mary Boshart who
worked at the Teevens Hotel. Both male and female immigrants from Germany worked in the homes of merchants, lumbermen, politicians, doctors,
and lawyers. The population of Pembroke in 1881 was estimated as 2,820,
and of this number only 128 were of German origin. The latter included the
families of a brewer, Karl Haentschel, a teamster, Robert Zerke, a carpenter, William Lastman, a gardener, Herman Witt, a cook, Robert Fitz-
mar, a shoe-maker, William Timms, and several sawyers, mill-hands, and
labourers.[14]

However, as the population of German-speaking immigrants increased in
Renfrew County, to 2,318 by 1871 and to 4,831 by 1881, it became possible
for craftsmen in rural areas to earn a living from their skills among their
countrymen. Some found that they could conduct their business just as well
from a rural setting, where their families could cultivate a vegetable garden
and keep a cow and hens. Several furniture-makers adopted this life-style.

As early as 1859, on the completed 70-mile portion of the Ottawa and
Opeongo Road, from the Ottawa River to Sebastopol Township, there was
scarcely a lot unoccupied. T.P. French urged the commissioner of crown
lands, Philip VanKoughnet, to extend the road through the wilderness for
another 15 or 20 miles, to Lake Opeongo. He claimed that many men had
visited the previous season with the intention of selecting a free grant, but
had been prevented by the scarcity of lots; otherwise, he was sure, the list of
settlers would have included another 100 names.

To obtain evidence on the soil in his area, French had visited every farm
on the road; the average value of the produce of each acre cropped in 1859
was $32.27, nearly $8 an acre above that of the previous year. Since the
land had been cropped in 1857 and 1858, he regarded his 1859 report as un-
answerable refutation of 'those persons who have so long and so mon-
strously endeavoured to prove by mere assertions the utter worthlessness of
the land along this road for farming purposes.' At least fifteen crops were
being produced (see Table 2); French admitted that he had forgotten to include milk, butter, sawn lumber, shingles, venison, and furs.

Cereals, hay, straw, and vegetables, which provided the greatest revenue, were being raised for sale, that is, for the lumbermen's shanties, and
this market would not last indefinitely; the cash crops of ashes and potash,
derived from the burning of hardwoods, were non-renewable. The markets
for the products that French neglected to itemize were not likely to expand,
unless transportation were improved for dairy produce and wood and con-
servation practised for the trapping and hunting. Neither happened. The
apparent success of farming 1,090 acres in 1859 (on land cropped the two

TABLE 2
Produce on the Opeongo Road 1859 (from T.P. French's report)

	Value (dollars)
8515 Bushels of Wheat worth $1 per bushel	8,515
8421 Bushels of Oats worth 50 cents per bushel	4,210.50
395 Bushels of Barley worth 60 cents per bushel	237
202 Bushels of Corn worth $1 per bushel	202
245 Bushels of Peas worth $1 per bushel	245
450 Bushels of Potatoes worth 50 cents per bushel	225
1580 Bushels of Turnips worth 15 cents per bushel	207
147 Tons of Hay at $16 a ton	2,384
308 Tons of Straw at $5 a ton	1,540
5650 lbs of Sugar worth 12 cents a lb	678.36
325 Gallons of Molasses worth $1 a Gal	325
164 Barrels of Pork worth $16 a Barrel	2,624
85 Barrels of Potash worth $22 a Barrel	1,870
4,667 lbs of Soap worth 10 cents a lb	466.70
9,102 Bushels of Ashes worth 5 cents a bushel	455.10
Making the total value of the crops for 1859	35,184.66

previous years) gave an illusion of prosperity that the immigration agent
employed in order to coax his employer to extend the road. In reality, it was
not a solid foundation for the future.

When construction was continued beyond Brudenell, the road had scaled
a fault of about 800 feet and led the traveller into stony and hilly country
for another twenty miles. In the undulating countryside beyond Brudenell,
opened up by an extension of the Opeongo Road, Polish immigrants were
willing to accept free grants in five townships in this area. The German
people were not.

When William Sinn, immigration agent, was asked 11 October 1860 'to fur-
nish the Government with some reliable information respecting the Prussian
immigrants who have settled within the past few years on the Upper
Ottawa,' he visited the district to record his impressions at first hand. [15]
Travelling along the colonization road, which he termed the Opeongo
Strasse, Sinn found that only three German immigrants had chosen to
locate on free grants: Gottlieb Slahr from Baden-Baden and John and
Heinrich Scheerer from Berlin. There were three German settlers in the

village of Renfrew: John Weber, Carl Bussow, and Joachem Grund; each
had enough property to keep a cow, pigs, and hens. The other fifty German
farmers had travelled north of the road and had settled in townships where
they had to purchase land if they wished to gain legal title. Most were in the
Bonnechere country, where pockets of good soil existed, as Alexander Murray had noticed in his survey.

Sinn's list of settlers was not a complete summary of the European immigrants who had reached the Upper Canadian side of the Ottawa Valley by
that year. He omitted the town of Pembroke, where the Methodist church
had recruited a German-speaking minister in 1860, to attend to those
members of the congregation who understood only that language. He also
omitted Fitzroy Harbor, Braeside, and Arnprior, on the Ottawa River,
where new arrivals of all nationalities might gain employment in the sawmills and allied industries of the lumber companies. The agent's knowledge
of the townships' boundaries was not always accurate; for example, some of
the German settlers listed by him in Alice Township were actually in
Petawawa Township. In view of the lack of roads throughout most of the
countryside that he visited, Sinn's report, prepared in ten days, was a considerable achievement.

Sinn found the following fifty German settlers in Renfrew County (his
spellings). In Bromley Township there were eight: Carl Krüger, John
Krüger, Carl Lenz, John Griese, Carl Somers, Carl Kleinholz, Gottlieb
Kusz, and Martin Marks. Admaston Township had two settlers, Ludwig
Schultz and Ludwig Ringe. Wilberforce Township had the largest number
(eighteen): John Witzel, J. Buchard, Friedrich Schütt, Carl Rühs, Wilhelm
Thur, Chr. Wassmund, Theodor Wassmund, Martin Budarich Sr., Martin
Budarich Jr., John Urenche, Joseph Rohloff, John Christen, Michel Mau,
Gottlieb Wassenberg, Wilhelm Luckow, John Luckow, August Friewald,
and Wilhelm Luloff. There were seven in South Algona Township: Wilhelm
Schröder, Friedrich Sell, John Bohn, Gottlieb Möller, Gottlieb Quast,
August Schröder, and Chr. Quast, and one in North Algona Township:
Nikolas Krantz. Fourteen men had chosen Alice Township: Martin Liesk,
Mathes Liesk, Ferd. Kaatz, Julius Ringe, Carl Ringel, Gottl. Volgeringer,
Edw. Weber, A. Diehl, John Boldt, John Biesenthal, Fried. Witt, Ludwig
Brosch, John Wienholz, and (again, but on a separate farm) Carl Ringel.

Sinn's report was designed to provide encouraging evidence for immigration agent William Wagner in Germany. Sinn assured him that at least
thirty more families had made payments on land in Wilberforce and Alice
townships but had not been able to take possession because of lack of roads
to reach their respective lots. Another dozen had settled in Petawawa and
Westmeath, a great number now in service were expected to enter on land

the following spring, and a further sixty families had informed their friends that they planned to emigrate from Germany in 1861.

Newcomers from Germany had experienced hardship, as William Sinn admitted. 'Those settled along the northwest shore of Indian River in Alice, and along the town line between Wilberforce and North Algoma [sic] have trouble in getting to the mills at Pembroke and Eganville because some old settlers have closed the shanty roads, which at present are the only means of access as no regular road is made as yet through the locality. They have to carry the produce upon their backs to market it, and as they are not able to plead their grievances in the English language, the townships' councils seem slow in granting and having the necessary conveniences constructed.'

Despite such handicaps Sinn believed that the German immigrants had made such progress on their own land that it would be foolish of them to hire out their services to others. 'They have reached the first step where they feel the sweetness of independence,' he claimed. 'What a contrast! two years only since they were servants of hard and exacting landlords in the Old Country.' Sinn was a man well qualified to make comparisons. A native of Prussia, he had earlier worked as an agent for the Emigration Department of Lower Canada, in arranging the assisted passages of immigrants from Baden in 1854 and from Württemberg in 1855, using the Hamburg shipping line Knorr and Holterman.

The farmers visited by Sinn had all arrived in Renfrew County within the previous two years. At every home Sinn listed the birthplace of the head of the household, the season of arrival in Canada, the number of acres cleared, the crops harvested, the livestock owned, and the location of the settlers. The earliest to begin cultivation were Martin Budarick sr and Martin Budarick jr, who located on adjacent lots in Wilberforce Township in the fall of 1858. (If a son was more than 18 years old, he could own land in his own name.) The Budaricks, from Drachhausen, Cottbus, Frankfurt-on-the-Oder, had neighbours in their new home, for the area near Green Lake had been pioneered by the Welsh-Irish family of Evan Edwards in 1841.[16]

Martin Budarick sr could report that he had thirty-six acres cleared for cultivation (more than any settler on the list). His crops in 1860 comprised 90 bushels of wheat, 26 of rye, 75 of oats, 7 of barley, 136 of potatoes, and 45 of flax. His livestock consisted of 2 cows, a pair of oxen, 4 young cattle, 5 sheep, 4 pigs, and 30 hens. The achievements of his son, with only four acres cleared, were much more modest, but perhaps he had been aiding his father. The Budaricks had certainly reached the first steps in independence.

T.P. French's belief that a good road was a necessary prelude to any settlement was clearly a fallacy, for the townships in which the German farmers had chosen land had no regular roads, as Sinn pointed out. It was in the interest of the crown land agent to encourage arrivals in Renfrew County to select lots on the Ottawa and Opeongo Road – his very job depended on it. In 1864, when his salary had been replaced by a commission of $2 extracted from each settler's fee of $5 (a later requirement), French resigned because the number of new grants on his road had dwindled to only nineteen that year. [17]

North of the Opeongo Road the land in Renfrew County was not dissimilar; indeed some of it was superior and largely unoccupied. Those who had come with funds could buy land immediately from the crown, or from those who had arrived earlier. Sinn noted in his report: 'There is also in the vicinity of the Ottawa River picked land for sale by private owners, or speculators.' When August Frivalt, a wagon-maker from Frankfurt-on-the-Oder, arrived in Alice Township with his wife and children in the summer of 1860, he purchased 109 acres of land for $60 from a settler, John Coburn. This was not cleared land, according to a granddaughter, [18] but still rough bush, and the removal of tree stumps was not completed until the third generation. August Frivalt had obviously come prepared with money to buy land.

Some German immigrants would have to work in the towns for a few years in order to make payments, while others would simply squat on the land until the Free Homestead Act of 1868 made it possible for them to obtain a legal title. The location of the churches founded by the German-speaking missionaries in the 1860s reveals that the townships of Alice, Wilberforce, and Petawawa were the most popular choices of the earliest German immigrants – and these townships did not even adjoin the Opeongo Road. It was in this region that Reverend L.H. Gerndt (Lutheran) [19] and Reverend Frederick Scharffe (Evangelical) [20] organized congregations. By 1869, a German Methodist congregation at Green Lake in Wilberforce Township could afford to pay $1,000 to purchase one acre for a church site, [21] an indication that the German farmers in this area were doing well.

Even in the townships that had poor land for farming, those who had ignored the offer of free grants were urging friends back home to join them. Wilhelm Schröder of Breitenstein, Friedeborg, Frankfurt-on-the-Oder, began cultivation of land in South Algona Township in the spring of 1859. Six other men from the same place joined him in this township in August 1860: Friedrich Sell, John Bohn, Gottlieb Möller, Christian Quast, Gottlieb Quast, and August Schröder. Sinn noted that they had arrived too late in the season to plant any crops.

For those who did not choose to settle on a free grant on a colonization road, there was a freedom from restrictions. These settlers did not have to perform statutory labour on a road that was regularly churned up by lumbermen, teaming as many as fifty wagonloads a day. They did not have to become responsible for 100 acres, but could buy acreage according to their means and their choice. (Some of them bought only 50 acres, considering this to be a large farm by the standards of the country they had left behind.)[22] They were not obliged to construct a house of a certain size; some of the log shanties were much smaller. They are few original homesteads that can be measured, but the one built by August Frivalt has not been altered in size, although it has been moved. Later used as a granary, and later still as a garage, it is sturdy still, with its dovetailed corners, two windows, and a door; the outside measurements of this 1½-storey log building are 16'4" by 21'4", very similar to the dimensions demanded by government regulations for dwellings on free grant lots. Those who settled on purchased land did not have to endure the regular inspection of a crown land agent who measured their cleared acres and asked questions about yield and value of crops. It was a much more independent life.

One unidentified early settler wrote in 1861 to William Wagner with a blunt comment. He praised Canada, but added, 'About your free grants of land, it is humbug!' Wagner begged Philip VanKoughnet either to extend the free grants or discard them completely, because, he complained, 'It gives only bad blood.'[23]

In 1862 the 100-acre lots on the Opeongo Road that were previously free now required the payment of a fee of $5. In his report on that year, French expressed the opinion that this charge had discouraged some applicants who did not have the means to pay. Of the sixteen people who had taken up lots on this road in 1862, half took the place of other settlers who sold their improved land and left the locality. At least a dozen of the new arrivals were German families, immigrants of 1861, who moved to the road in May and settled close to each other on farms granted earlier to Irish immigrants without fee.[24]

'They are all very intelligent and seemingly respectable and industrious,' commented French in describing the German newcomers. 'They have settled adjoining each other on the 4th, 5th, 6th and 7th Concessions of Sebastopol, and as they are not without some means to begin with, they will give a slight stimulus to the settlement, and I have no doubt will soon succeed in securing to themselves comfortable homes. One of them, Mr C.F. Hotterman, is particularly intelligent and energetic, and so satisfied is he with his own and his friends' prospects of success, that he intends others of his countrymen to come here next spring.' (Hotterman, or Halterman, purchased a farm from Patrick Neilan, a free grant settler.[25]) This community became known as Vanbrugh, the only place on the Opeongo Road where a German-speaking congregation was organized by the Lutheran missionary.

In the rural areas of Renfrew County new arrivals would often be invited to board with an established family until they had bought or built a home of their own. In the Augsburg area it was Mr and Mrs Gustave Tiegs,[26] at Golden Lake Mr and Mrs Johann Luloff,[27] and at Eganville, at the home of Mr and Mrs William Michaelis, the stagecoach from Cobden would sometimes deposit a load of guests after midnight.[28]

Hospitality from neighbours who spoke the same language encouraged the German immigrants to adapt to a new and uninviting environment. Augusta Klingbeil, the wife of Ernst Bimm, first seeing the wilderness of the Canadian Shield, burst into tears at the home of a cousin at Lake Clear.[29] Her husband resisted the temptation to return to his native land with his wife and five children and gained employment on the railroad. Later he was to establish himself in his trade as a blacksmith in Eganville. At one time this village was nicknamed Bimmsville because there were more descendants of this family than of any other.[30]

Although the steady stream of immigrants from Germany appears to have been assisted by letters from those in eastern Upper Canada who were satisfied, there must have been some sour notes from the disappointed ones. A government immigration agent, W.J. Wills, sent a letter of inquiry to some German settlers in Sebastopol Township, 28 July 1865, attempting to assess their progress. He received a reply from four farmers and a Church of England minister, Dr A. Schaffraneck, who had been hired to teach school there, as well as serve the Lutheran congregation at Vanbrugh.[31] The other four signatories were well-educated farmers who reported in detail on the facilities in their neighbourhood and their hopes for the future in a tone that suggested permanence.

On the whole the condition of our settlement may be considered as satisfactory, particularly as regards the present crops, which will turn out as very rich. With regard to the very different, even very unfavorable reports about our settlement, it is apparent to us how they have come into circulation. The reasons are as follows: We have had the misfortune to receive here several persons belonging to the educated class, who have been drawn hither by the circumstances that there are people among us at the same position in life as themselves and who have found themselves satisfied here. All these new people had certainly the desire to become Farmers, but were not possessed of sufficient power and endurance for

*the heavy work which the first commencement of the bush necessitates –
some have lost courage and have been obliged to return. They do not
however attribute their want of success to themselves or to their own
want of capability, but to the country. On their return they spread the
most extravagant and untrue statements to excuse their own mistakes.* [32]

The four farmers who signed this letter, F. Kosmack, Albert Kosmack,
Carl Walther, and Richard Koch, were living on that part of the Opeongo
Road where French had found German immigrants settling in adjoining lots
in 1862; Albert Kosmack had purchased Hotterman's farm. Successful
themselves, the four believed that three years of diligence and perseverance
had earned for them an independent future. Even those that had arrived
with modest means had equipped their farms with livestock and tools, and
most had surplus crops. Wheat, rye, oats, barley, millet, buckwheat,
potatoes, turnips, and timothy had been planted in 1865, and it was expected that 100 tons of wild hay would be harvested that season. Already
the men had felt the lack of hired help, and they certainly had no intention
of hiring themselves out to others. It was their opinion that unsuccessful
settlers were few in numbers and that the prosperous condition of the
majority had received far less publicity.

Since these immigrants had purchased their farms from other settlers, it
may be assumed that some of the forest cover had been removed from the
land before they acquired it. The list of crops expected that year did not include potash, one of the first sources of cash that could be gained from
felling timber, and one that had ranked fifth in importance on the Opeongo
Road in 1859.

Wherever and whenever land was cleared for cultivation on the Canadian
Shield in eastern Upper Canada, removing the trees, stumps, and stones
was an arduous task. French had devoted only one paragraph to this problem in his booklet, [33] describing the removal of the vegetation but omitting
to mention the burden of the stones.

After the brush and branches had been burned, large logs were collected
into piles and fired separately. The ashes were carefully gathered for the
manufacture of potash, usually in the winter, when the danger from fire
was less. This was one of the earliest crops that could be taken from the
land; it required no skill in its primary phases and was very remunerative.
Immigrants were advised that the necessary kettles and coolers cost about
£14, but were generally supplied on credit by the storekeepers in the neighbourhood, who were repaid in potash or other farm produce.

Large iron kettles, which might measure fifty inches in diameter, were made especially for the potash industry, because ordinary vessels could not endure the intense heat needed to boil down the lye and melt the salts.[34] It might take a week of steady stirring and heating before the lye reached the thick consistency of porridge. When a blue blaze appeared over the molten mass it was transferred into smaller iron pots, termed *coolers*, that had been heated to receive it. Hardening as it cooled, the potash 'cake' found a ready market. The potash produced in Upper Canada was usually forwarded to Montreal. From this port in 1861 the total quantity of potash exported was valued at $570,202, of which $503,217 worth went to Great Britain and the remainder to the United States.[35]

French had estimated that the ashes from two and a half acres of ordinary hardwood land should be sufficient to make a barrel of potash. It was not a crop that could be endlessly renewed, but it was an important source of cash needed for the purchase of livestock. An excellent farm cow cost about five pounds, according to French's estimates of 1857, and Sinn's survey of 1860 had shown that virtually every German household that he visited had at least one.

While the removal of the trees and bush was laborious, the uprooting of the stumps was even more difficult. William Wagner had suggested that the most suitable settlers for Canada would be those who were used to tearing out the stumps of the trees from the soil.[36] Some of their descendants were still tackling this job as late as the 1930s[37] in South Algona Township, using the same method.

A stump-puller, powered by horses, made the job easier. A long screw, positioned above the stump, rested on a framework of three sturdy posts in a tripod arrangement.[38] The exposed roots of the stump were cut through, the soil was excavated so that a chain could be passed down underneath the stump, and both ends of this loop were attached to a hook at the base of the screw. Above the screw a long pole connected the metal rod to a halter on a horse. As the animal was led around in a circle, the screw lifted and the attached stump was wrenched out of the ground.

Clearing stumps from the land might also be accomplished by the use of a stumping-jack, which worked on much the same principle as today's car-jack.[39] These tools were made of iron by blacksmiths such as Ernst Bimm of Eganville. The leverage on the jack was produced by human force exerted on a long handle. When the Bartscher family moved from South Algona Township to an Irish farm on the McGrath Road in Grattan Township, in 1916, they found that there was still much clearing of stumps to be done. They used both the stumping-jack and the stump-puller.

A bitter account of the obstacles facing settlers in Sebastopol Township was written by one of the Irish farmers, Martin Foy, who left it in 1871. Accompanied by his wife and five children, he travelled to the flat, treeless prairies of Minnesota where he became a successful pioneer. In 1890, he returned to Canada: 'Every place the ground was bare I could see the stones there still. The Mountains as high as ever. A great deal of the beautiful timber that covered or concealed the rocks had disappeared forever. When I went in on my old farm, to the Spring where we got our water so long, I stood, and I looked up the hill. You know I stood there contemplating its unequalled beauty. Oh, God, O God, I says to myself, What kind of a nightmare must I have, or what was I thinking of, to say that I remained there to spend, to throw away so many of my youthful Vigorous days.'[40]

Only when the forest cover was removed did the settlers see how much stone would impede the cultivation of their land. Unlike the stumps, which would rot in seven years if they were not removed, the stones would trouble the first, second, and third generations of German farmers, who sometimes still refer to the 'annual harvest of stones.' Stumps and stones were hauled away to build fences, some still in place. Mounds of rocks may still be seen on farm fields long since abandoned.

The largest rocks or boulders were moved with the aid of a stone-lifting machine, a sort of wagon with wheels of large diameter 'so as to pass over the largest stones,' explained Allan Kosmack, who can remember land-clearing operations in progress in the twentieth century, when he was a child. On the farm worked by his grandfather, Albert Kosmack, enormous stone walls range up and down the hilly fields. Albert's son, Frederick, was one of the few farmers who actually figured out an economic value for some of the stones – they were delivered to Eganville for use in stabilizing the muddy streets, in the years before paving.[41]

'A great deal of rock and loose surface stone is also to be met with, and while it must not be denied that such often proves a source of much annoyance to the farmer yet they do not prevent the proper cultivation of the land,' concluded French, ever the optimist.[42]

The stone walls on the Kosmack farm, which has been expanded from 97 acres to 1,300 acres, bound pastures meticulously cleared of rocks and fields of flourishing corn on dark soil. The first Kosmack to farm this ground knew the importance of renewing the nourishment of the soil with natural manure, a practice not followed by many of the settlers. Albert Kosmack had the advantage of a better education than many of his neighbours (for whom he wrote letters in three languages), and his farming practices were superior too. Now worked by his great-grandsons, Glenn and Morley

Kosmack, this property is one of the few productive farms still in operation on the Ottawa and Opeongo Road.

French, who gave a glowing account of the crops harvested in 1859, had not farmed his land long enough to realize that the soil would become exhausted if it was not fertilized. Henry Grahl of Wilberforce Township attributed the decline of agriculture in his area to this fault: 'German people did not know how to keep up land in those days – they kept ploughing grain again and again, without planting clover to renew the soil.' Although one study has concluded that this road enjoyed its greatest success in the years 1860-90,[43] a contemporary account in the Renfrew *Mercury* of 1880 indicates that it had lost its function and many of its free grant settlers by that time: 'The Opeongo Line, once the leading road to the lumbering districts of the Madawaska River, is now little travelled. The settlers in many settlements have nearly all deserted first located lots, and many have either moved back to better land or gone West.'[44]

Though the Ottawa and Opeongo Road had lost its appeal, the Bonnechere country, to the north, was becoming more densely settled. Throughout the three decades of immigration from Germany to eastern Upper Canada and later Ontario, the major preoccupation of the arrivals was the opportunity to own land. Their sons also wanted farms of their own.

In 1867 Johann Frederick Ernst Saar (nicknamed Aaron by neighbours who had difficulty pronouncing Ernst) purchased 100 acres in Stafford Township from the crown for the sum of $160.[45] Only 18 years old, he was the son of Carl and Caroline Saar who had come to Canada with their children in 1862 and settled in Alice Township. The young man made a good choice of land; it was level, well-watered, and close to Pembroke, ensuring access to markets and good communications. The fourth and fifth generation of Aaron's family are still working this farm with greatly increased acreage. If Aaron had waited until the following year, 1868, he would have been eligible to apply for a free grant of land under the new Homestead Act, although not in Stafford Township where he had chosen his site. In eleven townships in Renfrew County a settler could now obtain a free grant of 200 acres,[46] and if he wished to increase his property the price of crown land was reasonable. Freiderick Reiche added another 50 acres to his farm in Wilberforce Township in 1884 for $25, or 50 cents an acre.[47]

The agricultural possibilities of Ontario were assessed in 1880 by a provincial government report that still viewed the eastern part of the province with optimism: 'The counties of Frontenac, Lennox, Addington and Renfrew, are all, or will soon be, well supplied with railways connecting the rear settlements with the front.'[48] 'Some portions of Renfrew are still in process of settlement, while others have been occupied for forty years past. Although one of the most northerly of the counties, the warmth and dryness of the atmosphere in the summer months has a powerful effect on products depending on such influences. While some of the land is rough and poor, a considerable portion is good and fertile. Probably fifty per cent is still uncleared. The soil is mostly a sandy loam, and in places a gravelly loam.'

The Ontario Agricultural Commission report of 1881 concluded: 'Renfrew County has good markets at Pembroke, Arnprior, Renfrew Village and Cobden, but a large part of the farming population sell all their spare produce to lumbermen, and depend wholly on that industry.'[49] As the timber limits were stripped and the shanties moved farther up the Ottawa Valley, another colonization road, the Pembroke and Mattawan, became important to the economy of the small farms of eastern Ontario. This road, 98 miles long, was constructed along the shoreline of the Ottawa River; only 40 miles were open for year-round traffic in 1867, but the road was completed as far as Mattawa in 1875.

The purpose of this road had been outlined by the minister of agriculture (and premier), Sir Allan MacNab, in 1854: 'The formation of this road is highly beneficial to the Ottawa country for settlement and the lumber trade, opening up an extensive tract of fertile country, and greatly facilitating the transport of supplies for the lumbering establishments by affording land carriage where the navigation of the river is interrupted by bad rapids and the winter conveyance is difficult and dangerous as the ice is late in forming and never strong.'[50] The avowed reason for the road – to encourage agricultural settlement – was not believed by government officials, who were frequently petitioned by lumbermen to make repairs.[51] Even the plaque erected by the Archaeological and Historic Sites Board of the Ontario Archives in 1972 proclaims that the Pembroke and Mattawan Road was constructed primarily as a supply route to the lumber camps in the Ottawa Valley. Nevertheless a corridor of lots had been laid out, on either side of the colonization road, for practically the entire distance of its route through the townships of Petawawa, Buchanan, Rolph, Head, Maria, Clara, Cameron, and Papineau. Few were taken up.

A cohesive settlement developed in Petawawa Township, just west of the Petawawa River which had been bridged. Between concessions 9 and 15, free grants by virtue of the Homestead Act of 1880 were obtained by newly-arrived German immigrants and sons of earlier German immigrants who had grown up in Renfrew County.[52] (Up to 200 acres could be awarded to a bona fide settler.) Clearing land along the waterfront of the Ottawa River, and inland to a depth of thirteen lots, German families established themselves there in the 1890s. They tackled the same problems that earlier immigrants had faced, constructing their own homes, making their own furniture, building their own Lutheran church and the fourth school in Petawawa Township. It was a community that had no opportunity to mature because the land was chosen by the government for a site of a military camp in the early years of the following century.

For many of the farmers in eastern Ontario the Pembroke and Mattawan Road was not a new chance to own land, but a new avenue that led to the lumbering shanties. Whether they were driving supplies from stores in Pembroke, or teaming wagonloads of their own crops, many rural residents benefited from the 'Upper Ottawa Tote Road,' as it was called. Charles Bochert of Grattan Township could remember, in 1977, how he had driven sleighloads of hay along the Pembroke and Mattawan Road in 1917, pausing for the night at a hostelry in Deep River and at other stopping-places along the route.

The completion of J.R. Booth's railroad through the Wilno Pass in 1894 had ended the importance of the Ottawa and Opeongo Road as a route for the transport of lumbermen's supplies. The extension 1876–82 of the Canada Central Railroad (later the Canadian Pacific Railway – CPR) from Pembroke to North Bay did not compete with the Pembroke and Mattawan Road as a trail to the pineries of the upper Ottawa Valley.[53] The small farms in the townships of the Bonnechere country continued to enjoy a modest prosperity. In the 1880s and 1890s the number of residents in Renfrew County who claimed German origin had almost doubled, from 4,831 to 9,014, but census records of the individual townships in the northwest region of the county showed a pronounced change in the proportions of ethnic groups. The numbers of Irish were stable or decreasing, while the Germans had multiplied.

The growth of small and rural German communities in Renfrew County may be traced by the names of post offices, often German. Little change in nomenclature has taken place since the Department of the Interior mapped the area in 1914 and 1919; subsequent maps reproduce the names of hamlets that have disappeared or have dwindled in population so much that a centre would be hard to find. Places such as Alice, Augsburg, Budd Mills, Germanicus, Locksley, Rosenthal, Vanbrugh, Woermke, Woito, and Zadow were all centres of German settlement once, with their own post offices. Vanbrugh's post office was opened in 1863 or 1864, following an application by 'C.F. Holterman,' and new post offices were being established as late as 1916, when one was opened at Rosenthal, the postmaster being Charles Phanenhauer.

Detail about the lives of German immigrants and their families has been chronicled by a daughter of a Lutheran pastor who arrived in Pembroke in 1887. Having just graduated from Concordia Seminary in Springfield, Illinois, Reverend Ludwig John Schmidt, with his bride, accepted the responsibility of four congregations of the Missouri Synod in Renfrew County. At the parsonage at Locksley, Alice Township, their first child, Hedwig (Hattie) Dorothea Fredericka Schmidt, was born in 1888. In her seventies, Hattie Schmidt Cramer recalled the arduous years:[54] 'Most of the members of father's church were farmers. The land was light soil and very stony. If a farmer had 100 acres, about one third of this land would be too stony and rocky to cultivate ... Since the land was well adapted to sheep grazing most farmers had a fine flock of sheep. With their spinning wheels the women spun excellent yarn, unsurpassed in quality, from the wool of the sheep and lambs.' They were 'simple devout Christian people who had come from Germany to found a home in the New World. They had little money, but they literally deluged the young pastor with provisions from their farms. Milk, butter, lard, eggs, flour, meat, vegetables – also the wood for fuel. Feed, straw and hay for the horse were given them by the load, as well as oats.'

No matter how small the gift, Frau Pastorin Emma Schmidt thanked the giver graciously. 'Nun, ich danke ihnen auch, so ganz herzlich fuer ＿＿＿ und bitte gruessen sie auch schoen zu Hause.' [Oh I thank you so very heartily for ＿＿＿ and please give our kindest regards to those at your house.] The oldest daughter retained a life-long memory of German culture at its highest, 'even in this northern Ontario community,' as she described it.

In letters to her sister in Michigan, the pastor's wife describes his heavy duties, with preaching in four parishes, teaching German school two days a week, performing marriages, conducting funerals, holding choir practices. The annual salary was $300, paid in quarterly instalments.

'Here everyone is so industrious,' she wrote. 'Little girls, seven years old, knit stockings for the entire family. One little girl, seven years old has crocheted a whole bedspread. Working is the order of the day just as it is in Germany. Nearly everyone has a room with a loom where linen is woven, and dish and hand towels. Louis has received a pair of trousers of woollen material and I an apron of cotton. I already have a little God-child. Louis has baptized seven children and has had a marriage to perform. At these festivities rice soup with raisins and thick boiled rice are served as main dishes. Besides, there are meats, coffee cake, cakes and cookies.'

The Schmidts described the Canadian winter vividly in their letters. Since his parishes were miles apart, the pastor had to buy a horse, a harness, a top buggy, a cutter for winter driving, and a buffalo robe. He had to carry a

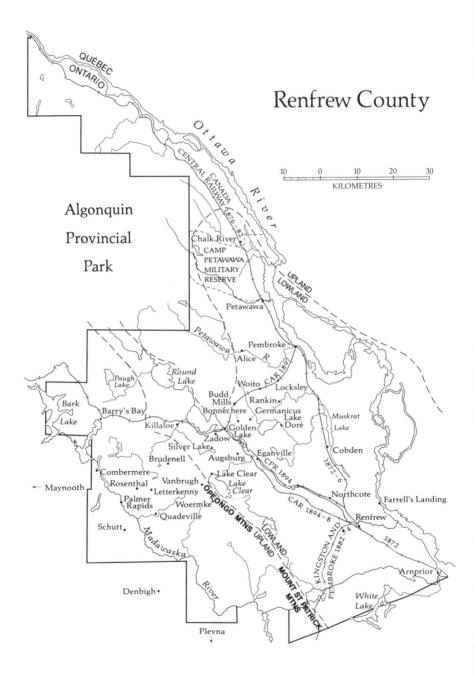

Renfrew County

QUÉBEC
ONTARIO

Ottawa River

Algonquin
Provincial
Park

CANADA CENTRAL RAILWAY 1876 - 82

10   0   10   20   30
KILOMETRES

Chalk River
CAMP
PETAWAWA
MILITARY
RESERVE

UPLAND
LOWLAND

Petawawa

Petawawa

Pembroke
Alice   R.
Woito   Locksley
Round   CAR 1897
Lake   Rankin
Paugh   Budd
Lake   Mills   Germanicus
Bonnéchere   Lake
Bark   Barry's Bay   Doré   Muskrat
Lake   Killaloe   Golden   Lake
Zadow   Lake
Silver Lake   Augsburg   Eganville   Cobden
Brudenell   CPR 1894   1872 - 6
Combermere   Lake Clear   Northcote
Rosenthal   Vanbrugh   Lake   CAR 1894 - 8   Farrell's Landing
Maynooth   Letterkenny   Clear   Renfrew
Palmer   Woermke   LOWLAND
Rapids   UPLAND   KINGSTON AND PEMBROKE 1882 - 4   1872
Quadeville   OPEONGO MTNS
Schutt   Arnprior
Madawaska   MOUNT ST PATRICK   White
Denbigh   River   MTNS   Lake
Plevna

shovel in the cutter to help in getting through snow drifts. Fur coats became a necessity, bearskin for him and black Astrakan for his wife. The only source of water in winter was snow, brought into the house for the washing of clothes. 'The home-made soap made by mother was very good soap, but without softening the hard well water with lye it was almost impossible to use, and the lye was so hard on the hands ... Only wooden wash tubs and a wooden wash board on which to rub the clothes by hand were her facilities. The water was heated in the boiler on top of the kitchen stove. Later, stoves were equipped with a water reservoir holding several pails of water, but not this stove. Mother took this drudgery as a matter of routine.'

Hattie Cramer never forgot the magic of the Christmas celebrations at Locksley, when the plain country church of Grace Lutheran would be decorated with a tall tree cut from the woods of one of its members and lit with wax candles. She remembered the Christmas Eve service when the congregation sang *Vom Himmel hoch, O du froehliche,* and exchanged the greeting 'Froehliche Weihnachten!' ('Merry Christmas!').

Mrs Cramer's saddest recollection is of leaving Alice Township. Her father became ill in 1895, and he resigned his pastorate the following year, having been advised by doctors to adopt an outdoor life. The Schmidts were persuaded by relatives to return to the United States and farm in Michigan. It was not an easy decision to make. The pastor had considered the purchase of a farm near the hamlet of Alice or the village of Pembroke, for during the nine years that the family had lived in Alice Township the value of farms in that area had risen. Farms that sold for $200 in 1887 had become worth $900 by 1896.

Polish settlers, who had begun their immigration to Renfrew County in the same years and faced the same difficulty with language, had not fared as well as the German farmers. In Ickiewicz's *Kaszubi w Kanadzie* (Kashubians in Canada), an account of the Polish settlement in Renfrew County, quotes a French Canadian employed by the Canadian government in 1872 to help a group of 300 Poles with wives and children to find lands for settlement.[55] As a fellow-Catholic, the guide admired the Poles' devoutness. He tried hard to convince them to choose unwooded, more fertile level ground. They sought instead hilly country where the soil was thin and sandy. 'Such they found further along in the county of Renfrew, in the township of Hagarty, and there they now labour in poverty. I felt sorry for these poor people, for there where I had pointed out land for them, today German settlers are receiving $300 an acre for their land, while the lands of the Polish settlers remain unproductive and next to worthless.' Ickiewicz was sure that the Polish settlers were hard-working, but commented that their desire for isolation had increased their difficulties.

William Sinn thought the same in 1860. The Poles had taken up free grants at the end of the road and even then were not progressing well. 'They have gone too far from employment, upon which they are yet dependent. They have no cattle for themselves, so necessary for logging and preparing the land properly. The land is also of the worst description.'[56] Some crops were so poor that they were not worth harvesting. A more recent study, by Father Al Rekowski, has concluded that the Polish immigrants were suspicious of government interference, eager to be left alone, and anxious to be a self-contained community.[57]

German immigrants who had arrived by October 1860 (according to William Sinn's records) had moved into Alice and Wilberforce townships, where people from Britain were clearing and farming land. Later immigrants from Germany settled on poorer ground in the northwestern townships, where Irish immigrants were pioneering. Census statistics and land records show that the German families stayed and multiplied, whereas the Irish declined in numbers, often selling out to their German neighbours before moving to urban centres.

Of all the ethnic groups in Renfrew County, the Scots most resembled the Germans; almost universally Protestant, these two groups appear to have had the thrifty ways and determination that wrought farms out of unpromising land – and a reputation for hard work that even today produces derisive remarks from the Irish and the Polish. Both Scots and Germans built spacious barns, for example, the 165-foot-long barn at Hyndford, known locally as Scotch Bush.[58] The huge log barns on a German farm in Grattan Township drew some comment from two members of the crowd at an auction sale in 1977. Speaking in the accent known as Ottawa Valley Irish, one said, 'Jesus, ye kin see that this is a German farm. Just look at the size of them barns.' His companion agreed. 'Ye'd niver see an Irishman building barns that big. Why, he'd have to half-kill himself, trying to fill 'em!'

The Reverend Ludwig Herman Gerndt, who founded most of the
Lutheran churches in Renfrew County 1861–70, and his wife, Mary
(courtesy K.G. Schutt, Killaloe)

Mr and Mrs Wilhelm Thur,
who arrived in 1859
(courtesy Dolly Maves,
Pembroke)

Mr and Mrs August Rutz,
arrived 1868
(courtesy K.G. Schutt,
Killaloe)

Mr and Mrs Wilhelm Budd,
arrived 1872
(courtesy Wesley Budd,
Budd Mills)

Mr and Mrs Ernst Bimm
arrived 1881
(courtesy Barbara Voss,
Deep River)

Adjustable fence plow plane
brought from Germany
by Rudolph G. Reinke, a
carpenter, in 1887

Egg basket brought from
Germany by Frederick and
Anstena Schroeder,
Raglan Township

OPPOSITE

top Bench-bed, North Algona Township

bottom Potash kettle on the farm of William Verch, South Algona
Township

left Stump-puller owned by Herman Stresman being used on the farm of Charles Holtz, Alice Township, in 1902 (courtesy William Stresman, Alice Township)

right Stump-puller on the South Algona farm of William Verch used by his sons as late as the 1930s

Martin Tiegs gathers a harvest of stones in Grattan Township in 1967.

Allan Kosmack on a fence of stones cleared from his family's land in Sebastopol Township between 1865 and the 1920s, and with his grandfather's stone-lifting machine

Fence-viewer Herbert Sell, appointed by Wilberforce Township, inspects the condition of a stump fence on land once farmed by Anthony Chusroskie.

Log house built by August Frivalt in Alice Township in the 1860s

CHAPTER FOUR

Buildings for a new life

Starting life again in a new land required the construction of buildings for living, for schooling and worship, for housing animals and farm equipment, for smoking meat, and for retail and manufacture. The earliest and more permanent homes built by German immigrants in eastern Ontario have few exterior features that distinguish them from houses constructed by other ethnic groups. Though studies of some other communities in Ontario have concluded that German cabins were rectangular while English cabins were square,[1] the proportions were sometimes prescribed on a Free Grant Lot and were unrelated to ethnic origin.

In the second half of the nineteenth century the common building material was the timber that covered the land so bountifully. There was plenty of stone, too, but this was seldom used for the first home; it never became the major building material as it did in the German communities of Pennsylvania.[2] Shelter was the primary concern of immigrants who arrived in a wilderness environment. If the immigrant could board nearby and work in a leisurely fashion, then a carefully built house of several rooms would result. More often new arrivals of any nationality would have to begin with the hasty construction of a simple one-roomed home, without a foundation, which would serve for the first winter at least. It was termed a *shanty* or a *log cabin*. Such a crude dwelling was described by Anna Leveridge, who brought her children from England in 1883 to join her husband in the backwoods in northern Hastings County.[3] The cabin she describes resembles the one occupied by Gotlieb Gierman and his two sons, from Prenzlau, Germany, who purchased a farm in Sebastopol Township in 1870 – and many others that exist only in the memories of descendants of the German immigrants.

Wrote Anna to her mother in England: 'Our shanty is a strange place, just a one-roomed house, made entirely of trunks of trees, 12 feet by 20, the trees just as they are felled, with the bark on. It is put up without nails or anything of the kind. The corners are hewed so that they fit one into another, mortised I think it is called. The roof is made of basswood logs hewed into troughs; the first lot laid with the bark inside and the hollow parts outside. Then over these, where the two troughs meet, other troughs are laid with the bark uppermost, so that the water cannot run through. The floor is lumber, as boards are called here; two little windows, one at each end, and a door facing south ... It is awfully cold; and the shanty being new and green, is not as warm as it will be. We are obliged to keep good fires, but firing is cheap, and it lies around the house.'

A 1½-storey log house became common throughout Upper Canada, later Ontario. It is often termed the *vernacular*.[4] The Germans of Renfrew County adapted traditional patterns of life to it. Unlike their ancestors in Europe, most of the Germans in North America separated the house and barn when they constructed the first building on the farm.[5] Though it was a long-standing tradition in Germany to have the animals and the family in the same building the custom was short-lived in the United States and Canada.[6] Of the explanations offered, one is related to the discomfort of heat from the livestock in the hotter summers of North America. Another cause for alarm may have been the danger from the fireplace, fuelled by logs that throw out sparks rather than by the smouldering peat used in Germany.

One example of this traditional style was built by Matthew Noack from West Prussia who cleared land in Hagarty Township in 1862, after deciding that his first location, near Mud Lake (a broadening of the Bonnechere River), was too low and swampy.[7] Having moved to land that was hilly and well endowed with stone, this immigrant built his first structure there 'in the Teutonic manner,' to shelter all his dependents under the same roof. Constructed of squared logs, neatly dovetailed at the corners, this rectangular building was divided into two sections of approximately equal size by an interior wall that did not reach to the rafters. It had double doors at the end that led into the stables and manger, above which was a hayloft. The half used by the family had small windows on three sides, a single door, and a chimney opening in one corner.

The fact that an owner of a house of less than two storeys paid appreciably less tax than the owner of a house with two storeys is believed to be responsible for the popularity of the 1½-storey house in the middle and late nineteenth century in Ontario.[8] With the exception of a few skilled stonemasons from Germany, such as Martin Schweig in Radcliffe Township and William Maves in Alice Township, German immigrants who built homes in the rural townships did not use the native stone; the building material was wood. They adopted styles used by others, such as the Irish, Scots, and English who were already well entrenched.

The still extant house built 1894–5 by August Tabbert in Alice Township was a simple example of this 1½-storey style.[9] It has been left in the centre of a cornfield by his descendants, as a reminder of pioneering days. This house of squared logs and dovetailed corners, with a central door at the front flanked by windows and gable ends that have windows allowing light into the upper storey, looks exactly like the log house built 1878–9 by Johnston Patterson in Admaston Township. Both young men were sons of immigrants, one from Frankfurt-on-the-Oder, Germany, and the other from Ballyhinch, Ireland, and both were able to live in their parents' homes while they worked on their own. Patterson left a record of the labours of house-building in his diary,[10] and a photographer recorded the appearance of his home in a tintype picture taken on 20 August 1880. Since the two houses look identical, the mode of construction and the sequence of tasks were probably the same.

Logs needed for construction were best felled in the winter, when snow smoothed the path of horse-drawn sleighs, one reason why summer arrivals seldom achieved a substantial house the first year. Johnston Patterson began on 14 February 1878 to haul logs to his property, and the four walls were raised on a foundation, the shingles were made, and the structure was enclosed by a roof by 23 October, before the snow fell. House-building would not have been comfortable in the cold Canadian winter. With his brothers' help, Patterson resumed work the following summer, chinking the spaces between the logs, putting in windows, partitions, and stairs, laying floors, digging out a cellar, and shopping around for a stove and pipe. The house was completed in time for his wedding, Christmas Day 1879; it was occupied, with some additions, by his descendants until 1952.

August Tabbert built his similar house fifteen years later, in 1894, and finished it in 1895. It had three rooms downstairs and three rooms upstairs and was inhabited until 1922, when the family moved into a larger house of brick.

The Tabbert, Patterson, and Noack houses had dovetailed corners, a feature that affects the durability and stance of a log building. In this type of corner the timber ends were cut in oblique notches, so that the end was nearly the original size, but sloped back along the log to a vertical cut. The notch also sloped from one side to the other. If the ends were shaped in this manner they would fit snugly together to make a tight corner, which could not be displaced in any direction. The corner was also self-draining because of the sloping form of the notches.[11] If a log structure is built on a stone foundation, as these were, the logs at the base are protected from dampness and the building is sturdy enough to stand straight for a century and more. Without a stone foundation, the building will eventually sag.

More light reached the upper storey when a window pierced the roofline of the long side of the rectangular house. With this dormer window over a central front door, this design of house was built for many years after Confederation in eastern Ontario by settlers of various origins, including Germans. One well-preserved (and slightly restored) example open to the public has been reassembled on the grounds of the Champlain Trail Museum at Pembroke. It was built by Anthony Chusroskie and his son, Simon, on Lot 6, Concession 22, Wilberforce Township, near Rankin. This was the third dwelling that this family had built and occupied on this site, the culmination of many years of toil; their story is probably typical of many German families.

Anthony Chusroskie and his wife, Henrietta Vonch, had immigrated with their first child, Simon, in 1858.[12] Since it does not appear on the 1860 list of William Sinn, the family was probably living in a community where it could earn money before it acquired land. On 1 December 1881, a Simon 'Kossoroski' purchased 47½ acres from Evan L. Edwards in Wilberforce Township for $200.[13] The Chusroskie family must have been living on this site earlier than the purchase date because it was listed in the (spring) 1881 census; the householder was Anthony, 55, and the oldest son, Simon, 25, was living with his parents. The Chusroskies would have been eligible for a free grant of 200 acres, under the homestead acts of 1868 or 1880, if they had settled in one of the townships where vacant land was available. Their choice of this location, about nine miles from Pembroke, must have had some advantages that outweighed the purchase price. It may have been the desire to live within a community of German-speaking neighbours (the Langs on one side, the Behnkes on the other) or the proximity to Pembroke, which could provide opportunities for work and worship. The Chusroskies were Catholic; there was no Catholic church in Wilberforce Township, or in the adjoining townships of Alice and North Algona, or in the more westerly townships of Renfrew County into which the German immigrants of the 1870s and 1880s were pouring. Members of the Chusroskie family walked to Pembroke to attend services at St Columbkille's Cathedral.[14]

'I don't think that they went very often,' confessed a granddaughter, 87-year-old Sister Clothilde. She recalled that the language spoken in the home had always been Low German and knew that the immigrant couple with six children had lived in a scoop-roofed shanty in their first year on the land. After her grandfather had built a more substantial log house, the shanty was used as a milk-house. The second home was later occupied by livestock after her grandfather and her father constructed the third home on the property, which was dismantled and moved to Pembroke in 1965.[15] Such progress had involved hard work and sacrifice. Sister Clothilde related that her grandmother had worked as a servant in the home of a Pembroke lawyer, Peter White, even when she had a family; she had walked the nine miles home on some occasions with a 25-pound sack of flour on her back.

The third house is a 1½-storey log dwelling with a central door leading to a staircase that divides the downstairs into two rooms and leads to the bedrooms above. An attached summer kitchen at the back is also made of squared logs; this was a common type of addition that produced either a T- or L-shaped floor plan, and the 'tail' might be further extended by the addition of a woodshed. The Chusroskie house, with its dovetailed corners, was so sound when it was moved that little replacement was needed; even the flooring in the upper storey is original.

Mr and Mrs Anthony Chusroskie continued to live in the home of their married son in their retirement years, a custom typical in German families. When the 'old age pension scheme' was introduced in Canada in 1929, it was noted in Renfrew County that North Algona Township had the unique distinction of having no applicants for pensions.[16] 'This township is peopled for the most part by German settlers or their descendants, an industrious thrifty class of citizens who, while perhaps not attaining great wealth, are for the most part comfortably situated and as a rule provide reasonably for the requirements of old age.

The transfer of the ownership and responsibilities of a farm from the immigrant to a younger generation, usually a son, was sometimes marked by the preparation of a 'maintenance mortgage.' This document was designed to ensure that the elderly parent or parents were maintained in the style and comforts to which they were accustomed; otherwise their successor would forfeit the farm. This practice was not universal. Some parents were content to sign over their farms for the nominal payment of one dollar 'and natural love and affection,' but others were not so trusting. They may have suspected that filial affection might not last as long as their natural life spans or that the death of one partner might result in hardship for the survivor. In some cases the maintenance mortgage required that an attached residence be built for the sole use of the retired couple, so that it could enjoy privacy and independence for at least the summer months. Such additions, known as doddy-houses (a corruption of the word 'grossdawdy,' meaning grandfather),[17] are in Renfrew County found only on German farms. This prac-

tice has also been found in other German communities in Ontario, such as
the Mennonite farmland in York County.[18]

It was not always necessary to build a separate residence for the mortgagees, especially if the owner of the farm was widowed. Charlotte Auguste
Kruger Zadow Zillmer was a widow when she emigrated to Canada in 1881,
at the age of 55, with four adult sons. She purchased a farm in South
Algona Township where she lived with her third son, Edward, then aged
25, who married the following year.[19] In 1892 'Gustie' Zillmer transferred
the property of ninety acres, comprising Lot 15, Concession 8, to Edward
and his wife, Henrietta, for the sum of $1 on condition that they performed
and fulfilled a number of covenants, terms, and stipulations outlined in a
handwritten mortgage prepared in duplicate.[20] The elderly woman was to
be allowed to occupy the room that she had always used, and the mort-
gagors promised to keep it comfortably warmed and furnished with the
necessary bed, bedding, and furniture. In the event of the house being
burned down, or from any cause becoming uninhabitable, the new owners
would construct another house on the same site, with a similar comfortable
room. The widow was to be furnished with board, clothing, care, and
medical attention. She was to be paid annually $6 in cash, the first instal-
ment to be made by 1 January 1893. She should be able to pass about the
house and premises and use the well in accordance with her own wishes,
and her friends and acquaintances should be allowed to visit her. One of the
more difficult duties to define or assess must have been the one that stated:
'The said mortgagor shall treat her kindly and act towards her as a dutiful
son ought to do towards his mother.'

If the 66-year-old Mrs Zillmer decided to leave the premises and live elsewhere, her son, Edward, was obliged to provide her with the cash and a
long list of supplies to be delivered to her new address. In fact, 'Gustie' did
leave the farm (sometime before the death of Edward in 1899) to live with
her youngest son, August, in Eganville. August had been the witness to the
handwritten mortgage and must therefore have been aware that this list of
supplies had to be provided in lieu of the board and care that she had received in Edward's home. From his ninety-acre farm the father of eight
children had to deliver to his mother every year the following items, 'of the
best quality': 500 pounds of roller wheat floor, 100 pounds of fresh pork, 50
pounds of fresh mutton, 50 pounds of butter, 15 bushels of potatoes, 50
pounds of salt, 5 pounds of tea not to cost less than 30 cents a pound, 25
pounds of white sugar, 10 pounds of clean, washed wool, 10 pounds of
soap, 10 quarts of coal oil, 5 dozen eggs, 5 cords of two-feet hardwood, and
5 cords of two-feet dry pinewood. After his death, Edward's family continued to live in the log farm-house, which was later occupied by his son,

with a wife and nine children. The matriarch of the Zadow family died in 1905 and was 'respectably buried' (one of the terms of the mortgage) in a Lutheran cemetery at Eganville.

Harmony between two or even three generations was never a problem with the Kosmack family in Sebastopol Township. 'We all lived under the same roof,' said Allan Kosmack, pointing to the large log house covered by boards constructed by his grandfather, Albert Kosmack, in the nineteenth century. A professional photographer from Denbigh, 6 September 1894, pictured the pioneer couple and daughters standing in a field of cabbages in front of a spacious home: opened windows have potted plants on every windowsill.[21] The name Vanbrugh appears on one wall of the house, signifying that this was the post office. Waiting in the driveway is a horse-drawn buggy, with the couple's son, Frederick, holding the reins.

When Mr and Mrs Albert Kosmack conveyed the farm to their son on 29 June 1905, the purchase price was the nominal sum of $10, and there was no long list of duties to be fulfilled.[22] The buildings, livestock, vehicles, harness, and farming implements were all transferred with just one stipulation. Frederick (a bachelor) agreed not to sell or dispose of any of these goods and chattels without his father's consent.

Some families decided that separate residences on the same property were a more sensible arrangement. So it was with the Boehme family of Raglan Township when August Boehme transferred his 200-acre farm on Lots 13 and 14, Concession 17, to his son, Carl, and his wife, 'Poline,' in March 1905.[23] 'It was considered wise to have separate houses,' remarked a grandson, Oscar.[24] The handwritten agreement was tailored to the needs of the people concerned. Living far from villages and stores, August Boehme was to be provided with one pair of 'schoes' (hand made) each year and every two years one 'suet' of cloth.[25] He could retain all his carpenter and blacksmith tools, important to a man who had earned his living as a furniture-maker before settling down to farm. He had already built a house to be used exclusively by the retired couple, a small two-storey dwelling parallel to the original home that he had occupied with his first wife and his numerous children.

When a retiring farmer had married a second time, and his wife was not a parent of the new owner, there was reason for caution. The stepmother's future could be guaranteed by a maintenance mortgage written in minute detail and by the construction of a doddy-house. Having a neighbour witness the mortgage (and perhaps retain a copy of it) might be a further safeguard. The handwritten mortgage had been witnessed by a neighbouring farmer, Martin Budarick, who made his oath before a Raglan Township justice of the peace, Charles Schutt.

August Boehme died 3 May 1907, little more than two years after the mortgage was signed. His second wife, Henrietta, was entitled to all the benefits due to the older couple. The yearly provision of food and fuel, access to a well, the cultivation of a garden, the promise of transport both in winter and summer, equal rights to an orchard, and the procurement of one cow and two sheep that had to be 'changed when necessary' were all hers to enjoy.

By the time Johann Gotlieb Lipke, aged 72, of Wilberforce Township was planning his retirement in December 1912, maintenance mortgages were typed on printed forms, and his was witnessed in Pembroke before a commissioner of oaths.[26] Once again a neighbouring farmer, Henry Kutschke, was present as a witness. Lipke was twelve years older than his second wife, Louisa,[27] by whom he had fathered six children. His first wife, Wilhelmina, had also borne him six children,[28] and it was to the oldest son, August, that he sold his 208-acre farm for the sum of $1, subject to a maintenance mortgage. Under the terms of a five-page document, the son and his wife, Bertha, agreed to provide for the older couple, on the same land and within the same premises, a long list of food, fuels, services, and labour. Because it is written in such detail, this mortgage gives a revealing glimpse of rural life in those years when small farms on the Canadian Shield were virtually self-contained. Johann Lipke had been toiling on his land since 1869 at least, for he received his free grant (under the Homestead Act of 1868 which required five years' residence) on 19 November 1874. The labour he expended on this patch of wooded wilderness in Germanicus can be seen still in the pastures cleared of trees, the fences made of stones and split rails, the hand-hewn beams of the barns, and the 1½-storey farm-house of squared logs where he raised twelve children. By 1912 the immigrant from Germany, who came to Canada in March 1863,[29] was ready to retire and hand on the farm's major responsibilities. His son agreed to look after the insurance and maintenance of the property; he also promised to provide the senior couple and the survivor with all the day-to-day essentials for a comfortable life, including the construction of an addition to the log farm-house for their sole use.
August had to supply the following necessities:

Each year: four barrels of wheaten flour of such quality as may from time to time be ground out of his own grist, 30 bushels of potatoes delivered by the Mortgagor in the cellar of the house in said lands – 50 pounds of beef on or before the first day of December – 200 pounds of pork on or before the fifteenth day of November – one fat sheep on or before the fifteenth day of October – eight pounds of wool per year – 18

*pounds of tea at a price not less than 25 cents per lb. – 100 pounds of
granulated sugar – one bag of coarse salt – 10 gallons of coal oil – 3
gallons of vinegar – Twenty ($20.00) dollars in cash – as much firewood
as the Mortgagees or the survivor of them may require cut ready to put
into the stove delivered in the wood yard on said lands – 1 dozen of eggs*
per week *between the first of February and the first day of November in
each year – 4 bars of Sunlight soap* per month *or of such other soap as
may be required by the Mortgagees or the survivor but not to exceed the
current price for Sunlight soap* (PROVIDED *that at the death of one of the
said Mortgagees only one-half of the above, except firewood, shall be
supplied to the Survivor).*

The mortgage would be satisfied if the senior Lipkes, or the survivor,
were allowed the following services and privileges:

*The use of one cook stove – 1 milk cow to be fed by the mortgagor to be
chosen if desired by the mortgagees or the survivor each spring from the
cows of the mortgagor – one-half of the dishes in the house at present,
and permit the mortgagees and the survivor to use one-half of the house
at present on said lands being two rooms upstairs and two rooms
downstairs on the west side of the house, and one-half of the cellar with
access thereto and therefrom for all purposes, and permit the mortgagees
and the survivor to keep on the said lands the bees now there which
shall continue to be the property of the mortgagees or the survivor, and
the use of two gardens one at the west end of the house called the Lee
Garden and the other north-west of the house alongside of the barn as
both are at present fenced, with free access thereto and therefrom and to
the barnyard either from the house or from the said gardens, and will
permit the mortgagee or the survivor to obtain water from the pump at
the house on said lands and from the well near the creek, thereon by a
convenient path through the front garden if desired.*

As long as they lived on this property, they were to be provided with a
horse and buggy, at least six times a year, for the purpose of driving to
Golden Lake or Eganville, presumably for shopping. These would be
journeys of two miles or ten miles respectively.

The mortgagor would plough or cause to be ploughed both gardens each
spring and manure them every second spring. He would give the mortgagees and the survivor six chairs of those in the house at the time and give
each of the unmarried daughters a wedding.

The labours of August included construction on or before 15 May 1913 of a frame cook house, 10 feet by 12 feet and 10 feet high with a shingle roof, for the use of Mr and Mrs Johann Lipke or the survivor. This, the doddy-house, was duly built, with a separate entrance and a stoop and a chimney that must have accommodated a wood stove. It still stands, attached to the summer kitchen of the original 1½-storey log farm-house, but the step-mother had little use of it.

Louisa Lipke died 3 December 1913, aged 60, just one year after the main-tenance mortgage had been signed. Johann Lipke continued to live on the property for another fifteen years, supplied with all his needs by a dutiful son and daughter-in-law and faithfully attending St John's Lutheran Church at Germanicus until 1927. The mortgage had specified that the mortgagees or survivor must be driven to church at least every second Sunday. Johann Lipke could have chosen to live with another of his children, according to the mortgage. It stated that if the survivor left this property to live with another child, then the mortgagor had to furnish the survivor at the other address with flour, potatoes, beef, pork, sheep, tea, sugar, salt, coal oil, vinegar, cash, firewood, cook stove, dishes, chairs, eggs, and soap, but only if the other address was in the county of Renfrew. With this proviso the choice was small. When Johann Lipke died 31 March 1928, aged 87, only three sons and three daughters were listed as mourners. At least four children had predeceased him, and many of his sons and daughters had moved out of Renfrew County – to southern Ontario and the United States.

August Lipke and his wife, Bertha, had worked hard to earn their inheri-tance. This small farm was almost self-sufficient, according to the recollec-tions of their son, Eric. 'Crops were many – wheat, winter rye, oats, peas, flax, buckwheat, barley, corn, hay, beets, mangels, potatoes and a kitchen garden ... Flocks [of sheep] were usually 25 to 30, two usually black, so no dye needed – used for socks, mitts, sweaters – fleeces were sold, lambs sold in the autumn were also a good source of income.'

Johann Lipke had built a loom. His grandson observed: 'The weaving was chiefly for their own use, and mainly for clothing, both wool and linen. Woollen blankets were double thickness and padded and extremely warm, usually a light golden brown with red stripes. These were also used for covers in sleighs during winter; they would use these to cover the horses, waiting in towns and in church sheds. Linen towels, pillow cases, sheets, beautiful red and white or blue and white bedspreads, tablecloths woven in patterns. Everyone had their own loom.'

On the Lipke farm there were no maple trees, but bees were kept, the number of hives ranging from fifteen to twenty-five, and sweetening was obtained from their honey. All farms had some cows for milking; the Lipkes had a herd of ten, which meant that they had a surplus of butter for sale.

Beef cattle were raised. Another source of income for such small farms was provided by timber. Poplar, spruce, and balsam were sold for pulp and fire-wood; cedar shingles, railroad ties, and fence and telephone poles were also harvested from the Lipke's 208-acre property.

Johann's oldest son, August, was the blacksmith in the family, working at a stone-walled forge built by his brother, Frank, at a safe distance from the house. 'He did all manner of ironwork, for himself and for many who came to him – horse-shoeing, farm implements, keys, hinges, tools, whatever,' recalled the grandson, Eric.

The 1920s were years of modest prosperity on the maturing small farms of Renfrew County, as evidenced by the churches and schools constructed then. In the western and northern townships, where the German immi-grants had settled in the greatest numbers, work on the farms continued to be performed by hand, by horses, and by steam-engine. Photographs taken on the Lipke farm during this period illustrate some of these tasks. The second owners of the farm, August and Bertha Lipke, were recorded pic-tured on the stoop outside the doddy-house, both looking much more care-worn than in their wedding photograph of November 1905. August, dressed in working clothes, stands besides a cream churn, the contents of which are protected by a rag which indicates that the farm still had a dairy herd. His wife is working at a spinning-wheel, most probably spinning wool, and be-hind her is a clock-reel wool-winder, made for her by her uncle, William Born, of Alice Township. Another picture from this period shows a steam-engine outside the granary, one of the log barns built by Johann Lipke, whose axe marks can still be seen on the squared log beams. The steam-engine, which visited farms to thresh the grain crops, belonged to the nearby Schutt family. 'We threshed at every farm in Wilberforce Township in the 1920s,' claimed K.G. Schutt one day when he was manipulating one of these monsters at the Petawawa Steam Club's annual show.[30] In the fore-ground of the picture is the water barrel, so necessary in keeping the boiler filled; the steam-engine is equipped with oil lamps, for they threshed from dawn to dusk, and dusk came early in the autumn months when crops were gathered. Only flax and navy beans were threshed by hand, according to the grandson.

The laborious methods of intensive cropping on small farms continued into the third generation, as did the tradition of looking after the elderly members of the family. It seldom happened that a property passed from an immigrant to a grandchild, if the owner had sons, but it did occur in the household of Karl Raglan and his wife, who lived in Wilberforce Township. The Raglans had welcomed home their daughter, Mary Lemke, after she

had been widowed with a young child, William. The boy, who grew up
with his grandparents and mother, assumed the responsibilities and maintenance of the family farm when he was 27 years old and still unmarried.[31]
He was obliged to promise that he would compensate four uncles, one aunt,
and his mother if they survived the original owners of the farm, who were
their parents. He also agreed to shoulder all the traditional obligations to
support the retired couple.

'The lawyer felt that I had paid a lot,' said William Edward Lemke, who
signed a maintenance mortgage on 24 April 1923.[32] There were the usual
provisions to allow the retired farmer and his wife to draw water from the
well, to be given firewood, to have a physician summoned when necessary,
and to be given a decent burial. The articles that the grandson had to supply
to the mortgagees while both were alive (and half the quantity to the survivor) were similar to the list of necessities required by the Zadow mortgage
of 1892 and the Lipke mortgage of 1912. Little had changed in thirty-one
years. Each year the Raglans were entitled to 3 barrels of good wheat flour,
15 bags of potatoes, 200 pounds of good pork, 100 pounds of beef, 10
pounds of mutton, 12 pounds of sugar, 4 pounds of tea, 12 pounds of wool,
and 12 dozen eggs; they were to receive 2 pounds of butter a week and 1
quart of unskimmed milk daily.

It had not been considered necessary for the grandson to build a doddy-
house or a separate dwelling for the retirees. By the terms of the mortgage
he allowed them to have the use of two rooms upstairs on the east side of
the house and the use of the kitchen stove until he married. Once he was
wed, he would have sole right to the stove, and the older couple would have
to provide their own cooking stove and place it in their own rooms.

The tradition of caring for the elderly was not always spelled out in a
document, with or without a lawyer. It continues today in a less structured
arrangement, and usually the different generations choose to live in
separate buildings on the same property. On Karl Raglan's farm there are
now three houses. Very few doddy-houses have survived the test of time.
Because they were constructed at least a generation after the main house,
the addition to the log farm-house was often a framework of sawn timber
and not as sturdy. If the old house was sold for its logs and demolished, the
three-sided doddy-house would be left to sway in the wind until the next
winter's snowfall caused it to collapse. A two-storey doddy-house of this
type was built by Otto Schroeder on a log farm-house on the Ottawa and
Opeongo Road, which he had bought from an Irish family named Kelly in
1917. It was constructed for the use of the owner's retired parents in the
summer.[33] There was no maintenance mortgage that obligated Schroeder to
build this extra wing for his parents' privacy, for he had bought the farm

and not inherited it.[34] Nevertheless, he followed a tradition that has been observed in other German communities in North America. Because the building materials in Renfrew County were primarily wood, not stone or brick as in Pennsylvania or southern Ontario, the doddy-houses built in the county have not lasted when their use became obsolete.

Those who have studied the architecture of barns in North America have concluded that they owe their form partly to the farmer's ethnic origin.[35] The German barn found in Pennsylvania and southern Ontario has been described as a two-storey structure, with stables on the ground floor and a threshing floor above, with a forebay. While this style, in which the upper storey protruded over the lower, is not typical of German farms in Renfrew County, there was one built on the farm of Ferdinand Biesenthal in Alice Township.

A single-storey structure of squared logs, which could be stacked in a variety of sizes and shapes, was a common type of shelter constructed for crops or livestock. Wood was plentiful and cheap. (Biesenthal's farm had at least one such log barn, which was older than the frame two-storey barn of the Pennsylvania style.) Small log structures, such as smoke-houses and sheds for wagons, hens, and hogs, could be added when time permitted, with lumber from the farmer's own property, essentially at no cost. The result would be a motley collection of log buildings that cluster around a farm-house.

One building that is characteristic of German farms in Renfrew County is the smoke-house, still commonly seen because it is still used or was until very recently. It is not an infallible guide to identification, for some farms lack a smoke-house, but when one is present it is sure sign that a German family has been living there. The popularity of pork was demonstrated by its prominence in the list of foods itemized in the maintenance mortgages. There was a steady demand for salted pork in eastern Ontario in the nineteenth century, from the logging companies that needed to supply food to their men in the shanties. But the pork prepared by German families for their own eating was preserved by smoking it, a process that could be used to improve the flavour of sausages as well as cuts of meat.

The smoke-house is a small, windowless building, always placed at a safe distance from the home or other farm buildings because of the danger of fire. It is sometimes located in the centre of the barnyard; it may be built in a field and surrounded by a fence to prevent the approach of livestock. Since the pigs are killed in the fall, the smoke-house is used during the months of cold weather (when a ground cover of snow also acts as a safety

precaution) for the curing of sausages, ham, and bacon. The supply of fuel,
the butchering, and the preparation of meat are done ahead of time.

A wooden sausage-stuffer,[36] made by immigrants such as August Ziebell
of Alice Township, consisted of a small and upright wooden barrel, the
staves reinforced by metal bands. Mounted on a four-legged pine stand, the
barrel was filled with ground meat; a hardwood plunger was swung down
into the barrel in order to force the meat out of an exit hole and into the
tube, to which was fixed the casing. The cleaned intestines of the pigs were
the casings or skins that would hold the sausages that were to be smoked
from hooks in the ceiling in the smoke-house. About five or six feet long,
the wooden sausage-stuffer was a bulky tool; it was supplanted by metal
grinders, patented in the 1880s, which were much smaller and were clamped
to a rigid surface when in use.

Two different styles of these metal grinders are used by branches of the
Zadow family who undertake sausage-making as a communal activity on a
farm in South Algona Township.[37] One man would be busy cutting up the
hams outside, while his wife and several relatives prepared the sausages inside the farmhouse. 'We do it the same way our grandparents did it,' said
Mrs Walter Zadow, who was showing a young son how it was done. From
a huge basin of ground pork, which had been seasoned with condiments
and summer savory, two groups of workers at each end of the kitchen table
were pressing the minced meat into metal grinders, from which the product
was squeezed through a tube into the casings, still made from washed
intestines.

A steel mincing grinder and stuffing attachment patented in 1886 and
1888 had been used by three generations on the farm of Mr and Mrs William
Lemke in Wilberforce Township. First used by Elizabeth Raglan, and later
by Mary Lemke, the tools for preparation of smoked sausages proved indispensable to the third generation during the Depression, when selling
sausages was much more profitable than selling meat. 'I had a pig that
weighed 360 pounds dressed that sold for only one dollar,' recalled Mr
Lemke; but smoked pork sausage could be sold for 20 cents a pound, with
the help of friends in Windsor who distributed it. The Lemkes' smoke-house
is of a style popular in the area where they live, on the Greenlake Road; the
small square building has a chimney in the centre of the roof. One of their
neighbours, Mrs Raymond Ashick, who has an identical smoke-house, is
sure that they were built by Martin Schimmens, a carpenter at Rankin.
Constructed from sawn timber, the boards either vertical or horizontal, this
style is found in many townships in Renfrew County and so was probably
built to specifications.

Some of the earliest smoke-houses were constructed from squared logs, wasteful of wood, but easy to assemble. One of these log smoke-houses is still used on the farm of Mr and Mrs Edgar Pilatske, South Algona Township, for the curing of sausages, bacon, and ham, in that order. Sausages are smoked in December, soon after the pigs have been killed in November, for otherwise the sausages will spoil; the fire is kept stoked four times a day, from early morning until bedtime, and may be continued for two weeks. The Pilatskes' smoke-house of notched square logs has no chimney, and when it is in use the smoke exits through the back of the building by a gap produced by the removal of a board in the gable end. The bacons have been rubbed with brine before they are smoked, usually in January, but the hams have been soaked in brine for two weeks or more before they are suspended from hooks in the smoke. The time required for smoking bacon and ham is much shorter than that needed for sausages. The Pilatskes prefer to use green maple as their fuel, that is, wood that has been freshly cut and still has sap in it; they feel that this gives a better flavour.[38]

The surest sign that a smoke-house is still in use is a pile of firewood beside it and the smoky smell that lingers in the shed long after the fire is out. The choice of fuel is an individual one, most people claiming that rotted maple is by far the best, while a few will argue that elm gives the best flavour. Hardwood sawdust is popular with Mr and Mrs Adolph Ott who live in Wilberforce Township, about two miles east of Eganville.[39] When they bought a farm there from an Irish family named McCabe in 1938, there was no smoke-house on the property, so the Otts built one. Inside their frame shed the fire is contained in a large iron cauldron sunk into the ground, and a spade is kept handy for shovelling out the ashes. Though the Otts built their smoke-house of sawn timber, some of the later structures were made of materials that would ensure more safety, such as bricks or concrete blocks. Such solid, fireproof buildings had the drawback that they could not be moved. When Mr and Mrs Herbert Sell decided to leave their three-storey farm-house and barns on Highway 41, Wilberforce Township, in order to move to a small and modern home a mile away in 1978, they were able to uproot their wooden smoke-house from the apple orchard and take it with them.[40]

Among the many smoke-houses on the German farms in Renfrew County that are no longer used are some fine ones made of squared logs which would also be difficult to move. One excellent example was erected by August Klatt from Pomerania on his farm in Raglan Township;[41] the squared logs are dovetailed at the corners as carefully as in any house. In addition to a central chimney, there are square holes in three walls to allow the escape of smoke, and the entrances to this two-tiered structure are protected by an overhanging roof. A similar log smoke-house, with an upper and lower chamber, was located in a bank behind the stopping-place, once run by Elwood Schmidt in Sebastopol Township; the entrance to the upper level was at the rear, at the top of the bank, but the central door, at ground level, that leads to the smoking chamber was again protected by an over-hanging roof. Present occupants on these farms are unable to confirm whether the upper storey was used for drying fruits, as on the German farms in Pennsylvania.

The use of squared logs as building material, to shelter families, livestock, crops, and food preparation on the farms, extended to the construction of places of worship and education as well. Once the basic needs for survival had been satisfied, and when a settlement of adjacent German-speaking families had reached a sizeable number, the desire for schools and churches was met by the erection of a log building or buildings for communal pur-poses. As the exploring Lutheran missionary had noted in his report for the year 1861: 'The settlements of Alice, Wilberforce and Algona, and the other townships in the County of Renfrew are making steady progress. Three congregations of the Evangelical Lutheran Synod of Canada have been established. The larger commune near Pembroke has received a free grant of fifteen acres as a site for a Church, School and Burial Ground; the other two congregations have also made application for a like grant.'[42]

Four years later, when a group of German farmers in Sebastopol Town-ship was queried by a government immigration agent about the condition of their community, the reply contained the following comment: 'We have now got our church and school established, which is very encouraging and gives much satisfaction to the people.'[43] In this community, called Van-brugh, where the Lutheran missionary had held the first services in a log school-house, the farmers were extremely well educated, and in 1864–5 they hired a German-speaking clergyman, Dr A. Schaffraneck, to give their children a public school education.[44] But this was unusual.

As one grandson of the German immigrant Gustave Tiegs was later to remark, 'Our grandparents probably never dreamed that their children AND their grandchildren would have a much poorer education than they did.'[45] Immigrants from the German states had come from a land where, even in their childhood, attendance at school had been enforced by law. Every child had to begin its education at the age of 5 years and continue until the clergy-man of the parish affirmed that a certain standard had been reached, generally by the age of 14.[46] Frederick the Great was credited with having introduced an organized system of national education which had started in Silesia and had spread into other provinces administered by Prussia in the 1850s. It was thought to be superior to that of the lower and middle classes of England and Scotland, from whom many other immigrants had been drawn to Canada.

Not until provincial legislation in 1871 established the office of public school inspector for every county in Ontario was there much attempt to introduce standards across Renfrew County. Then, as now, the headquarters of administration was in Pembroke. The vast majority of the German families lived on the land, where rural townships could afford only the basic amenities. There were problems that were common to all poor farming areas, where the population was thinly scattered and cash was a scarce commodity. Added to these obstacles was the problem of language for children raised in homes where the parents spoke only German. They had difficulty in understanding teachers who spoke only English, and their reading and writing skills were poor even when they became bilingual. The seventeen primary school superintendents appointed by Renfrew county council after it broke away from Lanark in 1866 were all English-speaking,[47] most of them clergymen of the Roman Catholic, Methodist, Presbyterian, or Anglican congregations that ministered to the settlers of British origin.

The county's first school inspector, 1871–6, was E.H. Jenkyns, and the second was Robert George Scott, 1877–1908. Their annual reports have left an account of an education system that was ill-equipped, badly staffed, and elementary in every sense of the word.[48] 'Trustees have hitherto considered that they have done all that the law requires if they have managed to put up a few logs to shelter the pupils from the rain or cold of winter,' reported Mr Jenkyns. 'They have only in two in three instances provided the necessary outside conveniences. I cannot mention one section in the County where there is any great anxiety manifested to make the schoolhouse neat, attractive and complete in all its arrangements.'

One school-house that comes close to this description is the one built in the nineteenth century in School Section 3, Petawawa Township. Constructed of squared logs, whitewashed on the exterior, it had the necessary outdoor conveniences in use until it was closed in 1965. The exact date of its construction is unknown; the deed for the land was registered by the school trustees 13 February 1892,[49] but the school may have been built earlier than that. Judging from the assessment rolls, Petawawa Township was settled almost exclusively by German immigrants. Henry Mohns, born there in 1895, was a grandson of a German immigrant and attended a log school in School Section 4 in that township. He recalled how one harassed schoolma'am used to travel home to recuperate every weekend. 'All the children spoke German, except for a few Indian children, and they didn't speak English either!' he remarked.[50]

Throughout the northern and western townships of the county, where the German immigrants settled, the proliferation of school sections was inevitable because of the distances that had to be walked by the children. Though Inspector Scott frequently grumbled about the expansion, additional school sections were organized. Some built during his career continued to be used until the closing down and final amalgamation of rural schools in 1968.

An old record book[51] reveals how cheaply and easily a new school was organized and built in the newly formed School Section 6 of South Algona Township, where the population consisted of German families. A meeting was held at the home of August Michaelis on 29 December 1897, and three trustees were appointed – Charles Frobel for one year, Fred Kerno for two years, and William Griese for three years. On 12 February 1898, the trustees met to choose a school site. A subsequent meeting of ratepayers approved the site chosen, Lot 11, Concession 3, and this half-acre was purchased from William Stahlke for $1. Another meeting of ratepayers, 7 July 1898, passed a resolution authorizing the trustees to borrow $350 to build a schoolhouse. It was constructed by volunteer labour, most certainly that year, for at a meeting in the school, 28 December 1898, the ratepayers agreed to donate stove wood. The first teacher was Tim McGrath of Ruby, a nearby hamlet; he was, of course, Irish. One of the school's first pupils recalled McGrath's tribulations. 'We all talked German at home and at school too, if we had the chance,' said Mrs Gustave (Amanda) Sell, celebrating her sixtieth wedding anniversary at the time that the school closed down. She had been one of the ten Stahlke children in the first enrolment.

With the exception of the First Baptist Church, Hagarty Township, which was built of local stone in 1899,[52] early German churches were constructed of wood, usually of squared logs. The simple style of these log churches, with an entrance at the gable end, was similar to that of the early schools; though many were replaced by brick buildings in the first quarter of the twentieth century, a number of log churches outlasted their congregations. As a result, some of them have been demolished.

St John's Lutheran Church on the Ottawa and Opeongo Road in Sebastopol Township is a log church that escaped the threat of demolition in 1978. The congregation there can date its history back to the years of Reverend Gerndt's ministry in 1862, but the church was not built until 1890.[53] Twelve members of the congregation aided the two contractors in erecting the structure, which was dedicated 17 August. The church did not have a resident minister but was part of a parish that included Eganville, Grattan, and Silver Lake, all served by the same man. At first the congregation stood to worship or brought small benches from home to be seated during the service; later it purchased benches made by August Quade which were plain and straight-backed. The altar and the pulpit were made by a German immigrant, Fred Morlock; a plaque reading 'Gott ist die Liebe' was carved by William Schroeder; and wooden candelabra held tallow candles poured by women in the congregation.

With only a small congregation to pay for the cost, extensive renovations were made in 1962 in preparation for the centennial of its foundation. The final year of regular worship was 1971, when the last report of the treasurer listed thirty-nine contributing households. The church was closed, and its members began to attend the churches in Augsburg or Eganville instead. The building became the property of the Grattan parish, and since it was constructed of squared timbers it attracted attention from those who make a business of taking down and reconstructing old log buildings. To save St John's from destruction a group of ten former parishioners raised the necessary money, $2,500, in 1978, to purchase the building and maintain it as a place of worship for occasional services.[54] Clapboarded and painted white since the early 1900s, this Lutheran church is still a landmark in the Opeongo hills of Sebastopol Township, one survivor of the numerous rural churches that German immigrants built from the trees that covered the countryside of Renfrew County.

In rural Pennsylvania the log churches built by German immigrants – and indeed the domestic buildings also – are now so rare that a few have been carefully restored and identified by a plaque. One such log church is the Byerland Mennonite Meetinghouse in Lancaster County, built about 1755 and used until 1848. The German settlement in Pennsylvania began a century earlier than in eastern Ontario, and the tax lists of 1788–9 reveal that the rural areas of the German heartland of Pennsylvania also were characterized by log houses and log barns in the early years of clearing the land and cultivation.[55] The 1½-storey house that was to become so well known in southern Ontario had been built in Pennsylvania too; in fact the German settlement in Upper Canada mimicked the styles of frame barns with overhanging forebay. In both these areas, the wooden buildings were replaced or improved when the farms matured and the owners became more prosperous; the lack of progression in Renfrew County, vis-à-vis other German settlements, may be explained by the limited success of agriculture, in the more northern climate on rough country.

Wood was the most easily obtainable building material in nineteenth-century Ontario, an attribute that made it attractive to settlers beginning a new life with little cash. Building with logs has been described as the

'Cinderella' of architectural history, because it was plain and functional, a style that would be abandoned when the occupant could afford something better. In York County the change from log houses to stone houses took place in the mid-nineteenth century, two or three generations after the initial period of settlement;[56] brick was considered even more desirable than stone, especially when transportation from brick yards in Toronto became feasible. In the townships northwest of Toronto, the census of 1861 showed that the number of log houses had declined since 1851. But at this time eastern Upper Canada was still in the throes of early settlement.

In its report of 1881, the Ontario Agricultural Commission noted that the rate of progress in farm buildings corresponded closely to the length of period of settlement, at least in those districts where the course of improvement had not been retarded by natural disadvantages. Inquiries by the eighteen commissioners in southern Ontario found that about 45 per cent of the dwellings of the farmers in that part of the province were of brick or stone or first-class frame.

The authors of *Rural Ontario*,[57] while admitting that they did not visit the 'rocky and forested wildness of the Laurentian Shield,' photographed some log farm-houses and out-buildings in southern Ontario that were no longer in use; they were shown as examples of the type of building that prevailed in each section of the province as it was opened up and for a generation or two afterward. The authors concluded that the ordinary inhabitant of Upper Canada in the nineteenth century did not admire log buildings and welcomed their passing as a sign of progress. In Renfrew County, many of the log farm-houses that are still inhabited have been concealed by a covering such as frame, stucco, or brick, chiefly to improve the appearance. The barns and other out-buildings have not received such treatment. The landscape is still characterized by buildings made of wood, a sign that the agricultural economy did not advance much beyond the expectations of the first settlers.

right Scoop-roofed cook-house (with split and hollowed logs overlaid concave – convex) on the farm of Wilhelm Budd, Wilberforce Township

Scoop-roofed shanty built 1870 by the Gierman family, Sebastopol Township

OPPOSITE *top and bottom*

Matthew Noack's house-cum-barn, built 1862 in Hagarty Township

Stone farm-house built 1882 by stonemason Martin Schweig, Radcliffe Township, and occupied by three generations of his family over the last century

House of squared logs built 1894–5 by August Tabbert, Petawawa Township

Johnston Patterson and his wife outside their home in Admaston Township, 1880 (courtesy Irwin Patterson, Forester's Falls)

Vernacular log house (two views, above) built by Anthony and Simon Chusroskie, Wilberforce Township, and now at Champlain Trail Museum, Pembroke

OPPOSITE

top Charlotte Auguste Kruger Zadow Zillmer. She gave her farm to her third son, subject to a maintenance mortgage, which stated that he had to act kindly toward her, as a dutiful son should. (Courtesy Mrs Elsie Zadow, Eganville)

bottom Large wooden farm-house of Kosmack family, Sebastopol Township

Log farm-house, Wilberforce Township, built circa 1874 by Johann Lipke, with doddy-house at right, added 1913 by son August for Johann and his wife

Bertha Timm and August Lipke (top), married November 1905. They inherited the farm of Johann Lipke (bottom), Wilberforce Township. (Photos courtesy Lorna and Dennis Peterson, Germanicus)

Steam-engine used by Schutt family to thresh at farms in Wilberforce Township, outside Johann Lipke's granary circa 1920 (courtesy Lorna and Dennis Peterson)

German immigrant Irving Christink (second from left) with family and friends enjoying music and refreshments in 1912, Alice Township (courtesy Orval Christink, Pembroke)

Fred Mohns and Ella Christink, 17 July 1912, in front of the bride's home of squared logs, Alice Township (courtesy Orval Christink)

Harvesting grain, around 1914. Family and neighbours help German immigrant Ferdinand Biesenthal (fifth from right) gather and store the grain on his farm in Alice Township. (Courtesy Mrs Richard Goltz, Alice Township)

top Doddy-house of sawn timber added to a log farm-house by Otto Schroeder in the 1920s in Sebastopol Township. Removal of the log building in 1978 caused the three-sided structure to collapse under the snowfall of the following winter.

bottom William Lemke with ox-yoke and grain shovel made by his grandfather, and remains of his grandfather's log house

Log house, smoke-house, and barns built post-1886 by August Neinkirchen, Petawawa Township

Squared log smoke-house, South Algona Township. *Above*, Ethel
Pilatske feeds pigs destined for this squared-log smoke-house when snow
arrives; *below*, Edgar Pilatske examines a smoke-cured ham.

Two views of a log smoke-house with upper and lower chambers, built
by August Klatt, Raglan Township

Sausage-stuffer: a hardwood plunger forces minced meat from the barrel through a horizontal exit tube; made by August Ziebell, Alice Township.

Four styles of smoke-house

Verch farm,
Wilberforce Township

Ashick farm,
South Algona Township

Witt farm, Alice Township

Zadow farm,
South Algona Township

OPPOSITE

One-room school-house of white-washed square logs at SS 3 Petawawa Township, used until 1965

Denbigh's white frame church, built in 1886 by congregation of St Paul's Lutheran Church

A 'work bee' at St John's Lutheran Church (built 1890), Sebastopol Township, in 1910 (courtesy Clem Ziebarth, Pembroke)

Pine altar, St John's Lutheran Church, Sebastopol Township, made by Fred Morlock

OPPOSITE

Drive shed with stalls for twenty-two horse-drawn vehicles, St John's Evangelical Church, Golden Lake; demolished 1967

Church at Vanbrugh rescued 1978 by parishioners of St John's Lutheran Church, Sebastopol Township

Byerland Mennonite Meetinghouse, built circa 1775, now located near Lancaster, Pennsylvania

Last service, 12 July 1925, at Bethelem Lutheran Church, Woito, Alice Township, constructed by members in 1886 (courtesy Norman Antler)

CHAPTER FIVE

Hand-spun comfort

'Nowhere is the importance of agriculture cash income more evident than in the case of textiles and clothing,' concluded one comparative study of the rural economy of Ontario and Quebec until 1870.[1] As general prosperity increased, after 1850, on the average farm there was a decline in the quantities of cloth and linen produced for home consumption. However, on the small and rocky farms of eastern Ontario, where cash income was small, the production of textiles at home continued much later than in other parts of the province.

The survival of wool-spinning in the western townships of Renfrew County, well into the twentieth century, is demonstrated by the advertisements of a carding mill at Killaloe in 1932.[2] At a time of year when fleeces would be sheared from the sheep, when the weather became warm in late May or early June, this mill invited farmers to bring in raw wool to be combed into fibres. For the making of rolls or batts the mill charged 12½ cents a pound, and for making the yarn the charge was 35 cents a pound. This custom work relieved the farmer's wife of the tedious chore of carding the tangled wool. With agents in Eganville (R.P. Mills) and in Pembroke (H.W. Wright & Son) the carding mill at Killaloe offered services to much of Renfrew County. Homespun yarn must have been especially welcome during the Depression for the knitting of socks, mitts, and sweaters, and loose wool was used to stuff quilts before cotton batts or synthetic fibres became common. It still is.

Until his death in 1979, Ernst Daber, from Pembroke, was a regular exhibitor at the annual Steam Show at Petawawa where he enjoyed displaying his grandmother's tools for the use of wool, brought from Germany. Daber,

born in 1900 and raised on a farm in Petawawa Township, actually used the
niddy-noddy wool-winder, the umbrella swift to unwind the skeins, and the
spinning-wheel to produce a two-ply grey yarn from black and white wool
– and he sold the balls of wool as fast as he produced them. However, the
production of textiles from wool and flax was generally the task of the
women on the farm, not the men. Both spinning and knitting of homespun
continues in a few German homes to this day, but the weaving of yarns into
cloth, using a loom, has ended. This pioneer skill is another one that had
survived late in this area, one loom being in use until 1945 at Rosenthal.

A factor in the survival of the woollen industry in the Ottawa Valley was
the continuing market for livestock that was provided by the lumber companies in the second half of the nineteenth century.[3] Long after other parts
of Ontario had accepted that they could not compete with American im-
ports of meat, the farmers of eastern Ontario still had customers close at
hand; the building of railroads along the Ottawa Valley at the end of the
nineteenth century compensated for the decline in the lumber industry by
allowing the producers to ship their livestock to the cities of Canada and the
United States. Carloads of lambs from Killaloe and Eganville travelled by
train to Buffalo, Boston, and New York.[4]

Even the optimistic land agent, T.P. French, had not envisaged the possibility that farmers in the neighbourhood of the Opeongo Road would produce their own wool and process it. (He had not advised immigrants to take
any tools for the manufacture of textiles.) He had urged them to take
blankets and warm clothing with them from their native land or else purchase them on arrival, the 1857 price for blankets being estimated at one
pound, five shillings, a pair.[5] Yet in many cases the only tool that a woman
brought with her from Germany was the spinning-wheel; more rarely the
accompanying tools for winding or unwinding the spun yarn were carried
across the ocean. Those expecting to live off the land must have known that
the ability to manufacture fabrics and knitted garments would add appreciably to the comfort of the family. In fact, the earliest records of the German farmers show that a few sheep were being raised, even though it was
necessary to have cleared land for pasture in order to provide grazing.

The numbers of sheep owned by German farmers visited by William Sinn
in October 1860 suggest that these animals were being maintained solely for
the family's own need for wool. Most households had only 2, but Martin
Budarick had 5 and Wilhelm Thur had 6. In 1861 the number of carding and
fulling mills in Upper Canada was 62, and the number of woollen mills was
82. These included William Logan's woollen mill at Renfrew, constructed
1857–8, probably the only one in Renfrew County when the German immi-

grants arrived. By 1866 there was a carding mill at Eganville, and by 1879 there was a fulling and woollen mill at Osceola.[6]

Removing wool from the sheep in the early weeks of the summer was essential. The decision to clip the wool was made when the danger of frosty nights is past. When flocks were large the heavy work of shearing the sheep was customarily done by the men, but the carding, spinning, dyeing, and weaving were considered women's work. Before the sheep were relieved of their fleeces, they were washed in a creek and their coats allowed to dry for a couple of days. Sheep that had survived the cold winters of eastern Ontario would have a heavy covering on their bodies. Hand shears sharpened on a whetstone were the early tools, and on some farms these have not yet been replaced by electrically powered shears if only a few animals are kept. On farms with few sheep the washing of wool could be done after shearing, rather than before. (One German housewife told the author that she soaked the wool in a bath filled with warm water and detergent and tramped it down with her feet.)[7] On farms with only two or three sheep, one would be black, so that a mixture of white and black natural colours would produce a grey shade.

The wool that was removed would be matted and prickly with burrs, and the first step in improvement was to comb the fibres in order to remove the unwanted debris. The process, as performed at home, was accomplished with a pair of carding boards, one with the teeth upward and one with the teeth down, drawing them back and forth across a clump of wool until the fibres were brushed straight. The use of power machinery for carding was one of the first innovations that reduced the labour of woollen manufacture; a water-powered carding machine with wire teeth fastened on a cylinder made endless carding possible. In eastern Ontario John Haggart of Perth had a carding mill by 1835.[8] A second invention was the fulling process, by which the cloth was made thicker, warmer, and stronger; this was done by soaking it in warm soapy water, causing it to shrink and mat. The fulled cloth was brushed with teasels (the head of a plant burred like a thistle) to raise the nap and later pressed. At a mill a length of cloth could be created more consistently and at less risk than if it were done at home by a fulling bee.

Carded wool was twisted into a roll or ball ready for the next step, spinning. The natural binding properties of wool allowed strands to be drawn out and twisted so as to produce continuous filament; the strength of the thread depended on the skill of the person fingering it.

The small spinning-wheels carried to Canada by German settlers could usually be dismantled for saving space when packing and reassembled on arrival. Mrs Gustave Michel, who left Silesia in 1867, took the drive wheel and the flyer-bobbin apparatus for a vertical spinning-wheel, but left the stand behind; her husband made a three-legged stool of pine for its support after they had settled in Petawawa Township. Most of the spinning-wheels taken by German families were of the more common style, with a three-legged sloping saddle, a drive wheel at one end, and the flyer-bobbin assembly (the spinning mechanism) at the other. This type has been termed a *Saxony* spinning-wheel,[9] but not because of its origin. In many of these German wheels there was a circular hole in the saddle that could hold a vessel of water, hinting that the wheel was used for flax as well as wool. Descendants of the immigrants have kept many of these spinning-wheels, even though they no longer use them, and beneath the darkened surface of the wood and the accumulated oil the grains of oak or walnut may sometimes be recognized.

Since the need for woollen yarn was imperative, either for spinning or weaving, there was a demand for wheelwrights to produce the tools that would enable the housewife to convert the fibres into wool. Some women had travelled to their new country without such equipment, while others had several daughters who were reaching the age to learn domestic skills before marriage.

Both regular and vertical spinning-wheels were made in Renfrew County from local woods; with elaborately turned legs, spokes, and supports, they were the work of skilled men. Passed on from mother to daughter or daughter-in-law and on to a third and fourth generation, some wheels have a history obscured by moves and marriages, until even the owners cannot be sure who made them. Some men, like Christian Born of Alice Township, made them only for relatives. Others made them to supplement their income.

The Saxony type of spinning-wheel was made in South Algona Township by an immigrant, Charles Hoelke (1854–1936), who left Germany 4 April 1881 with his wife, two sons, and a daughter.[10] He worked on a farm near Eganville for two years and later moved to Lots 18 and 19, Concession 8, South Algona Township. Working as a fence-viewer, as well as a farmer with cattle, sheep, and hogs,[11] Hoelke bought another farm from an Irish family, Lots 1–3, Concession 6, in the same township but nearer Augsburg, and there he set up a woodworking shop in a two-storey building adjacent to the farm-house. It was here that he made the parts for spinning-wheels, using a lathe with a bed eight feet long, powered by an iron wheel with a circumference of thirty-six inches; a foot-treadle enabled him to turn the lathe, leaving his hands free to manipulate the chisels that cut into the wood.

(When Hoelke's son, Henry, sold the farm in 1938 to Martin Lenser the tools were left in the workshop. Lenser sold them at auction 19 May 1984.) Black ash had been used in making the wheels, the spokes, and the foot-treadle. All the spinning-wheels known to have been made in Renfew County by German wheelwrights had a wooden foot-treadle; none were metal. One of the surviving Hoelke wheels with a firm provenance is the spinning-wheel bought by Emma Zadow Verch, the wife of a farmer in South Algona Township, who had twelve children; her youngest son, Gilbert, born in 1916, remembers her telling him that it had cost $8.

Although the vertical or upright wheel is considered rare in Canada[12] and is usually assumed to have been brought from Europe, it was common in the northeast corner of Wilberforce Township and the adjacent southeast corner of Alice Township, for an immigrant there made these wheels for women in the area, to eke out a living on the poor farm land that he had chosen. The identity of this spinning-wheel-maker, Martin Markus, was confirmed by his grandson, Solomon Kelo,[13] who still had one of the wheels, unused and in pristine condition. 'My grandfather was the *Stellmacher* [wheelwright],' said Kelo, who still lived on the sideroad connecting Concession 23 and 25 in Wilberforce Township where he was born in 1897.

On this same road Martin Markus had worked a farm and made spinning-wheels from black ash. Born in Drachhausen, Burchelidung,[14] Kreis Cottbus, 28 June 1834, Markus married Caroline Yandt in 1857. Leaving Germany in 1863, the couple walked out of the country, hiding by day and travelling by night; descendants believe that stealth was necessary because immigration was prohibited at that time. Although Markus was a brick-layer and stonemason by trade, he chose to settle on land near Rankin, Wilberforce Township, where a substantial number of German immigrants had already congregated. The eight children of this couple included a daughter, Augusta, born in 1866, who married William Kelo and lived near her parents on a farm subsequently inherited by her son, Solomon. Concession 23, Wilberforce Township, is signposted as Marsh Road; it leads through low-lying thickets of alder and bush and hardwoods, where no clearings are seen and any evidence of agriculture has been obliterated.

'Black ash grew all around here because of the swampy low land,' explained Solomon Kelo. Living on a fifty-acre property in retirement, he had once owned five farms in the neighbourhood for the express purpose of harvesting the timber, including thousands of feet of black ash. It was his opinion that this wood had been selected in pioneering years by several furniture-makers in the area. A skilled woodworker himself, Kelo had used black ash for his home's fitted kitchen cabinets and a blanket-box, choosing panels that displayed a decorative grain. Other properties of ash, its hardness and resilience, may have been more important in its choice by the men who made spinning-wheels.

'All the women around here used to spin,' said Kelo, who was quite sure that his grandfather had made spinning-wheels during the years that he lived on a farm, prior to his move to Pembroke in 1880,[15] and in the years before his grandson was born. His grandfather had lived until 1925 and had told him about his early years in Wilberforce Township. The hardware for the wheels had been made by the blacksmith in nearby Rankin, Fred Schiskoskie, who shared a household with a carpenter, Martin Schimmens,[16] who was married to his sister. Kelo had been shown the site in the woods where the charcoal had been prepared for the blacksmith. 'It was a large pit in the ground, about 12 feet by 16 feet, filled with dry pine logs which were set alight and then covered with sand so that they smouldered,' he said.

The spinning-wheels made by Martin Markus are easy to identify. The rim of the drive wheel, 18½ inches in diameter, consists of four curved sections (fellies) with their butted ends dowelled together. A pattern had been used to cut these sections from a dressed piece of black ash more than 1½ inches thick; each section was mortised to receive the tongues of two spokes which did not emerge onto the rim of the wheel. The assembly of the wheel must have therefore commenced with the insertion of the spokes into the hub. The eight spokes and the two uprights that supported the flyer-bobbin complex had been turned on a lathe. Kelo had seen the lathe which had been powered by a foot treadle and which had pulleys to increase the speed. The stool surface on which the spinning-wheel was mounted must have also been cut out of a pattern for it never varies; approximately half-moon in shape, it has a series of notches at the front and sides that identify it as the work of Martin Markus. The three legs on which this stool stands are curved and carved by hand, the two at the front sloping comfortably on either side of the foot-pedal which is attached to a stretcher at the front. Braced 'with a third leg at the rear, this is a sturdy spinning-wheel, and the appearance of those that have survived show that they have received steady use. The foot-pedal, made of wood, has often worn out and been replaced, or else it is in a splintered condition.

'The shuttle had to be replaced sometimes, and the women used to get one made by a carver in Pembroke named Abe Patterson,' volunteered Kelo. 'He used to make them of cherry.'

Even if the foot-pedal and the shuttle have been replaced, the identity of these vertical spinning-wheels made by Martin Markus is unmistakable. They were never painted; the original finish of beeswax and turpentine may have darkened with age, changing the honey colour of the black ash. Many descendants of German families in this area can remember them. Mrs Anthony Chusroskie, who died in 1918, had one, according to her grand-daughter,[17] who thinks that the wheel passed to her aunt, Susan. Mrs Ludwig Butt had one, and a great-granddaughter in Welland, Ontario,[18] has it still. Occasionally these wheels turn up at a farm auction sale miles from the township where they were made, but investigation of the ownership can trace it back to an early family living in the Locksley-Rankin area. Some of them are still in the possession of descendants and treasured as 'conversation pieces,' although no longer used.

Other tools needed for the winding and unwinding of wool required less skill; they were simple enough to be made by an individual farmer and were therefore less prized and fewer have survived. A swift is a type of reel of adjustable diameter on which a skein of yarn is placed in order to be wound off into a ball. One type that could be folded up and stored away when not in use was an X-shaped arrangement of parallel wooden bars that rotated on a horizontal axis supported on a stand. The two intersecting arms were pierced by holes into which bars were inserted; the length of the skein of yarn could be adjusted by inserting the bars into different slots of the cross-pieces. They are similar to a type of swift found in Quebec, with the difference that these are taller in height and would be used by a person standing up.

The type of wool-winder termed the *clock reel (Skeiner)* was made by German immigrants with varying degrees of skill. At its simplest, it could be a cross-piece of two intersecting bars mounted on an upright, so that the woman could turn the 'wheel' which had been strung with wool yarn until she had measured the required length. A more sophisticated type of clock reel, as made by William Born of Alice Township, was backed by a mechanism of wooden cogs; after forty revolutions of the wheel the release of a wooden slat, causing a sharp noise, announced that forty strands of wool had been wound – equivalent to one skein *(Fitz)*. A skein wound in this way could be used for knitting. If the yarn was needed for weaving it had to be wound on spools for making the warp or on bobbins to fit in the shuttle.

A bobbin-winder was another tool that could be made at home or by a man possessed of more skill. Bobbin-winders were among the products made by Martin Schimmens, the carpenter at Rankin who built houses and smoke-houses and who shared his home with a brother-in-law who was a blacksmith. Little ironwork was needed for a bobbin-winder apart from the spindle and the handle used to turn this wheel. The bobbin-winder had a drive wheel set at one end of a stand, with a box at the other end where the

bobbins or spools were placed on a spindle; yarn was wound from a skein
while the large wheel was turned by hand. The two rotating devices were
usually attached to a plain saddle supported by three or four legs, but the
style made by Martin Schimmens had an X-shaped trestle. The shuttles were
carved out of hardwood, by the men or boys of the house, and were sometimes incised with decoration.

Though the mixing of black and white woollen yarns could produce practical shades of grey, other colours could be produced from plant material
that grew wild.[19] Commercial (aniline) dyes in every hue were available in
the years before the First World War, and some surviving pioneer clothing
and quilts made of wool made ample use of them. All woven fabrics are
constructed of two series of yarns – the warp running lenghwise of the cloth
and the weft running crosswise. The interlacing of these two threads is
called the weave. A frame, or loom, holds the warp threads taut and
divides, raises, and lowers them, to permit the shuttle to pass from side to
side between the threads. Large and cumbersome, it was put together with
pegs, so that it could be taken apart and stored when not in use.

The need for warm clothing was especially urgent when families had little
cash revenue and lived from the produce of their land. If wool were used for
warp and weft a thick cloth would result. Cotton thread could be bought at
the general store and made a warp that was easy to handle; if the weft were
the homespun wool and the two threads were tightly woven together the
result would be a finer plain flannel that could be tailored to make clothes.
Dyed wool permitted the weaver to produce coloured strips in the fabric,
rather than solid shades; dyed warp and weft threads introduced small
checks.

Both warp and weft were woollen threads when winter blankets were
being made, the plain natural colour often being relieved only by stripes on
the borders. Horse blankets were also woven entirely of wool, darker
colours being used in their manufacture. Since most looms could weave a
cloth in a width of only thirty to forty inches, it was necessary to sew two
handwoven pieces of material together to obtain the desired width; that
central seam (or several seams) is a trademark of a piece of weaving produced on an early loom.

Professional weavers, who used more complicated looms to produce
complex patterns termed *Jacquard coverlets*, do not appear to have found a
market within the German settlement in eastern Ontario. In other parts of
Ontario, the work of professional weavers has been found in considerable
quantity in the Niagara peninsula and in Waterloo County, both areas of
extensive settlement by German families. Most samples of local weaving

that have survived in this area are of plaincloth, simple warp and weft, such as the red and grey striped woollen fabric from the farm of a family named Remus displayed at the Champlain Trail Museum in Pembroke.

The weavers in the German families in Renfrew County were all women, judging from the 1881 census records. The ones described as such are usually unmarried daughters who have passed the eligible age for marriage and thus were literally spinsters. However, those who were married and were the mothers of growing children might be both spinners and weavers also, according to the recollections of their descendants. Unlike the German weavers in southern Ontario, the workers in eastern Ontario did not have sixteen to twenty shaft looms and the skills that produced the more complicated cloths. The majority of weavers produced fabrics solely for the use of their own families and relatives. One exception was Emilie Henriettie Augustine Frederick, a widow with a family to support; with her husband, Johann, and four children she had immigrated from West Prussia in 1859 and settled on a 100-acre farm on Concession 19, Wilberforce Township. After she had been widowed ten years later, she sold her farm for two barrels of flour and purchased another home at Golden Lake. There she was surrounded by German-speaking families and made her living by weaving and spinning for others.[20]

The Griese family did custom work, i.e. took orders for their weaving, in Bromley Township, where the population was predominantly Irish.[21] The 1871 census lists only five German families in this township, all with surnames misspelled by the English-Canadian enumerator. One of the three industries there was described as a 'Loom' owned by John 'Gruci,' a farmer from eastern Germany; the farmer's wife, Elizabeth, 47, and their daughter, Augusta, 19, were both 'weavers.' These two women, who worked for six months that year, wove in that time 540 yards of cloth and flannel valued at $378. Their joint wages were estimated at $60 annually. Since the 223 households in Bromley Township produced a total of 5,327 yards of homemade fabrics that year, the industry of the Griese family accounted for less than one-tenth of the total. Obviously the German immigrants were not the only families weaving their own cloth.

On most farms weaving was practised for only a few weeks each year, for the loom was a large object that filled most of the space in a room. It might be assembled for use in a warm house in winter, if space permitted, or else it was installed in an outside shed and used only in the summer. Mrs William (Martha Wolfgram) Karau, who married in 1900, made as much as forty yards of cloth in one season, according to her daughter, Mrs Solomon Kelo: some was all wool, some linen, and some wool and cotton mixed.

The loom was the work of the home carpenter, an arrangement of vertical and horizontal timbers that enclosed the weaving shafts and were made from local woods with no attempt at decoration. At the Champlain Trail Museum there is one made of pine from the Bucholtz farm in Alice Township. At Madonna House Museum in Combermere, there is a similar loom, made from black ash in Rosenthal as a wedding present in 1890; it was made by a man named Schraeder, a member of a family that left Germany in 1864.[22] The latter model is said to have been in use until 1945, but only in museums now is it possible to see a loom assembled in a workable state. On farms the remains of the looms are stored in pieces out in the barns if they have been kept at all.

Since both Renfrew and Eganville had woollen mills in the early years of German settlement in Renfrew County,[23] nearby residents could have their textiles manufactured from their own sheep's fleeces, long before subsequent generations abandoned the production of home-made fabrics. Yet it continued. Eganville, in the centre of the German settlement in Renfrew County, had a carding mill as early as 1866 and a woollen mill that made blankets for the Canadian army in the First World War. Nevertheless, on the farms in the surrounding townships, the home production of woollen materials persisted. Esther Lemke, who sold the contents of her Eganville home in the summer of 1983, watched the woollen blankets made by her and her sister, Emma, sell for as little as $2 each. She recounted how they had been made on the Schraeder farm in Grattan Township, about 1920, on a loom that produced a width of thirty inches. Some had been made in the natural cream colour of the wool, with black stripes woven at the ends; some had been dyed pink or green after the blankets had been finished. Mrs Lemke remembered the hard work involved in carding, spinning, and weaving when she was a girl, skills thought to be necessary then.

Among the textiles that have survived with the identity of the weaver undisputed, a large number of articles can be attributed to Mrs Edward Luloff, the former Anna Junop of Rosenthal in Radcliffe Township. The selection includes a sleigh cover, carpeting, blankets, quilts, and clothing that ranges from a petticoat to a man's jacket, a remarkable legacy that shows just how important this skill was to the comfort of the farm family.

There has been some misunderstanding among textile researchers concerning the 'Annie Luloff' of Renfrew County to whom so much weaving has been ascribed. In fact there were three sisters-in-law with the same name, and in order to dispel the confusion within the family they were nicknamed Ferny's Annie (Mrs Ferdinand Luloff, the former Hannah Yourt), Eddie's Annie (Mrs Edward Luloff, the former Anna Junop) and Mud-Lake

Annie (Mrs John Luloff, the former Annie Luloff, who married a cousin).[24] The last was widowed early, in 1909, and lived on a farm in Grattan Township, beside a widening of the Bonnechere River known as Mud Lake. It was at this farm in 1977 that a picker purchased some quilts made wholly of wool, following the death of Mrs John Luloff's widowed daughter, Tessie (Luloff) Heiderman, in the spring. The farm was being readied for an auction sale, to be held in September; at this event the items sold included a knitting machine and the X-shaped swift, but there was no sign of a loom.

'Aunt Annie never did any weaving,' declared her niece, Sarah Luloff, who lived with her sister, Teresa, on the farm in North Algona Township where, they claimed, the weaving took place. Teresa was more blunt. 'Annie did everything with tongs,' she remarked drily, meaning that Annie, a spoiled only daughter, was accustomed to having other people serve her needs.

The sisters were adamant that the weaver was their mother, Mrs Edward Luloff, and could produce both tied and stitched wholecloth quilts identical to the ones from the Mud Lake farm, one of which is now in the collection of the National Museum of Man.[25] They particularly cherished a wholecloth quilt that their mother had made before she was married, in 1900, which had won a prize in a contest at Rosenthal. Like other quilts that she made later, during her married life, Anna Junop's prize-winner had been constructed from home-spun, home-dyed, and home-woven fabrics; triangles and squares of solid colours had been assembled in a geometric design on the upper surface, the filling was loose wool, and the two layers had been stitched together in parallel rows of fan-like contours. In her other quilts the design of the upper surface, either bold stripes or small checks, had been produced during the weaving. The making of quilts from woollen materials woven especially for this purpose may be unique to some German families in this part of Ontario, and possibly in Canada, according to Dorothy Burnham, research associate, Royal Ontario Museum, who visited the area in September 1982. Other examples have turned up at German farms. One such quilt, made by Mrs William Karau, has been folded lengthwise to make an upholstered surface for a daybed. It was more customary for early quilts to be made from scraps of unused material and pieces of worn-out clothing, and these too could present a vivid pattern, as well as a warm covering for a bed. In this form of construction, however, the quilts made by German women in Renfrew County do not differ from those made by other groups of settlers.

Already a practised weaver before her marriage, Anna Junop was one of the oldest of fourteen children born to Mr and Mrs Christian Junop, who lived on a rocky farm in Radcliffe Township. She was born in 1878, one of four daughters, and it is believed that she learned domestic skills from her mother, née Hannah Louise Luloff, who immigrated to Canada in 1873 from Pomerania.[26] At 22, Anna married Edward Luloff, a childless widower thirteen years her senior and the youngest son of Mr and Mrs Johann Luloff. Edward inherited the farm in North Algona Township and the care of elderly parents. While his young wife raised five children and cared for home and husband, she also had to share the house with her father-in-law until 1910, her mother-in-law until 1914, and a bachelor brother-in-law until 1922. Despite her load of responsibilities this was the period when Anna Junop Luloff produced a variety of textiles in bright colours, using commercial dyes obtained from the general stores in Golden Lake about a quarter-mile away. The loom was set up in a corner of the spacious kitchen in the winter months, and 'she wove for everybody in the family,' according to her daughters. Bold stripes of orange and grey, red and green, or red and purple were woven for the top surfaces of quilts; bright green edged with red was chosen for a petticoat.

Her daughters thought that their mother was the only one in that area they knew who used four shafts on her loom and so could weave twill. The twill woollen blankets that she made had coloured stripes at each end, pink and black on a white or brown background. As in the quilts, the blankets have a central seam where the two lengths of thirty-six-inch-wide woven cloth were stitched together; the exact meeting of the stripes at each end is a measure of the weaver's skill at maintaining the same tension throughout. Sarah, who was born in 1910, could remember her mother making one of these striped blankets for her in the 1920s.

Some of the cloth woven by Mrs Edward Luloff was sent away to a fulling-mill in either Eganville or Renfrew, so as to thicken the fabric. One of these thick, tweed-like woollen materials was sewn into a jacket for her husband and lined with a gay, checked homespun, for this weaver was a skilled needlewoman as well.

No flax was grown on this Luloff farm, and no linen was woven by Anna Junop Luloff, only wool. Sheep-rearing was still popular in Renfrew County in the first quarter of the twentieth century, judging by advertisements seeking wool in the weekly newspapers, but hand-weaving on the loom had gradually lost favour. When Ferdinand Kuhl, a tailor, immigrated to Eganville from Germany in 1888, the farmers of the surrounding area would bring him their own cloth, woven on their farms, to be made into suits.[27] In the early years of the twentieth century, Kuhl obtained material manufactured from woollen mills for use in his tailoring business. According to one of his daughters, Helen Sack, this was more profitable.

When flocks on the farm produced more wool than was needed for the family, the surplus could be exchanged for merchandise at the local general store, everything from shoes to lace curtains, or it could be sold for cash. The *Eganville Leader* ran advertisements of merchants who were eager to buy large quantities of wool. In 1905 one merchant advertised (9 June) that he wanted 20,000 pounds of wool to fill an order; the Eganville Woollen Mills, which was making blankets, tweeds, flannels, and yarns, advised its customers (11 August 1905) that it would allow 27 cents a pound in trade or 23 cents in cash. The next year (18 May) the mill offered 30 cents a pound and wanted 50,000 pounds of wool, but the same Eganville merchant who had contracted to supply a large firm with '10 tons of wool' offered to pay more. Sheep were still being driven through the streets of Eganville in 1911 to the two railroad stations (20 October 1911), especially in the fall when farmers wanted to reduce their livestock and logging companies were accumulating supplies of meat at their shanties at Massey and Kippewa in northern Ontario. The First World War brought orders from the militia department (14 September 1914) for 1,500 pairs of blankets from the woollen mill in Eganville, an item it had made regularly for the lumbermen.

Blankets and woollen fabrics had become the staple items of manufacture at the woollen mills. Home-weaving had become the exception, rather than the essential skill that enabled a family to withstand a cold climate. Very few coverlets have been found in Renfrew County, a fact that may be linked to the absence of professional weavers in this area. Unlike Waterloo County, which in the 1840s received trained and apprenticed weavers displaced by the industrial revolution in Germany, Renfrew County received settlers from rural areas who brought with them their household skills.

There was at least one German farm in Petawawa Township where a type of brocade weaving was still produced by Mrs Carl Gutzman (née Emilia Lindemann) and her daughter-in-law, Mrs William Gutzman (née Elizabeth Gutzman), about 1920. Although this style of coverlet looks as if it has been embroidered, because the coloured designs are raised above the neutral background, the pattern of the green, blue, red, and yellow threads is laid down as the weaving progresses.[28] This type of weaving is performed by two workers combining their talents at the same time, one weaving the warp and weft in the regular fashion, while the other lifts up coloured threads of weft to lay them above the background weft. The grandson of Mrs Carl Gutzman, Edgar, could remember that his mother and grandmother argued about the colours.[29] The uneven tension of the weaving, shown by the difficulty of matching the patterns along the central seam, suggests that the two women may have taken turns in the production of the neutral background of warp and weft, in shades of light brown and dark brown.

The only comparable technique that has been noted in this area is the use of raw wool inserted on the weft when blankets were being woven; this was added to the normal woolen fibres that constituted the warp and weft as woven by Mrs Frederick (Augusta) Biederman of Wilberforce Township, in the early years of the twentieth century.[30]

Raising sheep for the sale of meat was gradually abandoned in Renfrew County in the years following the First World War. Wolf packs from Algonquin Park were blamed for the number of sheep killed; it was alleged that in 1924 wolves had been seen within ten miles of Pembroke.[31] The Ontario government had reduced the bounty on wolves that year from $40 to $15, a change that produced a storm of protest in the Pembroke and Eganville papers. Fewer flocks meant that the amount of wool produced in Renfrew County declined. That was also the year that the Childerhose Woollen Mill in Eganville decided to move and relocate in New Liskeard, under the impression that the Temiskaming district held great promise.[32]

Spinning wool for the purpose of knitting continued, though the numbers of sheep were few. In *Selected Canadian Spinning Wheels in Perspective* (1980), Judy Keenleyside comments that in the 1920s and the 1930s great numbers of Canadian men and women probably spun their own yarns. Fall fairs in eastern Ontario still include categories for wool and wool products; the Denbigh Fall Fair invited entries in 1979 for a display that had to include every process that wool goes through, from sheep to garment: sponsored by the local agricultural society and the Ontario Department of Agriculture, the five prizes were awarded 50 per cent on workmanship and 50 per cent on promotional and educational value.

Most farmers who continue to raise sheep in eastern Ontario send their wool to a clearing-house in Carleton Place; from there the wool travels directly to the export market unscoured, to countries with greater textile technology.[33] The housewife, such as Mrs Alfred Lipke of Alice Township, who knows how to use the swift, the clock-reel winder, and the spinning-wheel is becoming a rarity.

Another textile produced and used on farms in eastern Canada in the nineteenth century was flax; obtained from a plant, it provided tough fibres for cloth used in garments, household linens, grain bags. The yarn was produced by spinning from combed fibres, and all the flax materials were woven on the loom. This pioneer skill has not survived.

One estimate of its former importance may be gleaned from William Sinn's report of 1860.[34] He listed harvests of six types, all of edible plants except for flax *(Flachs)*, grown at that time principally in the township of Wilberforce. The largest crops had been secured by Friedrich Schutt, who had garnered 60 bushels, Christian Wasmund, 50 bushels, and Martin Budarick, 45 bushels – possibly they had had more time to clear land than the several other farmers who had harvested 20 bushels. Estimates of the harvest of wool were not collected, for Sinn recorded merely the numbers of sheep kept; it is therefore not possible to make a direct comparison of the value of the two fibres to the early settlers. Both were important in the Prussian states from which most immigrants had come. An observation of 1852 regarding the peasantry of Prussia then (East and West Prussia, Pomerania, Posen, and West Brandenburg) stated: 'Clothing was made from flax of their own growth and wool spun in their cottages.'[35] In 1889, when Prussia embraced nearly the whole of northern Germany, linens were considered one of the principal manufactures, Silesia, Saxony, and Brandenburg being particularly noted for their quality.[36] In 1860 every German immigrant in eastern Upper Canada who grew flax also kept sheep, but although the two fibres might be interwoven – for a combination of warmth and strength – the preparation of flax involved special techniques and tools. The flax fibres from which linen was made were long fine ones, known as bast bundles, arranged in the stem of the plant between the outer bark and the central woody core. Separation of these bast bundles was a laborious task after the harvest of the plant in August.

Only a small area was needed for the growth of sufficient flax plants to meet a family's needs. Arnold Radke of Pembroke, who grew up in Alice Township, can remember his grandmother using flax, although he thinks that the growth and harvest of this plant ceased when he was a young boy, sometime before 1914.[37] 'It was sown in the spring,' he said, 'not a whole field, but about three-quarters of an acre. When it was ripe the flax was pulled and bunched and dried in the field. There were outside ovens used for baking bread in those days – and these were also used to dry the flax. There was a tool called a *Brauk* or flax-breaker which was used to smash up the stems. Then my grandmother would use the *Schwinge* in the summer kitchen.' At this point Radke made a chopping motion and described the use of a long-bladed instrument wielded with some force. These wooden knives used in breaking the fibres had been termed *scutching* or *swingling* knives in English. After his grandmother Mrs Charles Radke, had combed the tangled fibres on a bed of nails, the filaments of flax would be ready for spinning. On a loom the flax was woven into towels, bedspreads, and even pants for the men.

Radke's account of placing the flax plants in the outside bake ovens to dry was repeated by Henry Grahl of Wilberforce Township, who also recalled that the flax seeds were first removed from the plants by flailing the sheaves on the floor of the barn.[38] The seeds were given to cows who had given birth, so as to contribute extra nourishment to the milk for the calf. Grahl described the flax-breaker as having two jawbones that clashed together to break the outer fibres of the flax stems that covered the white heart. His mother, Mrs Daniel Grahl, had a spinning-wheel for making flax yarn, and her children, in winter, made the wooden spools upon which the yarn was wound before its use on the loom.

Grahl's sister, Mrs William Lemke, reiterated that it was important to pull up the flax plant, roots and all, for if the plants were cut by a scythe, like other field crops, as much as six inches of the stem might be lost.[39] Mrs Lemke, who could still wind a niddy-noddy of yarn from an X-shaped swift most skilfully, could not recall the flax plants ever being 'retted', i.e. allowed to soak in moist surroundings so as to hasten the breakdown of the unwanted outer stem, but she remembered that her mother had a habit of storing the flax plants on the potatoes, in the cellar.

Mrs Solomon Kelo of Wilberforce Township agreed that the procedure for harvesting the flax was to pull it up and set it in single sheaves so that it would be well aired.[40] Whether the flax on her parents' farm was threshed or flailed, the seeds were used as provender for fattening young cattle, and the stalks were dried inside a barn or by the warmth of the sun. The dried stalks were crushed by the flax-breaker and carded by a bed of nails, known as a hackle or hetchel. At this stage the flax fibres might be bleached by leaving them on fresh green grass in the sunshine, or else the flax yarn (which had been spun) could be exposed as skeins in the same way. By the time that Mrs Solomon Kelo was training as a teacher in 1920, the use of flax was so outmoded that she prepared a display of its step-by-step manufacture as one of her class projects. Her mother, Mrs William Karau, had woven cloth from flax to make sheets, tablecloths, towels, men's clothing, and the ticks used to enclose bedding. It was a skill needed by the second generation of German immigrants, but not the third.

Any home handyman could have made the tools used in the preparation of flax, except the spinning-wheel. The latter resembled the spinning-wheel used for wool, with the addition of an elbow-shaped extension upon which a bundle of flax fibres could be attached, at the top. Moisture was needed for the spinning of filaments from the plant fibres; as noted earlier, the spinning-wheels brought from Germany have a circular depression in their sloping saddle that could have held a container of water. The flax-breaker was made of hardwood blades, a pair hinged together at one end, with the lower blades mounted on a stand and the upper ones moveable. When the meshing of the two blades had broken the tough fibres of the stems of the flax plants, the crushed pieces still adhering to the resilient fibres were scraped away with the aid of a scutching (or swingling) knife, followed by a final cleaning when the handfuls of beaten stalks were combed through a bed of nails (hackling). The hackles made by German farmers in Renfrew County consisted of a rectangular bed of nails set in a piece of wood pierced by holes at each end; presumably the holes allowed the hackle to be secured when work was in process. A double set of hackles, either on the same piece of wood or on separate foundations, would have a coarse bed (i.e. nails set far apart) on one and a finer bed (nails set close together) on the other. Drawn repeatedly through the teeth of hackles, the bast bundles used to produce linen would be cleaned of the loose bits of bark and woody fibres known as shive.

These tools have seldom been treasured by the third or fourth generation of German settlers. Some, like Henry Grahl, can recall that they were thrown away in the 1930s; others, like the granddaughter of William Gierman, did not remember what a flax hackle looked like until one was found in the barn. Although several descendants, like Arnold Radke, knew that the flax plant was grown in a damp, low-lying location, none had any memory of 'retting.' The absence of this stage is all the more remarkable because the growth of flax in Renfrew County was most popular in the townships of Alice and Wilberforce, where patches of swamp are abundant.

According to the diary of William Gutzman of Petawawa Township, flax was still being grown on his farm in 1921.[41] The harvest of this plant had been encouraged in Canada by the demand for linen during the war.[42] (One of the wartime needs was for airplane wings.) Some third-generation families can remember from childhood the scratchiness of home-woven towels made from flax grown on the farm, but the tedious work of harvesting the plant and preparing the fibres was phased out during the lifetime of the second generation.

Ernst Daber displaying his grandmother's spinning tools brought from Germany

Spinning-wheels from Germany, Wilberforce Township

Hand shears used to clip fleeces by Mrs Hertha Ott, Wilberforce Township

Mrs Michael Linde spinning wool
circa 1910 outside her farm home,
Admaston Township (courtesy
Robert Corrigan, Barry's Bay)

Spinning-wheel made by Henry
Hoelke, South Algona Township

Vertical spinning-wheels
made by Martin Markus for
Mrs Herman Scheueneman
(top) and for
Mrs William Hein (bottom)

left X-shaped swift, on a vertical stand, used for unwinding skeins of yarn, Grattan Township

right Clock-reel wool-winder made from maple by William Born, Alice Township

OPPOSITE

top Bobbin-winder: drive wheel and bobbin box supported on a bench, a common style; Wilberforce Township

right Bobbin-winder made by a carpenter, Martin Schimmens of Rankin; the drive wheel and bobbin box are placed on an X-shaped trestle. Wilberforce Township

Home-spun quilts filled with loose wool might be tied with individual knots or secured with rows of hand stitches. North Algona Township

OPPOSITE

top Loom from Bucholtz family, Alice Township, Champlain Trail Museum, Pembroke

bottom Loom from Schraeder family, Radcliffe Township, in Madonna House Museum, Combermere

Wholecloth quilt made from handwoven woollen fabrics by Anna Junop
Rosenthal, who won a prize for it before 1900

Star quilt made from remnants, Wilberforce Township

Home and store, 1903, of tailor Ferdinand Kuhl of Eganville, who left
Germany in 1888 (courtesy Mrs Helen Sack, Eganville)

OPPOSITE

Brocade weaving. Coloured pattern is laid on plain ground by extra
strands of weft as the weaving proceeds. Made by Mrs Carl Gutzman
and Mrs William Gutzman, working together, Petawa Township, and
displayed by Mrs Edgar Gutzman, whose husband was Mrs Carl
Gutzman's grandson

Mrs Solomon Kelo with flax-breaker, Wilberforce Township

Scutching knife and blade, Lipke farm, Wilberforce Township

Flax hackles

Reiche family,
Wilberforce
Township

Kelo family,
Wilberforce
Township

Gierman family,
Sebastopol
Township

Michel family,
Petawawa
Township

Mrs Ernst Brose spinning flax circa 1910, Wilberforce Township
(courtesy Mrs Erna Hein, Pembroke)

CHAPTER SIX   # In the German immigrant's home

Unlike some German immigrants in southern Ontario, who had travelled overland from the United States, those who journeyed to eastern Ontario could not carry pieces of furniture from their previous homes. They had moved to a new country across an ocean, and the amount of luggage was limited to items that could be packed within a chest. Whether the maker of furniture in Renfrew County was skilled or unskilled the native forest cover determined the choice of woods, a more limited choice than could be found in other parts of the province and one that is an important feature in identification.

The logging companies during the first half of the nineteenth century had worked along the tributaries of the Ottawa River in eastern Ontario.[1] Lumbermen had harvested white pine, red pine, and oak along the Petawawa, the Bonnechere, and the Madawaska, water routes that made access easy for the logging companies and exits easy for the timber they felled. By the time the Ottawa and Opeongo Road was begun in 1854 and the Pembroke and Mattawan opened in 1867, these roads were being used as avenues to the sites of logging operations that were moving farther away. Despite massive exploitation of the forest resources, there were stands of timber untouched by lumbering companies. On the uneven terrain of Renfrew County there were pockets of forest that would not have been profitable to harvest, and there the trees grew large. (An eastern white pine felled in Maria Township in December 1967 had a height of 112 feet and an average diameter of 41 inches. Its age was calculated to be 242 years. A cross-section is on display at the Champlain Trail Museum in Pembroke.)

In the centre of Renfrew County, rising from the eastern shore of Lake Dore, is a 120-acre tract of virgin forest believed to be unique in eastern

Ontario. Dedicated 19 June 1979 as the Shaw Woods Forest Reserve, this protected area has been described as typical of the region before widespread logging took place. The undisturbed trees, said to be 'the largest to be found in Canada east of the Rockies,' will allow present and future generations to see the variety of trees that faced the earliest settlers before they cleared their land.[2] This forest reserve contains white ash, beech, hemlock, sugar maple, red maple, yellow birch, white oak, black ash, and white pine.

The range of deciduous woods was therefore not as great as in southern Ontario. Black walnut and chestnut do not occur naturally in eastern Ontario, and there was no black cherry large enough to supply boards for furniture-making. There was pine aplenty for the use of the skilled and un-skilled woodworker. The free grant acts of 1868 and 1880 both acknowl-edged that the 200-acre lots being allocated for farming would have pine trees growing on them; the locatee was at liberty to cut them down and use them for building, fencing, and fuel, as needed for well-being. No mention was made of using pine to construct furniture, but this soft wood was the most commonly used. Another soft wood, light in colour and fragrant, was the eastern cedar, which grew well in swampy areas unprofitable for farm-ing; it was most often used as the secondary wood in furniture, out of sight or in places where strength was not needed.

As in other parts of eastern Canada cleared by pioneers earlier in the nineteenth century, the making of furniture at home was a necessity as long as frontier conditions prevailed. The newcomers were far from stores, had little cash, and depended on their own ingenuity. In her description of furni-ture in Upper Canada Village, where household furnishings from St Law-rence River communities have been assembled, Jeanne Minhinnick com-mented, 'Later pieces, available today, often look exactly like the earliest primitive furniture, though their actual date is probably later than 1860.'[3] By that date the communities along the St Lawrence had matured and pros-pered; access to water enabled residents to purchase sophisticated furnish-ings, imported or domestic, for their homes. Furniture factories had begun to replace the individual craftsmen who flourished when communities were isolated and in their infancy. Imported woods, such as mahogany, were available.

When German immigrants began to arrive in Renfrew County in 1858, there were still individual craftsmen at work there. Pembroke, with a population of 700, had a cabinet-maker, Samuel Halliday, as well as several carpenters. Renfrew, with a population of 450, was the starting-point for many newcomers attracted to Canada by the promise of free land on the

Ottawa and Opeongo Road; in this community there were three cabinet-makers, Robert Drysdale, Robert C. Mills, and James Wait, as well as a chair-maker, James Watt, and several carpenters. Even the small village of Arnprior, population 250, had its own cabinet-maker, William Tough.[4]

When an extension of the Canada Central Railway reached Renfrew in October 1872, heavy machinery arrived for Thomas Hynes' Cabinet Factory,[5] to enable it to run by steam-power. Born in Fitzroy Township, Hynes had served his apprenticeship as a furniture-maker with D.C. McMartin of Bristol Corners, Quebec, and subsequently worked at his trade in Ohio before settling in Renfrew in 1868.[6] The steam-powered machinery, a 15-horse-power engine firing a 25-horse-power boiler, was installed in the third shop that Hynes occupied in Renfrew, each move being an expansion. The local newspaper was impressed with this factory and salesroom on the main street of the town and described the equipment for making furniture: 'The machinery on the lower floor consists of turning lathes, cross-cut and rip circular saws, a tenoning machine, a large surface plane. In the upper storey there are a cross-cut circular saw, a boring machine, and one of Dobson's newly patented scroll saws. The cost of the machinery which is of the newest and best styles, is $3,000.' This business thrived and in 1894 Hynes purchased another site in Renfrew. There, in partnership with a son, he constructed a brick building housing 'commodious warerooms in which furniture from the large factories is temptingly displayed.'

Thus by 1895 the era of the village furniture-maker, who used hand-powered tools to fill orders from customers, was obsolete in towns like Renfrew. There was also a furniture factory in Pembroke by 1880, advertised by A.H. Horn.[7] In the townships along the Ottawa River, in the eastern part of Renfrew County, families could afford to replace the original furnishings of the farm with manufactured goods, for the farms were prosperous and well served with roads and railroads. The products of local furniture factories, a city store, or Eaton's catalogue were within the reach of any family that could pay in cash and arrange for the transport of goods by horse-drawn vehicle from the nearest railroad station.

There were no such amenities in the townships of Renfrew County where the German immigrants began to settle in 1858. Those who ventured on to land with few assets would have to make their own furniture from the wood that they found on their own property. Most simple functional pieces would be discarded when better furniture could be afforded, and few examples of crude workmanship have survived. Rarely has a household of furniture made by an immigrant not a furniture-maker by trade been kept, but there are a few known. There were a number of farmers whose furniture made only for their own home was constructed so well that chairs, tables, and cupboards, even beds, were still useful and used in the life of their grand-children. Invariably such furniture was made of pine, for softwoods were easier to work than hardwoods.

Only those skilled in furniture-making used hardwoods, but these trees had been cut down and burned in the preparation of potash by the first set-tlers to clear the land. (The ashes of softwoods were not of use for this pur-pose.) Birch, beech, maple, and white ash are virtually unknown in the hand-made furniture of eastern Ontario. Oak was used, but rarely. The most sought-after hardwood was black ash, the least strong but the most decorative of the four species of ash native to eastern Canada.[8] The black, blue, red, and white ashes are all found, and the green ash (a variety of the red) also occurs. *Fraxinus nigra* (black ash), popularly called 'swamp ash,' most closely resembled *Fraxinus excelsior*, the European ash. Its vivid, almost coarse grain would be employed to good effect by the German immi-grants who made the best furniture. It had been the choice of at least two of the men who made spinning-wheels. These woodworkers would not hide it with paint or varnish, for the grain of the ash was meant to be seen, to be appreciated. Their skilful choice of grain, however, would sometimes be concealed by layers of varnish applied by later owners or by the inevitable darkening that occurred within a farm-house heated by wood and lit by oil-lamps.

The frequent use of the black ash in Renfrew County, as the primary wood in the largest and most important pieces of furniture, may be unique in Eastern Canada – judging by the published accounts of early hand-made furniture in Ontario, Quebec, and the Maritimes.[9] Authors and well-known antique dealers Henry and Barbara Dobson have described a rare Quebec-made Regency table, circa 1820–30, thus: 'This is the only piece of furniture known by the authors that uses black ash as the primary wood, that is, for all the external visible surfaces. The secondary or unseen woods are birch and white pine.[10] The German furniture tradition, based on the use of un-painted hardwoods with surface carving, where the decorative effect was achieved by the natural qualities of the wood, has not been much in evidence in other studies of German-Canadian furniture.[11] Yet it survived in the isolated communities of eastern Ontario. The use of black ash was so prodigal that even backboards or shelves are made of the same wood in some cupboards, though it was more customary for pine or cedar to be used where the wood could not be seen.

When a contrasting wood was applied to the surface of the ash, the choice was usually basswood or white wood; one of the softest of the Canadian hardwoods, it was valued for its hand-carving and has good gluing characteristics. In the late Victorian period the bland surface of the basswood was painted black to heighten the contrast with the figured ash – and this surface, painted black, might be further decorated with gold. Black paint was sometimes used to outline the cornice (the moulding or group of mouldings at the top of a cupboard), and there was a central symbol, such as a heart or a cross, this too might be emphasized further by gold paint.

Black ash grows on wet swampy ground, pockets of which are common in the townships of eastern Ontario that do not border the Ottawa River. Even so, the use of black ash by furniture-makers of the first, second, and third generations of German immigrants (and by at least one who immigrated from Poland in the 1890s) has no simple explanation. Its grain is certainly more attractive than that of other hardwood species growing in the area. In western Renfrew County the black ash is plentiful and in favourable conditions can reach a height of about 90 feet, though 40–60 feet is more common. Its trunk may grow to a diameter of 1 to 2 feet, and boards of eighteen or twenty inches are seen in the furniture.

One reason for its continued use offered to the author on several occasions was: 'Black ash doesn't burn.' White ash, which grows on stony well-drained soil, is also found abundantly on the ridges of the Canadian Shield. It was highly valued as firewood, and farmers who lived close to Pembroke recall how they would take wagonloads of white ash into Pembroke's market and wait patiently to get their price. Some would not reduce their price at day's end, preferring to take their wares home, rather than give in to bargain-hunters. If this explanation has validity, then it may have been a reason why the black ash escaped the fate of other hardwoods cleared from the land and burned in order to make potash.

Men without any particular training in the skills of furniture-making had to make the first necessary beds, chairs, tables, and other functional items for sleeping, sitting, and eating. Hand-planed wood sufficed before sawmills were within easy reach, and hand-carved legs were made before lathes were available. When the first German immigrants arrived in eastern Upper Canada there was at least one water-powered sawmill in action, at Balaclava, Grattan Township, which served the settlers on the Opeongo Road.[12] Most of the German settlers lived in townships that did not have sufficient water-power to run a sawmill, so the earliest boards were planed by hand.

Few of the simple pieces made by pioneers show any style that could be interpreted as a tradition carried from Europe to the wilderness of a new country. One exception is the two-board chair or *Bretstuhl*, where the back and seat are joined by two through mortise-and-tenon joints secured with tusk tenons under the seat.[13] The legs are straight and tapered, mounted free

TABLE 3
Glossary of furniture-making terms

---

bead moulding   a small, half-round, projecting moulding that looks like a
   string of spaghetti
blind doors   doors that do not contain panes of glass
butt joint   the joining of the squared edges of two boards at right angles
cartouche   an ornamental scroll, often with curling edges
chamfer   a right-angled corner cut away to form a flat surface
cornice   the moulding or group of mouldings on the top of a cupboard
crest rail   top rail of a chair back
dentils   small square blocks used in a series on cornices
dovetail joint   a strong corner joint achieved by cutting two pieces of wood
   in a pattern resembling a dove's tail and interlocking them
ebonized   stained or painted black
finial   an ornament at the top of a post or of a cupboard, usually turned on
   a lathe
glazed doors   doors containing panes of glass
lathe   a machine for turning wood or other materials, by rotating articles
   against the tools used
mortise-and-tenon   joint created by a rectangular tongue that fits into a
   corresponding cut-out slot
ogee curve   sometimes spelled 'OG'; common name for S-shaped curve
pediment   a triangular or arched section at the top of a cupboard
rails   horizontal members of chairs or beds
splayed   slanted out
stretcher   rail that supports or braces the legs of a chair

---

of stretchers, and may be squared or octagonal in cross-section or even
rounded. Examples have been found in eastern Ontario. The essential and
identical feature of the construction of this chair has been followed, but ela-
borate carving and cut-out scrollwork on the back are missing. They resemble the sketches of the chair outlined in *The Cassubian Civilization*, a study
of the ethnography of northwestern Poland. They are not encrusted with
detail similar to the chairs illustrated in *Bauernmöbel*, a book that shows
finely carved chairs from different parts of Germany. [14]
   An even simpler version, found more often than the two-board chair, is
the stick stool, which has no back. In this crude seat or bench the four legs
are splayed and enter the single board without any supporting structure,
though they are obviously tapered (tenoned) to fit into a hole. Many old
stick stools are still sturdy because their makers combined green and

seasoned woods to ensure a tight fit; if legs made of dried wood were inserted into a thick seat of green wood, the latter would shrink as it dried. However, many surviving stick stools have a cluster of nails driven into the joint, indicating that the meeting of the two boards had to be secured. Softwoods such as pine were popular for seats, but legs would be fashioned from hardwoods such as maple and ash. The use of different woods is another reason why joints have loosened in many old chairs (because of different shrinkage) and also why so many old chairs were painted to give cohesion to the design. Paint was not a typical finish given to hardwood furniture made by skilled German immigrants. On pine, home-made paint created by mixing a powder with oil was commonly used and produced a reddish-brown finish of varying degress of opacity. If the furniture was too close to a stove or a heating pipe the finish will have a bubbled scabrous appearance.

Other styles included the spindle-back (or rod-back) Windsor chair, the spindle-back Boston rocker, and the slat-back chair. All were made by professional chair-makers and home carpenters in the years before 1850 in southern Ontario.[15] They were made after 1850 in eastern Ontario where families lived far from furniture factories. Examples in the possession of families descended from the men who made the chairs have an established provenance. All could be made with hand tools.

The spindle-back or rod-back Windsor chair is an improvement on the stick stool; it has a back consisting of two plain posts connected by a crest rail at the top, with a number of spindles that connect the crest with the seat and provide support. The four legs are splayed but are reinforced on three or four sides by stretchers. The shapes of posts, legs, seats, and spindles may vary; the earliest ones had single-slab seats, while later ones had multiple glue-jointed boards.

The spindle-back Boston rocker has a high back in which the spindles and posts curve before they meet the rail. The legs on either side are set into short rockers, the mark of an early chair; the saddle-shaped seat may have been constructed from several boards that may have become unglued with time. The typical Boston rocker has arms, but the armless variation, usually referred to as a sewing or nursing rocker, is also found. The legs and stretchers may have been turned on a foot-powered lathe, but the spindles are slim and plain. Rockers of this type were made in Ontario until the last quarter of the nineteenth century, by which time they were being produced by furniture factories.

The slat-back chair has horizontal rails at the back. The seats were woven, most often of elm bark, and had to be replaced. Some had arms and some had rockers or both or neither. The two back posts usually ended in a decorative turning, but otherwise the chair showed little evidence that any

sophisticated tools were required for its production. They were sturdy
chairs with slats two to five in number, but those that have survived have
usually had the seat replaced by a more modern alternative.

In a pioneer's home the first table was likely to be plain and utilitarian. The
frame was composed of four legs joined by four rails, which were called a
skirt; this frame supported a top that might consist of one or two wide
boards. If the top were made of a softwood, such as pine, it would have to
be replaced eventually. The legs and skirt, customarily made of hardwoods,
would endure longer, especially since they would be protected by paint or
varnish. The table surface was most often left unfinished and could be
scrubbed clean. Once in use it might occasionally be planed to remove signs
of wear. In the earliest tables, the skirts had no drawers and the hand-made
legs were generally squared or gently rounded. Plain old kitchen tables still
found in German farms often have a distinctive curve at the bottom of the
leg; some have hinged drop leaves that in a horizontal position are firmly
supported by wooden blocks or butts that slide out from underneath.

Treadle or foot-powered lathes made it possible for even the farmer without training to make turned legs. Making four legs the same required more
expertise. The addition of drawers, as well as turned legs chamfered at the
junction of the upper squared sections to fit into the skirt, made a kitchen
table of pleasing appearance that served several generations. In some cases
the table top fitted over the frame and was joined to it by detachable
wooden pegs. While peg-top tables in the German communities of southwestern Ontario might be made of walnut or cherry, those in the German
farms of eastern Ontario were made of pine. Since this softwood is easily
scarred and worn, the surface on many of these tables has been protected
with twentieth-century oil-cloth glued to the wood. Alternatively, it has
been replaced, and with narrower boards.

The draw-leaf extension table, compact and ingeniously constructed, has
been found in Ontario only in regions where German immigrants settled,
e.g. Waterloo County.[16] In eastern Ontario this style was made by at least
one skilled furniture-maker and by many settlers who fashioned furniture
only for their own family. The placing of a drawer on an end that has an extension leaf is common and curious, since the drawer is not easily accessible
when the table is opened to its fullest extent, which may be nine or ten feet.
This draw-leaf table may be square or rectangular, and in either style the
position of a drawer on a side with no extension is more accommodating,
and the drawer is larger.

Judging from the number of German families who know that one of their
ancestors gave birth during the long ocean crossing, the making of a cradle

must sometimes have been a priority. Some were hastily made of un-seasoned wood that later cracked. In an age when large families were ex-pected and appreciated, the cradle was a project that many young fathers had to tackle in their wilderness home, and a careful piece of workmanship often resulted. Since it is small, easily stored, and easily transported, and since the maker's identity is usually known, the home-made cradle is the piece most often retained within a family's possession. After it had been used by the children of the first couple, it might be passed from sister to brother as the progeny of the second generation appeared. It was sometimes claimed by the first one to get married and begin a family. In rare cases the babies were produced so rapidly that two cradles were needed by the same mother. After the third generation had been rocked through babyhood, the cradles were seldom used. Now they are most often found, coated with chaff and cobwebs, stored in a barn with other obsolete or seldom-used items.

The home-made cradles of the German immigrants in eastern Ontario were made in two styles, both lacking a hood or canopy. A rectangular box, constructed from five boards secured either by dovetails or dowelled butt-end joints, with deep crescent-shaped rockers positioned at the head and foot, was a popular shape. Usually the headboard and footboard were iden-tical in design and depth and may each have had a pierced decoration that made the cradle easy to grasp; some had hand-holds at the side instead. Two or three holes on both long sides enabled a string or cord to be passed across the cradle, so that it could be rocked manually, from a distance. If the rockers were made of pine the wear and tear on the softwood edges would be considerable in families with many children. Some rockers are almost flat from wear, while others have an extra curved piece attached later. Those made of pine were coated in the common red-brown oil-based paint mixed at home, while those made from the black ash received only a clear varnish. This box-like style was characteristic of the area of northwest Poland, Cassubia, whence some German-speaking immigrants came. (It was also the style most often used in making dolls' cradles, probably because it was so simple to make in a scaled-down version.)

In the box-like cradle, four sides of solid wood or panelled wood might be joined at the corners with squared hand-made posts – sometimes termed *pencil* posts – into which the sides fitted with mortise-and-tenon joints. The tops of these posts might end plainly or with hand-made finials. The wood used was pine. From this style of cradle it was a natural progression to the larger 'youth bed,' suitable for a child or a young teenager. Again the head-board and footboard were identical in height and design, but the side rails were low, for there was not the same danger of the occupant falling out. Since it had to accommodate a heavier weight, the single baseboard had been replaced by a series of slats that rested on the side-rails in a ladder-like formation. (Exactly the same style was used for adults' beds, some in painted pine and some in black ash.)

Cradles that rocked too easily and spilled their contents were said to be the reason for the construction of a swinging cradle owned by descendants of Louis Frederick Verch, who left Germany in the 1870s and had eight sons and two daughters. The swinging cradle is uncommon.[17] In this one the frame has four plain and immovable posts, braced by side-rails on all four sides, and has no pretension to elegance; the cradle, though, has been designed with a row of spindles above three panels and with fresh paint is still in use.

When lathes became more common a patient craftsman might make a large crib fenced by turned spindles, but in general the turning of wooden posts was confined to the four corners of a more demanding style of bed or cradle. This type had panels fitted into four squared posts with ends turned on the lathe. These panels were made of hardwood and had slender rockers to which were attached the ends of the corner posts. Some posts were inserted into holes in the rockers, and some grasped the rockers on both sides. In the German styles found in eastern Ontario the posts were not high enough to be a practical aid for rocking, unlike the ones made in Quebec. The sturdy pine rockers constructed on the box-like cradles could be conveniently moved up and down by foot, but in the four-posted style the slim rocker was susceptible to damage, if this was tried.

The use of panels that fitted into each other by mortise-and-tenon joints was some assurance against the likelihood that the wood might split. It also permitted the use of woods not available in such generous widths as the omnipresent pine. Rarely, panels were glued together to form smooth boards of hardwood for the cradle. A hardwood cradle could be decorated by adding intricate panelling or beaded moulding; no painting or stencilling was needed.

In some cradles the bottom board was secured firmly to the four sides with no allowance made for shrinkage – and it split. The problem was solved most simply by allowing the bottom board to rest on ledges; another method was to make a row of parallel slats or spindles that provided a base for a mattress. In either case the base of the cradle could be replaced without damage to the rest of the structure. Again the styles of beds paralleled the styles of hardwood cradles, resulting in the low four-poster.

Other types of home furnishings were also fairly simple to make. One of the earliest furnishings on a farm was the pail bench. For use in the kitchen or summer kitchen, this tiered bench generally had two or three shelves and was made of pine. Though it was a utilitarian piece rather than furniture, made by the home handyman rather than a skilled craftsman, it was sometimes topped by curved arms or a scalloped gallery that gave it a graceful shape. Those later exposed to the weather or damp ground have deteriorated, and this reminder of pioneer days, when water was carried from a well and when every rural home had at least one cow for milking, has usually been chopped up for firewood. The one made by Johann Krohn of Germanicus, who was listed in the 1881 census as a 50-year-old father of seven children, was a clumsy construction of thick pine and large nails that did not excite admiration when it surfaced in a yard sale in 1982. Pail benches were still being constructed as late as 1930 by carpenters in the Golden Lake area and can still be found in use on some farms.

Shelves could be attached to the walls of a log farm-house by anyone who could hammer a nail. By the time that eastern Ontario was being settled by German immigrants, clocks made in Connecticut and Massachusetts were being sold cheaply throughout North America.[18] With their moderate height and shallow depth, they were suitable for a shelf or a mantel top, and they became known as mantel clocks. A wooden shelf supported by a perpendicular brace could serve to house a clock. In some German homes a two-tiered shelf was built; the lower accommodated the Bible, equally indispensable to the daily routine of a devout family. A Bible in their own language was one of the most treasured items that immigrants brought to a new land; many families used the early blank pages as a diary of births and deaths.

A wash-stand was a convenience in homes that did not have bathrooms. In the bedroom it could contain a crockery wash-basin, a jug for hot water, a shaving mug, a soap dish, and all the accessories needed for keeping clean. It enabled family members to wash in the privacy of their own bedroom. With a splash board at the back, to protect the wall, the wash-stand might have a cupboard with one or two doors to conceal the utensils; a sophisticated version would have rungs along the sides to serve as towel racks.

In eastern Ontario, where the growing season is short and the winter long, the storage of food was imperative. Root-houses for vegetables and dug-out cellars under the house were an essential feature of the farm, accommodating barrels of sauerkraut and pickled herrings, eggs in water-glass, tubs of butter under brine, smoked hams, sausages, and salted pork. Shelves were built along the walls of the cellar, and some foods were suspended from the ceiling. Bottles of preserves, jams, jellies, and perishables such as fruit were stored on sturdy pine shelves, more than an inch thick.

More precious delicacies were stored in a food cupboard, or *Milch-schrank*. Although it might see duty only in the cellar or a nearby shed, it was made with care and even with decoration. In both the Rankin area of Wilberforce Township and the Augsburg area of South Algona Township it was a regular product of a skilled furniture-maker; these men must have had a steady demand, judging from the number of cupboards that have survived. The styles are readily identifiable. The one-door style of Augsburg and the two-door style of Rankin both have ventilation in the doors provided by a series of vertical posts. Curtains, usually of porous fabric, were attached to the insides in order to prevent invasion by insects. In cupboards made by farmers the doors are solid; they may be panelled, scalloped, even topped by a pediment, although the only admirer of the workmanship would be the immediate family. They were made so stoutly, with useful shelves, that they were frequently kept by family members who sold a farm and moved away. They were invariably made of pine and painted, even by the skilled men. Later generations are rescuing food cupboards from the obscurity of the basement, realizing their worth as a souvenir of the early years of subsistence farming.

In contrast to chairs and tables, cradles and beds, and shelves and benches, cupboards designed for the storage of dishes or clothes were more likely to be made by skilled men. Cupboards made by amateurs lack the fine detail. Trained craftsmen had been taught how to construct 'case furniture,' with dovetailed drawers that slid easily in and out and chamfered doors that closed firm; these were furnishings that were made to last and merited surface carving or fretwork that pleased the eye. Some furniture-makers would design a distinctive pediment, with or without symbols, which still identifies their cupboards.

There were some trained cabinet-makers whose descendants no longer live in the area. For example, Charles Freidrich (Karl) Timm, born 1869 at Samoklink, Bromberg, Posen, married Bertha Wilhelmine Reglin at Rankin in 1892 and lived near Carson Lake in the Barry's Bay area, where he was known as a cabinet-maker until his death in 1912.[19] His widow remarried, and none of their children live in western Renfrew County. So no one can identify a piece made by Karl Timm.

There were cabinet-makers whose work cannot be attributed because there are no pieces in the possession of their families. One example is Christian Remus, who arrived, aged 59, in the Pembroke area in 1864. In company with friends, Remus, his wife, and their four children left Hansfelde, Kreis Satzig, Regierungs Bezirk, Stettin, and travelled to Canada.[20] At Ottawa the group hired a team of horses to transport them to Cobden, at the end of a good road. There they embarked on a small boat, which must have travelled along the Muskrat River toward Pembroke. The group finally arrived in Pembroke, and with $10 in his purse Christian Remus settled in nearby Upper Alice. He made furniture for the settlers and coffins when anyone died. He sometimes would get up in the night and say, 'I must make a coffin. Someone is going to die.' In the 1881 census he was listed as a 76-year-old widower, living with his married daughter, Louisa (Mrs Frederick Huebner), in Alice Township. Neither Christian nor his son, Frank, a 28-year-old married man with his own family, was listed as a furniture-maker. Although Christian's skill is known to his descendants, not one piece of work has been definitely attributed to him.

In the home of Elmer Maves, on a farm close to where Remus had lived in Upper Alice, there was a square draw-leaf table made of black ash, a pine sideboard with a scalloped gallery, and a glazed kitchen cupboard with panelled doors as well as a drawer that could be locked by a wooden peg. All were the work of a skilled man, but no piece was signed. And all were destroyed when this farm-house burned to the ground, 22 December 1980. It was a sad loss for Mr Maves, who had turned down offers as high as $1,000 a piece from an antique dealer.

In houses heated by stoves, chimney cupboards were sometimes constructed underneath the chimney as a support;[21] these did not have any back boards. Similarly, it was easier for men with limited skill to build a flat-to-the-wall cupboard without any back. Corner cupboards might also be constructed in this way, for a corner in a log building would seldom be a true right angle. Perhaps for this reason, corner cupboards do not seem to have been often made by any of the trained furniture-makers of German origin in eastern Ontario.

One German immigrant who succeeded in filling the rooms of his farm-house with a variety of durable furniture was Gustave (or Gustav) Michel, a stonemason from Silesia[22] who arrived in Petawawa Township in 1867. With his wife, who had suffered the death of all three children during the ocean crossing, he lived in a field at first and boarded with the William Gutzman family during the first winter. In 1868 his name appears on the assessment rolls of Petawawa Township as a farmer who owned 100 acres of land, 2 of them cleared. He was working in Pembroke, earning money as a stonemason. By 1872 he had completed a large log farm-house and had furnished it with cupboards, couches, benches, tables, chairs, beds, and a cradle, all made from pine. Many of these pieces were still in use when his unmarried grandson, Oscar Michel, died there 1 April 1981. It was a rare example of a family that had kept the interior furnishings of a farm-house virtually intact throughout three generations of occupation. Following Oscar Michel's death the contents of the home were dispersed and the property was sold.

In a home furnished by the work of an immigrant, household effects may stay in place only as long as direct descendants live there. Furniture made by August Schwartz from Strasbourg, who settled in Fraser Township about 1881, was distinguished by the chevron carving that followed the outlines of drawers and doors, a feature identified with the German Palatinate.[23] The last of the four unmarried sons who lived on the family's farm decided to leave it when he was 90 years old and board with a neighbour. The hand-made furniture was sold by him for $5 and $10 a piece to an antique dealer, except the tall clothes cupboard; made of pine, this cupboard was rather large to move, but when cut in half horizontally, the bottom half served as a dresser for Schwartz in his new home.

In the first generation that lived its adult life on the land, there would customarily be only one clothes cupboard made for the parents' bedroom. In farm homes today with two or more, inquiries reveal that the extra ones have been acquired by inheritance or purchase. Towering seven to eight feet high, with a drawer at the base, they have back boards bearing traces of a sawmill's circular blade. Clothes were suspended from wooden hooks, either fixed in rows or swinging on projections from the back.

In contrast to the dish cupboards and other smaller collectibles such as wash-stands and dough-boxes, clothes cupboards have not been purchased from the farms by 'pickers' who go from door to door, offering cash for old furniture. The type built by German immigrants in eastern Ontario was made in one piece, unlike the wardrobe or *Schrank* found in the German communities of southern Ontario which could be dismantled and moved to another room. The type of eastern Ontario appears to have been made in the bedroom itself, for in some homes it cannot be moved out of the bedroom or down a narrow twisting staircase. It may still be in place when owners sell a farm-house – and it stays where it is.

The survival of clothes cupboards through several generations may be the most revealing evidence for the identity of some skilled, first-and second-generation German furniture-makers. The distance that the furniture-maker travelled to practise his trade was limited in the days of poor roads and horse-drawn vehicles. If a cupboard has not moved from its first home and if a descendant of the maker or a customer can provide an identification, positive attribution can be given to various pieces by one man.

A series of events demonstrates this well. One fine cupboard emerged from a farm because the fourth owner altered the stairs and the cupboard was taken to a franchise that strips varnishes and paints from old furniture. Its origin, on Concession 25 in Wilberforce Township, was linked with two other cupboards from that road purchased by collectors. All three were crowned by a striking scrolled cornice that contained surface carving below the thorny and scalloped top. One of these cupboards, entirely of pine, was distinguished by a heart, and subsequent research showed that it had been made for Mr and Mrs William Druve who married in 1873. (Identification was provided by Ethel Michel of Ottawa, their granddaughter, who went to live at that farm in 1906.) A second, glazed cupboard, made of pine with applied pieces of basswood, had a carving that looked like five thumb-prints (or ears of wheat). In the case of all three pieces, the last owners could not provide identification of the maker. Several more cupboards and one couch with similar surface carvings were present on farms that the author visited in Petawawa, Alice, and Wilberforce townships. Again no one could supply the name of the maker, though some were positive that the par-ticular piece had belonged to the first members of the family to live in eastern Ontario.

Not until David Raddatz visited his grandparents' homestead in the town-ship of Sebastopol was the maker revealed. The home once occupied by Mr and Mrs Reinhold Raddatz, later by Mr and Mrs John Raddatz, their son and daughter-in-law, had been vacant for years when the grandson, David, entered the house in 1980 and discovered that thieves had attempted to steal the clothes cupboard, the only piece of furniture not taken away by the family. Made of ash, the cupboard was topped with a scrolled cornice. The thieves had managed to get it out of the bedroom but had found it impos-sible to move it down the stairs, and there the cupboard was lodged. David fetched his chain-saw and cut off the bottom section of the cupboard, removing the drawer and freeing the piece of furniture. He took it home to his farm in Bromley Township, where his widowed mother lived.

'That was made by my mother-in-law's father,' said Mrs Raddatz, who had no trouble remembering the name of the furniture-maker, August Boehme (1841–1907). August's grandson, Oscar Boehme, lives on the homestead cleared and farmed by August in Raglan Township, in south-west Renfrew County. Oscar Boehme not only owned pieces of furniture that confirmed the identity of the cupboard-maker in Petawawa, Alice, and Wilberforce townships; he could also supply details of the immigrant's life and back up this history with a crown grant, dates, and certificates. No other furniture-makers of German origin in eastern Ontario has been described with such detail and such conclusive evidence. August Boehme's legacy included not only furniture but also his influence on others.

Basketwork, which did not require special equipment, was another skill brought to eastern Ontario. Indigenous vegetable fibres useful to the pioneer settlers included bark, strips or splints of wood, rushes, and roots, which could be woven into containers. Few early examples have survived. Oscar Boehme of Palmer Rapids knows that a German family whose members were blind made baskets in the area of Raglan and Radcliffe townships; he has one of their round, flat-bottomed baskets, somewhat tattered at the edges.

One German immigrant known to have been skilled as a basket-maker was Jacob Gunsinger (1842–1919), who arrived in Canada in 1882 with his wife and four children and settled at Plevna, at the end of the Frontenac Road.[24] His granddaughter, Lizzie Gunsinger of Plevna, remembers him making baskets out of slats of wood, possibly basswood, about 2 feet by 2½ feet and 15 inches in depth. These baskets were used for carrying chaff or garden produce. Although Jacob Gunsinger was skilled in this work, his granddaughter is sure that he did not earn a living from it in Canada, his main occupation being farming.[25]

One who did supplement his income from basket-making was Friedrich Liebeck, who had a workshop at his farm in Wilberforce Township.[26] Born in Germany in 1860, he had immigrated to Canada nine years later with his parents, Mr and Mrs Mathias Liebeck, who farmed at the end of the Marsh Road in that township, where swampy areas provided a supply of black ash. For years, at least until 1940, Liebeck drove his horse-drawn buggy or sleigh fifteen miles to Pembroke's market, where he sold his baskets and accepted orders. He used wood splints in their manufacture and painted the finished work. When his grandson, Wilfred Liebeck, married in 1937, he and his wife received a laundry and a shopping basket from his grandparents as wedding presents. Painted green, the shopping basket, which has a central handle that enables it to be carried easily over the arm, is still in their possession. The laundry basket has been lined and used as a baby's bassinette for their grandson in London; with handles at both ends, it is exactly the same as that made by another German immigrant, Frank Born, in adjacent Alice Township. An example is in the museum at Pembroke.

Roots of the willow, the 'diamond' willow, were used by William Woermke (1863–1955) to make a basket one day in the 1930s, when he was visiting his relatives on a farm in Wilberforce Township.[27] Having immigrated from Germany as a young man, William had moved from his mother's farm in Sebastopol Township to Saskatchewan to live and work. On a visit home he called on his niece in Germanicus and entertained her children by constructing a basket in a flat bowl shape in two colours; the red roots were split in half, exposing the white interior, and both whole and split roots were combined to make a container of pleasing appearance in two colours.

Although basketwork is more ephemeral than woven fabrics or woodwork, sufficient examples of the styles made by different immigrants to

Pennsylvania have survived to provide models from which duplicates can be made. Baskets made from roots, woods, and grasses by Dutch, Swiss, German, Scots, and French settlers in that state have been reproduced by a teacher of that craft, William Oosterman. In the summer of 1983, he was present one day a week at the Landis Valley State Museum, where he worked and answered questions. Among the collection of finished baskets that surrounded him were two shapes identical to baskets made by German immigrants in Renfrew County. Without prompting, Oosterman identified these two as styles made in Pennsylvania only by German people, not by others. One was a two-handled laundry hamper similar to that made by Fred Liebeck, and the other was a single-handled shopping basket of the type made in the Palmer Rapids area by a blind German family. Both baskets were made of wood splints, in Oosterman's case made of oak because that was the wood most readily available to him. The Pennsylvania teacher remarked, however, that German people had been fond of using a particular type of ash for their basketwork; he remembered that it was called black or swamp ash.

The same hardwood, black ash, was popular in the production of home-made tools used to harvest the cereal crops. Hay rakes, chaff forks, grain shovels, flails, and straw cutters (the last-named known in Pennsylvania as *Streuschneider*) were made by individual farmers from ash and maple. Since the principal grain crop grown by first- and second-generation German farmers was wheat – judging from the list of provisions in the maintenance mortgages – the baking of bread played a vital role in the house-wife's work in feeding the family, and families were usually large. To ease her work in pounding and kneading the rising dough, which had to be kept warm near the wood stove, a dough-box was made so that she could tackle the task in a standing position. Plain and utilitarian, these dough-boxes consisted of a rectangular container mounted on legs or trestles. Usually designed to hold about fifty pounds of dough, the box was about three feet long and about one foot deep; it had sloping sides, perhaps twelve inches wide at the base flaring out to fifteen inches at the top, and its removable lid served double duty because when it was reversed it provided a flat surface for moulding the loaves. Simple handholds on the sides made it easy to grasp the dough-box in order to turn it beside the fire and ensure that an even heat reached the dough inside.

In eastern Ontario most dough-boxes were made of pine, and though the outsides were often painted the inside surfaces were planed and left bare. They were simple enough to be made by the individual farmer; they were also made by skilled men for sale. Dough-boxes made by the more experienced German woodworker typically have an S-shaped side trestle with a cut-out arch. Obsolete now, they were made by village furniture-makers as late as 1930.

Occasionally a man skilled in crafting objects from wood turned his attention to making a toy such as a rocking-horse, and those that have survived show that they were greatly enjoyed; runners are so worn that they may have been replaced, and ears made of leather have become tattered from the tugging of children's hands. The fondness of German immigrants for horses – because they could be ridden, unlike oxen – is told in many a family legend. Typical is the story of Gottlieb Quast, one of the earliest settlers in South Algona Township in 1860; his great-grandson, Mervin Quast, tells of how Gotlieb could still gallop bareback at the age of 75.[28] The number of German settlers who had served in cavalry regiments during military service before they immigrated may explain it. As Frank Keuhl once told his grandson:

> *Erst komt dein phert,*
> *Denn der lieber Gott,*
> *Unt den komst du.*[29]

> *First comes your horse,*
> *Then the Dear Lord,*
> *And then you.*

Horses were also featured in windmills or whirlygigs, complex creations of wood and wire which displayed miniature models of human beings performing the tasks of pioneer life. When a breeze moved the blades of the windmill the attached wires caused life-like movements of the jointed figures. The women churned butter or scrubbed on a washboard. The men sawed or split wood, rode a horse, or milked a cow. Since these windmills were intended to be placed out of doors, they did not have a long life, despite coats of paint, for dampness and changes in temperature slowly eroded the work.

One surviving, complex windmill, with sixteen figures, demonstrates the skill of Johann Gottfried Weissenberg (1834–1910), who made them to earn extra money. Born in Wietzehorst, Posen,[30] in 1859 'Fred' Weissenberg emigrated and in 1860 in Pembroke married Pauline Radtke from Podewels, Pomerania. Shortly afterward he travelled to the United States and enlisted in the union army; he was later wounded and discharged.[31] The Weissenbergs' second son, William, was born in 1863, so the immigrant's foray into action cannot have been lengthy. But he was disabled by his wounds and walked with a limp; from the farm where he boarded on the Black Bay Road in Petawawa Township, he made windmills and furniture to earn a living. His plight came to the attention of a Pembroke lawyer, Peter White, who summoned Weissenberg to appear at the Renfrew County court house in Pembroke. According to William Stresman, a nephew's son, Weissenberg complied with the request with some trepidation, fearing that he was about to be accused of some misdemeanour. Instead, he was asked to sign papers that affirmed that he was disabled as a result of service in the United States Army, and he received a pension from the American government for the rest of his life. His granddaughter, Mabel, remembered how her father, August (born 1860), drove him into Pembroke (a journey of about ten miles) by horse and buggy or horse-drawn sleigh each month to collect this pension.[32] Mabel's grandfather never farmed, and the payment of the pension was continued to his widow, until she died in 1916.

Before Weissenberg's death on 17 September 1910, he had given one of his windmills (which could be turned by hand as well as by the wind) to a young boy. It was a fine toy for children, and the family kept it sheltered under a verandah where it could be protected from the weather. All the sixteen figures were painted white except for the chimney-sweep, holding a brush, who is black from head to toe. The two women, engaged in the traditional jobs of butter-churning and laundry, were garbed in scraps of fabrics, which have been renewed, but the men are not clothed except for the suggestion of jacket and pants and headgear incorporated in the carving of the wooden figures. Not all the figures move. At the summit of this four-tiered structure is a man riding a goat. At the base is a man sitting on a barrel, holding a bottle. At the side a guard with a rifle stands on the steps leading to a watch-tower. The focal point of the arrangement is a pit-saw, operated by one man above and two men below. The other figures that flank this action could have been added later at the whim of the woodworker. There are men chopping wood and two fellows step-dancing; a man is bouncing a child in the air while beside him there is a man with a sword, the purpose of which is unclear. When the windmill is turned there is a flurry of action as these figures spring to life. Descendants of Fred Weissenberg know that he made many windmills, but they do not know if any others survived.

Whereas few toys have outlasted ownership by one or more generations, the tools used for sheer survival or added comfort in a harsh climate have endured. Some still hang in the barns. They were in use in rural Renfrew County long after they were obsolete in urban settings or more prosperous agricultural regions. Hand-held grain cradles were employed on ground that was too littered with boulders ever to benefit from machinery, and scythes still cut the long grass on uneven land. The bleak poverty of the 1930s may have caused the owners of dough-boxes and spinning-wheels to doubt that the future would make them unnecessary. A thick wool blanket is still a warm covering even if it does have a central seam, and so is a woollen quilt; in some old farm-houses that lack central heating the artifacts of the past are making life more comfortable for the present occupants. As a matter of pride, the flax runner woven by a grandmother, from plants harvested by a grandfather, may be brought out to show a visitor, and in some homes the spinning-wheel, newly varnished, occupies a place of honour in the living-room, where it is not used – but admired.

Basswood shovel made by Karl Raglan, Wilberforce Township; forks of
maple and ash made by Ernst Brose, Wilberforce Township

William Walther using neck-yoke to carry potatoes from garden to root cellar, Sebastopol Township

Salt box
still in use,
North Algona
Township

bottom right Rectangular wooden bowls carved by Fred Schultz, Alice
Township, for making butter and mixing meat

Boot-jack still in use,
Sebastopol Township

Streuschneider: straw clamped in wooden trough is cut by hinged iron blade for animal bedding. Petawawa Township

Four dough-boxes

Bill Luloff,
North Algona Township

Albert Zadow,
South Algona Township

Gierman family,
Sebastopol Township

Walther family,
Sebastopol Township

Rocking-horses
left North Algona Township
right Lyndoch

OPPOSITE
Weissenberg's Windmill, by Johann Gottfried 'Fred' Weissenberg,
Petawawa Township

Lathe used by Charles Hoelke, South Algona Township, to make black ash spinning-wheels

OPPOSITE
Sideboard of black ash, made by Fred Morlock, Sebastopol Township

top Panelled doors in black ash, North Algona Township

bottom Black ash cupboard, North Algona Township

Chest of drawers in black ash said to have been made by Edward Weber

Four home-made chairs

Michael Luloff,
North Algona Township

Ferdinand Biesenthal,
Alice Township

August Boehme,
Raglan Township

Gustave Michel,
Petawawa Township

Draw-leaf table made by Ferdinand Biesenthal, Alice Township

OPPOSITE

Type of footed leg believed made exclusively by German settlers,
Wilberforce Township

Draw-leaf table made by Johann Lipke, Wilberforce Township

Box-like cradles

Pine, painted, made by August Mueller, Grattan Township

Black ash, made by August Boehme, Raglan Township

Box-like cradle with pencil posts made by Herman Verch, North Algona Township

Mrs Elsie Zadow rocked fourteen children in this panelled cradle with pencil posts. South Algona Township

Hardwood cradles with turned posts

Ash,
Kathen family,
Pembroke

Oak,
Ashick family,
Rankin

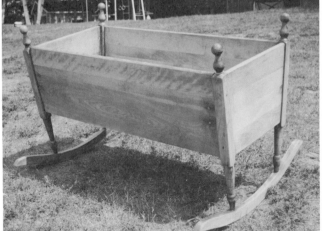

Maple,
Kuhl family,
Eganville

Black ash panelled youth bed with pencil posts, made by August
Mueller, in use by great-grandson, Grattan Township

BELOW

left Black ash cradle with pencil posts, spindled, made by August
Bohme, Raglan Township

right Bed with pencil posts, spindled – post of black ash and panels of
pine; made by August Boehme, Raglan Township

 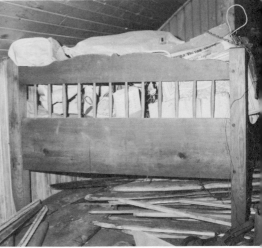

Pail-benches

Made by Karl Hildebrandt, Wilberforce Township

Made by Albert Zadow, South Algona Township

Pail-bench of thick pine
with large square-headed
nails, built by
Johann Krohn

Pail-bench made for a couple who married in 1930 and still in use fifty
years later, Hagarty Township

left Bible-shelf (Bible stored behind curtain), Wilberforce Township

right Clock-shelf made by August Boehme, Raglan Township

left Amateur's cupboard (painted pine and varnished black ash), without drawers, South Algona Township

right Wash-stand, made by August Gust, Petawawa Township

Kitchen cupboard made by a skilled man, with a locking device on one drawer, Alice Township

Kitchen cupboard and couch made by Gustave Michel served three generations, Petawawa Township.

Amateur's kitchen cupboard, with clumsy dovetails (detail), Blemkie family, Grattan Township

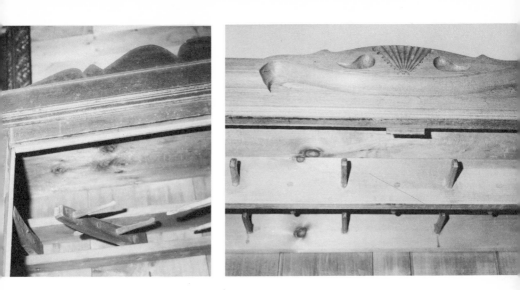

left Wooden pegs attached to a set of projecting arms that pivot from the back, Sebastopol Township

right Rows of wooden pegs in fixed positions, North Algona Township

Chevron border made by German immigrant (from Strasburg), Fraser Township

William Oosterman identified two types of Pennsylvania baskets as uniquely German: a laundry hamper and a shopping basket, both in styles also made in Renfrew County.

Laundry hamper   Shopping basket

Laundry basket made by Frank Born, Alice Township

Peg basket made by Frank Kumm, Wilberforce Township

Basket made by
blind members of
a German family,
Raglan Township

Sawmill at Rankin (courtesy Locksley-Rankin Women's Institute)

OPPOSITE

top Julius Budd's sawmill, Budd Mills, Wilberforce Township (courtesy Wesley Budd, Wilberforce Township)

bottom Circular-saw marks in wood sawn into boards at a sawmill, South Algona Township

Reinke's factory, Eganville (above), founded 1895 by three men, including R.G. Reinke, a ship's carpenter; interior view (below), circa 1900 (photos courtesy Waldemar Reinke, Eganville)

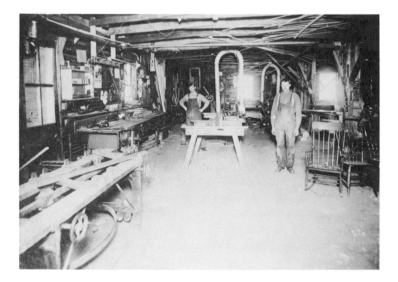

CHAPTER SEVEN

Furniture-makers in a new land

August Boehme 1841–1907

In 1865, when August Boehme and his wife, Mary Kielow, immigrated from Brandenburg to eastern Upper Canada, the community of farmers in north-west Wilberforce Township, Renfrew County, was well established. Along Concessions 22 to 25, and the cross-roads that intersected them, a colony of German immigrants[1] had made Rankin the commercial centre of its settlement. The village had grown up around a few stores, including a blacksmith's shop, where the first Lutheran services were held, and a stream that provided water for a succession of steam-powered sawmills. This area, about twelve miles from Pembroke, had first been cleared and settled by the Irish-Welsh family of Edwards, who penetrated the wilderness in 1841.[2] By 1869 a group of German farmers was sufficiently prosperous to pay $1,000 to Evan Edwards for one acre of land for the site of a Methodist church. Presumably the farmers could also pay for furniture to be made for their homes.

Married 21 June 1862, the Boehme couple had been bereaved by the loss of their first child, Louise, during the ocean crossing of six weeks. The year of their arrival is confirmed by a trinket-box that 23-year-old August made for his wife, bearing her initials and the year 1865. Though a blacksmith by trade, Boehme was also a skilful woodworker who could make his own planes and construct furniture ranging from cradles to couches, but his most notable legacy is a number of cupboards that have turned up in bewildering number of townships in Renfrew County.

Since he did not farm, a furniture-maker did not need to own land. Boehme arrived before the Homestead Act of 1868 made the acquisition of

200 acres easy. It is believed that Boehme and his teen-age wife boarded with other people in their early years in eastern Ontario. ('probably trying to get a bit together,' as his grandson phrased it). Somehow, the family escaped the attention of census-takers in 1871, though undoubtedly living in the Rankin area, where one child, Carl Gustav, was buried. Judging from the distribution of large clothes cupboards in Boehme's style, which often cannot be taken out of the farm bedroom because of their sizes, Boehme must have moved around the countryside, working in customers' homes.

Not until he moved to Raglan Township did Boehme apply for a crown grant of 200 acres under the 1868 Homestead Act, choosing Lot 13, Concession 17, and Lot 14, Concession 18. His application, 24 April 1874, was processed by John S.J. Watson of Rockingham, a commissioner of oaths, and witnessed by Frank Densin, a neighbouring farmer in Raglan Township. In the 1881 census household no. 106 listed August Boehme, 39, as a farmer, with his wife Mary, 29, and 7 children born in Ontario: William, 15, Bertha, 12, Mary, 10, Charles, 8, Anna, 5, August, 3, and Herman, 2. Four of 12 children had died young, including the twelfth, Fredericka, who died at birth, 10 March 1881. Boehme was granted title to his land in 1883, which means that he must have fulfilled his duties of settlement, including the construction of a house sixteen by twenty feet.

The movement of a number of German farmers from the Rankin area to Raglan Township, including the Budaricks, the Richters, and the Manteufels, took place in the 1870s and has no simple explanation. August's grandson, Oscar, thinks that his grandfather moved in order to find uncrowded land. Certainly the hilly 200 acres he chose is isolated, about two miles from his nearest neighbour; it consists of rough grazing land and bush, more suitable for sheep and poultry than for cattle and crops. It is good for hunting and trapping, an avocation that the grandson has continued to pursue.

August Boehme's family lived at first in a scooped-roof shanty, a vanished dwelling that served them only until a log house was constructed. Most of this two-storey home remains, and the detail of its beams, floors, and doors reveals the craftsmanship of a fine woodworker. The lintel of the door that led to the upper storey has a tulip design; the door latches were carved from wood and still work; and the beams have been edged with a moulding plane and serve as a support for racks to dry apples, a suspended pole for drying socks, and a sturdy buttress for a hanging bookcase pegged on either side. In the kitchen area much original furnishing remains, including a pail-bench, a dough-box, a table with squared legs and a drawer, and a farmer's flop-bench. An old wood-burning stove occupies the centre of the downstairs room, for the owner of the property finds this old house useful as a centre for his trapping operations. A cupboard and two chairs sold years ago have been illustrated in three books on early furniture, with the name of August Boehme in the captions, so Oscar is not surprised by visitors who track him down and express an interest in his old furniture. While he is not tempted by offers of ready cash, he is amused by the values placed on objects which he regards as family possessions too personal to sell. (In the summer of 1981 he was offered $700 for the trinket-box by a picker who started at $50 and kept increasing his offer while Oscar feigned reluctance. In the end, refusing to sell, he said, 'Two fools met here today. You're a fool for offering $700 and I'm a fool for refusing it.')

In *The Furniture of Old Ontario* (1973), Phillip Shackleton described August Boehme's kitchen cupboard as displaying folk-craft tradition, owing nothing to the style books. In *The Heritage of Upper Canadian Furniture* (1978), Howard Pain described the same glazed dish dresser (also illustrated) as a direct reflection of a common form in the German rural tradition; two chairs by Boehme are also featured, one a simple *Bretstuhl*, considered a traditional German design. That same chair and the kitchen cupboard appear again in *A Splendid Harvest* (1981), by Michael Bird and Terry Kobayashi, accompanied by a photograph showing the Boehme family posing, about 1900, in front of part of the farm-house that still stands.

When August Boehme had become an owner of land, farming became his main occupation. The making of furniture was no longer his major activity, though he obviously furnished his own home. Still in use is a harvest table eight feet long, with a pegged top that can be lifted and reversed; this and several items of painted pine still furnish the house. The upper room contains a bed and a cradle made in a similar design, both unpainted and both made from black ash. Boehme chose this hardwood, which grew on the swampy parts of his property, for the cradles and cupboards that he made for his daughters when they married. For the clothes cupboard for his own home he chose ash and put a heart on top – a vital clue. The cupboard rescued from the Raddatz homestead was also of this ash; the cornice had the unmistakable scroll, with a heart and two ears of wheat or thumb-prints on either side.

The cradle that Boehme made for his daughter, Mary, who married Reinhold Raddatz, is the box-like style, with three cut-out holes in the identical footboard and headboard, making it easy to grasp. Four sides (joined with wooden pegs) are made of black ash, with vivid grain centred along each side, but the bottom piece is of pine. The rockers are so worn from use that a crescent-shaped piece has been attached underneath each one. In the fall of 1981 the cradle was being readied for the fifth generation to use it. It had never been painted.

The cradle, the clothes cupboard, and the bed that August Boehme made for use in his Raglan Township home were made from black ash, but he used pine for a food cupboard, a clock shelf, a pail-bench, a hanging bookcase, a dough-box, a hired man's bed, a stool, and other furnishings. His choice of black ash for large and important pieces is significant. No other hardwood appears to have been worked by him, although maple, oak, and white ash grow nearby. His earlier work in the Rankin area, 1865–74, cannot be fully documented, but those cupboards and one couch that bear his style are all made of pine, with occasional use of basswood as a secondary material.

The German immigrants who lived in the northwest corner of Wilberforce Township and who belonged to the Evangelical church did not have their own place of worship until 1891. The Lutherans were holding services in a blacksmith's shop, and the record of one service conducted by Reverend Gerndt, on 13 April 1868, lists several members of the Evangelical church among the thirty-two people present, including 'Wilhelm Druve & Frau' and 'August Boehme & Frau.' Some Evangelicals such as Martin Markus travelled from Rankin to the nearest church, at Golden Lake, about eight miles over rough trails.[3] If Boehme (an Evangelical) attended the Evangelical church (St John's) or the Lutheran Church (St John's, Bonnechere) in Golden Lake during his stay at Rankin, then he would undoubtedly have met Mr and Mrs Johann Luloff, owners of a stopping-place in that community. Two cupboards at their home in Golden Lake, made entirely from black ash, were topped with the scrolled cornice and symbols carved in the surface of the wood. Possibly the choice of wood was dictated by the customer's ability to pay. The Luloffs, who arrived in 1867 with sufficient money to buy cleared properties and hire servants, would have been able to afford the best.

Identification of a piece of work by Boehme is sometimes aided by a pencilled notation, written in old German script. Unfortunately for posterity, he did not write his own name. He had a habit of writing the name of the customer and the completion date on the inside of the top of the left door of the clothes cupboard. One surviving inscription indicates that his clientele was not confined to his neighbours or fellow-worshippers. His scrolled pediments are so distinctive that they can be recognized on sight. When one of Boehme's cupboards was displayed in an Ottawa antique store,[4] its provenance was described to a customer as French Canadian, for it had been purchased from Quebec, in the Gatineau area. Having been brought up in Rankin, the visitor, a granddaughter of Wilhelm Druve,[5] promptly opened the doors, pointed to the scrawled message in German which translated as 'This cupboard was made for William Duck,' and retorted: 'They did NOT speak German up the Gatineau.' William Duck was the crown attorney and clerk of the peace, appointed by Renfrew County council when it was first formed in 1866;[6] one of his tasks was to approve applications for naturalization, whereby immigrants from non-British countries could acquire all the rights and capacities of a natural-born British subject. (His name is on the certificate of naturalization for Frederick Schutt in 1868.) By the time that Duck left his position in Pembroke, the railroad, which reached that town in 1876, had made it possible for passengers' household effects to be moved to another place of employment.

Following the death of his first wife, August Boehme remarried – this time to a Densin from a nearby family that was not German. He must have absorbed some of the values and attitudes of his English-Canadian neighbours in the Palmer Rapids area, for he became a member of the local loyal Orange lodge, which in late-nineteenth-century Canada was less an ethnic institution than a social club for Protestants in frontier communities.[7] His certificate of membership still hung in 1981 in the small house where he died in 1907. As in many German families, when he retired he had transferred the property to a son, on condition that he and his wife be allowed to live on the same premises with the promise of support. The elderly couple had a separate house, which was a simple two-storey structure, with two rooms downstairs and one above, the staircase shielded by a door with a finely carved handle. A new roof has preserved the structure and the contents, including large framed portraits of August and his first wife.

The present owner of the property, Oscar Boehme, lives in the fourth house, built in the 1920s, surrounded by a number of his grandfather's furnishings, still in use. From the clock-shelf above the harvest table to the stool on the kitchen floor, August Boehme's talented work is an enduring testament to the skill of German pioneers who made their own tools and then created a comfortable environment.

Carl Gutzman 1850–1936

Born 27 March 1850 in Pomerania,[8] Carl Gutzman immigrated to Canada to join his two older brothers, William and August, already settled in Petawawa Township with their wives and children born in Germany. Descendants believe that Gutzman was only a teenager when he left Germany, a story confirmed by the presence of his name on church records at Petawawa in 1868 and 1869, as godfather to nephews. Family legend has it that he journeyed across the ocean alone under the guardianship of Carl Dannhauer, the captain of a sailing vessel that docked at Halifax. An older brother, William, born in 1834, had already established himself as a tailor

in Petawawa Township before 1867 and appears on the assessment rolls as a
land-owner in 1870. Charles 'Goodsman' is listed in 1871 and described as a
carpenter, but men with a skilled trade did not need to farm. By 1873 Carl
Gutzman still had not cleared any of the land on his 100 acres, at Lot 21,
Concession 4, and owned no livestock.

On the agricultural frontier of poor land in Petawawa Township most
settlers built their own homes from timber on their property, and their first
crude furniture as well. A carpenter could make cupboards and furnishings
on order for a customer and would work where his skill could earn him a
living. Gutzman's whereabouts during the early 1870s are unknown, for his
name is not recorded on the township records again until 1879. In that year
he was the owner of 157 acres on Lot 11 on the Lake Range, the irregular
shoreline of the Ottawa River west of Pembroke. He had married Emilia
Lindemann of Alice Township 13 April 1877, and by 1879 their first child,
William, was a year old. Gutzman was now described as a farmer, and,
with five acres cleared, he owned one horse, two hogs, and four cows. The
couple eventually had nine children, and four generations (including Mrs
Gutzman's mother) continued to live on the property.

When a family group was photographed outside the farm-house in 1906,
Gutzman and his wife, with children and grandchildren, look comfortably
prosperous. The farm-house itself had been faced with concrete block over
the logs, and the farm, soon to be inherited by the oldest son, was not
threatened by expropriation by the Department of Defence which had been
quietly purchasing waterfront lots in Petawawa Township. The parents
moved to a separate house when they retired, and several children had left
permanently for California. William, who married in 1901, carried on the
farm and eventually left it to a son, Edgar, who purchased the neighbouring
Lindemann property in 1958. It was there that his widow held an auction
sale, 7 September 1981, that displayed some of the work of Carl Gutzman,
though much had already disappeared into the hands of pickers and lost its
identity.

Since Carl Gutzman had found a bride in Alice Township and may have
travelled from farm to farm as a furniture-maker in his early years, he may
have made some of the fine cupboards that emerge from that area. The pine
food cupboard sold at this auction was unlike the double-doored cupboards
with apertures protected by a series of vertical bars so typical of the Rankin-
Locksley community. It had a blind door with a right-hand opening on the
bottom half and a frame of wire mesh that had a right-hand opening on the
top half. It was simple, functional carpentry, with no decoration. The pine
clothes cupboard was plain in structure and notable only for the grain-
painting on the doors. The furniture-maker's son, William, used to hire

himself out as a grain-painter in the winter, and one of his well-educated sons may have converted the clothes cupboard into a bookcase. At first glance, it appeared to have a single bottom drawer, as was customary, but, even though there were a couple of porcelain pulls, the 'drawer' was only a false front. This type of fake representation is found also on some clothes cupboards in Pembroke and in the Locksley-Rankin area.

Among the items attributed to Carl Gutzman still in the family's possession were the small and heavy footstool, with the S-scroll cut-out on the top and flanking apron, a picture frame carved from hardwood, and the panelled headboard and footboard bed rescued in pieces from a shed. The style of this bed, with its scalloped top edges and pencil posts, has been described as Polish in derivation,[9] but it has turned up in German homes across Renfrew County, in different townships. Several other wooden articles that emerged at this auction elicited little admiration, such as the clock-shelf consisting of three boards placed at right angles and the food cupboard, so battered that it sold for only $6. A beautifully crafted grain shovel carved from butternut was attributed to Carl Gutzman; though cracked and repaired, it earned $100.

Carl Gutzman had made some fine furniture for his retirement home. Unfortunately its contents were dispersed after his death, with the result that there is little evidence to back up his reputation.

Gutzman was one of the twelve founding members of St John's Lutheran Church (of the Canada Synod) in Petawawa Township when it was formally organized 6 April 1873.[10] Church records mention that he used to walk from his home on the Ottawa River to teach Sunday school at a small log building more than a mile away in 1896. In 1899 he was elected lay-reader, a position that required him to take over the preaching duties if the minister were unable to be present. While his reputation as a staunch supporter of the church is well documented, his character was stern and unbending. When one of his daughters pined over a lost love, she was instructed to go to her room and read the Bible. Distraught, she never recovered.

Gutzman's efforts in support of the church included work on the furnishings, such as the font. It was so heavy that it was difficult to move when young parents wanted to rearrange the setting for photographs of their children's baptisms. According to Oscar Michel, who lived opposite the church on the Black Bay Road, this was the reason why the font was sold and replaced by a lightweight structure.

From all accounts and appearances the furniture in Petawawa Township was made of pine, even by skilled men; black ash, which grows in low-lying swampy areas, does not seem to have been used in this township, which is primarily level and sandy.

John Noack 1839–1919

When John Noack died at his home at Locksley in the township of Stafford, 8 January 1919, at the age of 79 years, his obituary filled only one paragraph in the *Pembroke Standard* (16 January) and made no mention of his skills or occupation. He was survived by his wife (Wilhelmine Mielke), two sons, and three daughters. One of these daughters, Matilda, born 26 May 1887, confirmed that her father made many fine cupboards owned by descendants and by families that once lived in the Locksley area. A food cupboard made for his daughter Wilhelmine, born 6 April 1878, is still owned by her grandson, who was able to provide firm attribution and an invitation to examine the style.[11] The food cupboards and clothes cupboards made by John Noack are identical in exterior features. The clothes cupboard owned by a member of the Mielke family has the same recessed panelled doors of pine, beaded moulding top and bottom, chamfered corners at the front, simple feet, and simple cut-out crest to decorate the top as the food cupboard owned by Noack's great-grandson.

Born at Schmelvitz, Kottbus, Frankfurt, Prussia,[12] in 1839, John Noack immigrated to Canada in 1869. His brother, Martin, eleven years older, may have already been settled at Locksley. His cousin, Christian Noack, born in 1841, located in the same parish. All three Noacks married, had children, and farmed.

Although John Noack owned a 100-acre farm in Stafford Township and his main source of income is believed to have been derived from farming, he made furniture for friends and neighbours as well as immediate family members, of whom there were many. His brother, Martin, was married to Anna Schettke, and his cousin, Christian, was married to Elizabeth Regel; their children married sons and daughters of other German immigrants. In the last year of his life, John Noack made a crib for a newborn in the Biesenthal family; it is in the Champlain Trail Museum in Pembroke. It has turned spindles on all four sides, revealing that Noack must have had a lathe.

In his cupboards, Noack's work shows a decided liking for right angles and squared proportions. The only glazed cupboard attributed to him (from the home of a Radke married to a Noack) has a central decoration – like the three sides of a rectangle – above the mouldings that trim the top. An identical 'squared' decoration has been repeated on at least two clothes cupboards. Noack, an adult when he immigrated, was not trained as a furniture-maker, according to his daughter, Matilda, who believed that he was naturally endowed with this talent. This may explain why his furniture was not decorated with ornamental scrolls or surface carving and why he did not use hardwoods.

Karl Raglan 1848–1936

Born at Gramenz, Neustettin, Coeslin, Pomerania,[13] in 1848, Karl Raglan accompanied his father, Ludwig Raglin, to Canada when he was only ten years old. He later married Elizabeth Kielow, who had 'arrived in Am- merikar August 2, 1867,' according to the entry in her Wendish Bible, and the couple had their first child, Carl William, 26 April 1868.

They were living on Lot 15, Concession 22, in Wilberforce Township, a property of 142 acres for which 'Charles' Raglan received title 12 March 1873. (German spellings of names were often replaced by English versions in government records.) Free grants under the Homestead Act of 1868 were being sought by immigrants from Germany along this road to the exclusion of any other ethnic group. On one side of his farm, Raglan's neighbours were Carl Greif, on Lot 14, Henry Lemke, on Lot 13, and Herman Yandt, on Lot 12; on the other side were William Druve, on Lot 16, Gustave Ziebell, on Lots 17 and 18, and Christian Kruger, on Lot 19. Most of the ar- rivals from Germany in this area had satisfied the requirements for a crown grant, which included five years' residence on the land by 1874. Some sold their properties and moved to uncleared land in the western townships, but Raglan stayed. Although he prospered as a farmer, enlarging his property by the purchase of William Druve's adjacent farm in 1914 from the Radtke family, he is most remembered as a furniture-maker, not only by his im- mediate family, but also by descendants of his neighbours.

Karl Raglan's father was a musician, who had immigrated to Canada for health reasons, and the identity of the person who taught the young man to make furniture can be only a matter of speculation. Members of the Raglan family attended the same services of worship in the German language as August Boehme, the furniture-maker, who lived for several years in this northwest corner of Wilberforce Township. The pine cupboard by Boehme illustrated in Bird and Kobayashi's, Pain's, and Shackleton's books on early Canadian furniture bears a close resemblance to kitchen cupboards made by Raglan; both have a well-defined pie shelf that separates the upper two doors from the drawers and doors below and a simple curved crest of fret- work on the cornice that is virtually identical and of similar proportions. Boehme's cupboard has purely decorative hex signs and hearts which may be construed as a folk-craft tradition from his homeland, while Raglan's cupboards are plain.

Like many other furniture-makers, Raglan made coffins. Like them, too, he made some of his own tools, and a number of these are still in the posses- sion of his descendants[14] who continue to live on the land that he cleared and acquired, in harmony under separate roofs. The vise that Raglan used was a portable pair of wooden jaws, with one vertical grip firmly inserted into a stand; unlike the customary vise used by a woodworker, which would be attached to a work-bench, Raglan's vise could be taken along to the site of his work. A pine chest, with an interior drawer, was large enough to contain a variety of planes for smoothing wood and fashioning grooves. The log farm-house in which Karl Raglan and his wife reared their family of nine children was demolished in the 1930s, after the family had built a more modern home, but its contents were stored in a barn.

Articles rescued from the old log house showed that the pioneer family had appreciated music and books. A concert roller organ, a compact device that bore a patent date of 28 March 1894, had come from Germany; its many player rolls could reproduce tunes such as *Amazing Grace* and other hymns, as well as waltzes that were enjoyed for dances in the confined quarters of the earlier house. A hanging cupboard, which had never had a door, had been in use as a bookcase originally; with a simple peaked pediment and wide back boards, it had hung from the log walls on nails. A later generation found another use for it, placing it on the floor. Hanging cupboards are not suitable to ornament a wall encased in gyproc.

Over the years some of Raglan's cupboards were given away to neighbours who were 'burned out,' a common risk with old houses made of wood and heated by wood. The clothes cupboard that Raglan made for his own home is still used for the storage of clothes in another home; the wooden hooks are attached to projecting pegs that swing from the back of the cupboard. At the base is a single drawer, outlined by beading produced from one of Raglan's moulding planes. The simple crest on the pediment is the same as that found on a kitchen cupboard in use in another home. The double-doored food cupboards discovered on so many farms near Rankin may be his work also, for the pediment is similar.

Apart from a hardwood ox-yoke and a basswood grain shovel, Raglan appears to have used only pine in the articles that he made for his own family and for others. His business as a furniture-maker may have been stimulated by the departure of August Boehme from the Rankin area to western Renfrew County in 1874. Yet Raglan must have been successful as a farmer, for he enlarged his property to 342 acres and on this land raised cattle, sheep, hogs, poultry, dairy products, and vegetables.

Frederich August Gutzeit 1849–1926

By the time Fred (or Fritz) Gutzeit migrated from Pomerania[15] to Canada, in 1874, the German-speaking settlers in western Renfrew County were sufficiently numerous and well established to support skilled tradesmen. (That

was the year William Michaelis, a tailor, went there to live.) Born on 18
March 1849, Frederich August Gutzeit was a 35-year-old bachelor and a
trained furniture-maker when he left Germany with his chest of tools. His
uncle, Ernst Gutzeit, had migrated to Canada in 1863 and had settled in
South Algona Township with his wife, his daughter, and his son, Paul. [16]
Fred Gutzeit obviously sought out his relatives, for he married his cousin,
Hannah (Joanne), soon after his arrival.

Those who had settled on land in this township in the earliest years –
there were seven German immigrants farming there by 1860 – were obliged
to be farmers, whether or not they had any training or aptitude, for there
was no other type of employment except for seasonal work in the shanties.
There were no good roads for travel to the villages where store goods could
be purchased. Not until 1894 was there a railroad to bring in merchandise
ordered from catalogues. It was a self-sufficient life in every way. The
township was well forested, so there was an ample supply of wood for the
settlers to make furnishings for their homes, but the more ambitiously ex-
ecuted cupboards that have been discovered in the possession of families
that once lived in the Silver Lake–Augsburg area of South Algona
Township were the work of Fred Gutzeit. In the 1881 census Fred 'Goodsite'
is described as a carpenter.

The furniture-maker and his bride lived on land close to the farm of Ernst
and Paul Gutzeit. Paul, soon nicknamed 'Shoemacher' Gutzeit, because of
his trade, eventually built a small log dwelling close to the road. Fred also
constructed his home close to the road, but only a clearing remains today,
for the log building has been sold and re-erected on a hill overlooking Eganville. The area of School Section No. 6, South Algona Township, where the
Gutzeits once lived, received an influx of young people from Toronto in the
1960s, and few descendants of the original families remain. Most, like Paul's
oldest son, born in 1893, moved off the farm to live in retirement in a
nearby community, but they had clear memories of the man who made furniture.

'He planted potatoes, kept pigs, had cows for butter and milk, just like
the rest of us,' recalled his oldest nephew, Bill Gutzeit, who lived in Eganville, 'but most of the time he worked on his cupboards.' The furniture-
maker's personal life was tragic; his wife was struck by lightning in her for-
ties and remained an invalid until her death on 6 July 1916. The family still
has a photograph of a gaunt haggard woman, whose misfortunes included
the death of her only child by drowning in a ditch on the family's land,
while he was still an infant. Thus when Gutzeit died 10 October 1926, at the
age of 77, he had been a lonely widower for a decade. There was no gravestone erected over his burial place in the Missouri Lutheran cemetery at

Augsburg, and no obituary appeared in the *Eganville Leader*. He left behind
only the evidence of his craftsmanship, including one cupboard that has
travelled from the custody of the Hoelke family of South Algona Township
into the National Museum of Man in Ottawa.

Although Gutzeit had no direct descendants, he had plenty of relatives.
His brother-in-law, Paul, and his wife, the former Bertha Dwyer, had
eleven children who lived to adulthood: William, Conrad, Arthur, Walter,
George, Herbert, Ida, Martha, Hattie, Lizzie, and Annie. Bill lived with his
uncle for a couple of years before the old man died. Accustomed to filling
orders from bereaved relatives, Gutzeit had made his own coffin ahead of
time, and his nephew added a coat of black paint before the burial. Bill
Gutzeit, then 33 years old, inherited the farm property, the buildings, the
contents, and one cow. Later married and the father of four daughters, he
continued to live on the property until his family was grown and independent. When he retired and moved to Eganville in the 1950s, his uncle's log
house and piece of land were sold, but the furnishings that had been made
by the immigrant were retained, as well as the chest of tools from Germany.

The pine tool-box with handles is itself a skilled piece of work, with dovetailed corners and a skirted base. Having spurned offers from collectors, Bill
Gutzeit was firm in his intention to bequeath the collection to a grandchild.
'I shall not be doing any more carpentry now,' he said at the age of 86. At
one time he had used the tools for tackling jobs in his own home. 'There are
18 planes in this chest,' he said, as he pulled out some of the large bench
planes used for reducing, smoothing, and levelling wood and showed them
to the author. A succession of moulding planes followed as he reached
deeper into the box, bringing out a centre-bead moulding plane in two sizes,
a quarter-round moulding plane, and an Ogee moulding plane. There was a
wooden mitre box with a complexity of diagonal incisions, a wooden bevel
for checking angles, a marking gauge, a carpenter's square, and a dovetail
saw. Inside the chest there were two fitted drawers, one on top of the other,
which both stretched across the length of the chest and slid to and fro on
runners, so as to make the interior of the tool-box accessible. The upper
drawer had a slot into which was inserted a set of wood-carving chisels. 'He
used them all his life,' said his nephew.

The presence of wood-carving chisels in the tool-box is a reminder that a
characteristic of the owner's work included a surface carving of a symbol
placed in the centre of a fretwork decoration attached above the moulded
pediment of the cupboards that he made in the later years. His earlier work
bore only a simple crest on top, judging by the kitchen cupboard that he
made for his own house and others like it. Bill Gutzeit inherited examples of

both styles. His uncle used both pine and ash, the hardwood being obtained from R.G. Reinke, the lumber dealer in Eganville.

The pine cupboard that Fred Gutzeit built for his wife, with glazed doors above and solid doors below, was made in one piece and has received so many coats of paint that its original colour has been masked; its two blind doors conceal a pair of drawers, one on each side, dovetailed back and front. The simple scalloped pediment on this flat-to-the-wall cupboard is identical to the design on the pediment of a corner cupboard that has served three generations on a farm in Sebastopol Township. The latter, a massive one-door food cupboard, equipped with shelves from top to bottom, was most probably made on the property, some ten miles from Gutzeit's home. Moved from its original squared log farm-house, which was occupied by the family until 1935, it is used for storage in the summer kitchen of the 'second' house. It too was made of pine and has been repainted.

The ash cupboard in Bill Gutzeit's possession was made in two parts, the two glazed doors enclosing a shelved cabinet – a separate case that rests on a deeper chest of drawers and panelled doors. The pierced fretwork that rests on the pediment of these seven-foot-high cupboards is so unmistakable a sign of Fred Gutzeit's work that it can be identified even when it has been detached and used (upside down) as a support for a shelf. This decoration was used on some of the flat-to-the-wall pine cupboards made for storage of food in a basement; it relieved the severity of the one-doored structure which had an upper panel of vertical bars to allow ventilation.

The black ash furniture was not painted, only lightly covered with a varnish so that the symmetry of the grain could be seen. The moulding around the top of the ash cupboard was ebonized, and the carved symbol in the centre was highlighted by gold. At least that was the intention of the furniture-maker, and the one in Bill Gutzeit's possession was in this condition. The nephew recalled that the most popular orders from customers were for 'dress cabins,' 'dish cabins,' and 'common cabins' (cabinets?). He described the latter as food cupboards equipped with shelves for the containers of milk and preserves. The clothes cupboards, always built in one piece, were made at the home of the family that ordered them, but the two-part kitchen cupboards were made by Fred Gutzeit in his own workshop at his home and later delivered.

Mrs John Dament of Pembroke, born on a farm in South Algona Township in 1900, was only a child when Fred Gutzeit arrived at her parents' home one day with a two-part cupboard on his horse-drawn wagon, but she remembered it. It was made of black ash ordered by her mother, Mrs Charles Ristau, wife of a second-generation member of a family from Pinne,

East Prussia. Gertrude Ristau married John Dament, and while her older brother, Herbert, eventually inherited the farm property and sold it, Gertrude acquired the personal possessions such as the spinning-wheel, the portraits, and the hand-made furniture; these she dispersed among her children before entering a senior citizens' home.

The ash cupboard made for the Ristau family bears the symbol of a cross, whereas the fretwork on the Gutzeit cupboard was adorned with a heart. Otherwise the two cupboards are identical in proportions and design. Mrs Dament's cupboard too had not been 'restored,' and the old home-made varnish was blistering. (Bill Gutzeit could remember that a 'paint oil' was mixed with a powder obtained from a local store.) Again the pediment was coated with black paint, and traces of gold clung to the central motif.

As children, Gertrude and her brothers, Herbert and Bernhard, used to pass by the furniture-maker's home on their way to school, in School Section No. 6, South Algona. 'He was the only one in that area who made furniture for others,' she remembered, 'and his wife was never seen without a shawl over her head, even when she was calling in the cows for milking.' Mrs Dament particularly remembered the tables made by Gutzeit, which were extended from the centre when the end-leaves were tugged from underneath. From her description, these tables must have resembled the style used by amateur furniture-makers in eastern Ontario, such as Ferdinand Biesenthal in Alice Township and Johann Gotlieb Lipke in Wilberforce Township.

'We used to call him Tischler Gutzeit or Carpenter Gutzeit,' said Barney Ristau of Golden Lake, the last active blacksmith in Renfrew County in 1979, despite being past his eightieth birthday. Taken on a drive through the winding dirt roads of South Algona Township that summer, Ristau pointed out where the Gutzeits and the Ristaus had once lived. Log houses were surrounded by sacks of cement, concrete blocks, and other building materials, evidence that newcomers were planning to live in the wilderness. All signs of agriculture had long since been obscured by the growth of bush, but boulders and uneven ground were still apparent. The trades of shoemaker, tailor, and furniture-maker might have looked more hopeful when land was cleared and the lumber shanties provided a market for feed and vegetables. Yet even those who could make a living from a skill cultivated some land to provide their families with food.

Fred Gutzeit was a member of the Zion Lutheran Church of the Missouri Synod at Augsburg, which erected a new brick building in 1893. There is no memorial to him in the cemetery of this congregation, but a curious piece of furniture made to hold the long vestments of the pastor may have been his work. This tall narrow cupboard of pine has a separate compartment at the top believed to have been designed to hold books. The whole structure, with its broken arched pediment, is strongly reminiscent of a grandfather clock. It was obviously made by a person with skill and training. Gutzeit was the only furniture-maker known to belong to this church.

Albert Zadow 1854–1941

Among the German immigrants who settled in South Algona Township in the last quarter of the nineteenth century, there was another who had been trained in Germany as a furniture-maker. Julius Albert Zadow arrived in eastern Ontario 3 June 1881,[17] having left his native land one month earlier with his widowed mother, his wife and two children, his three brothers, one sister-in-law, and a niece. Ten Zadows embarked on the Ship *Curia*, but eleven disembarked in Canada, Albert's wife having given birth to a son, Robert Curia, on 15 May during the crossing.

The matriarch of the family, Charlotte Auguste Krüger Zadow Zillmer, aged 55, was responsible for the family's move. In her first marriage, to Karl August Zadow, she had borne four sons and a daughter. Her second husband died of typhoid fever, as did her daughter, and with the money she inherited from the affluent Zillmer, she suggested and paid for the entire trip. 'Gustie,' as she was known, was related to Ernestine Krüger Luloff who had settled in Golden Lake in 1867, and this tie may have influenced the choice of destination, for the attractions of the western provinces of Canada usually superseded those of eastern Ontario by 1881.

All four adult sons – William, 29, Albert, 27, Edward, 25, and August, 23 – had performed their obligatory military service before leaving Germany. The youngest had been trained as a wagon-maker, and he established himself in the business of Eganville, where his house and stables still stand on the Wilberforce side of the Bonnechere River. The other three sons chose to settle on land in South Algona Township, in the area of School Section No. 2, close to Golden Lake. In this township where the population reached its peak about 1901, according to the census figures, the land is poor for agriculture; either low and swampy or hilly and stoney, it offers only a bare subsistence type of farming. More than half the soil in this township is 'class 7,' i.e unfit for any agriculture.

As a trained furniture-maker, Albert Zadow had brought his tools with him to Canada. Although he made coffins on demand, his descendants agree that he did not earn his living from building furniture. On his arrival in South Algona Township, he may have been deterred by the presence of other established furniture-makers, both British and German, eking out a precarious living.

A young Englishman, Frederick William Lord, had opened his own cabi-
net-making shop in the village of Rockingham, in the adjacent township of
Brudenell, in 1876. In 1925 Lord visited Eganville to see his parents' graves
and spoke to a reporter for the *Renfrew Mercury*. His recollections shed
some light on the conditions of that time for a furniture-maker. 'Mr. Lord
says he saw no money but his patrons gave him plenty of food in exchange
for the furniture. Raw material for the furniture was obtained at the late
J.S.J. Watson's mill. ... Speaking of the Opeongo country, Mr. Lord said
there had been sold to immigrants sand farms that wouldn't keep a cow.
Sometimes a farm instead of being all sand was all rock. On the Opeongo
Line there was no activity except in winter; in summer it was absolutely
stagnant. Wheeled vehicles in the upper country were few and far
between.'[18] Lord travelled in a Willys-Knight sedan and regretted that there
was not a passable road to Rockingham, the site of his first furniture store.

With the limited opportunity for cash customers in 1881, the outlook for
furniture-makers like Zadow was not bright. Instead of beginning a
business for which he had been trained, Zadow bought and sold farms, improving them and selling them at a profit; the locations of the births of his
offspring show that he did not stay in one place. Furniture-making,
however, occupied him during the winter, when he made pieces for his own
home and those of his three married brothers. He himself married twice and
fathered 23 children, 16 by his first marriage and 7 by his second, to
Auguste Ernestine Michaelis, whom he wed 1 August 1899 in Eganville.

Throughout his life he continued to make furniture, with hand tools, in
the ways he had learned in Germany. He died 5 October 1941, at the age of
87, in Wilberforce Township.[19] He was survived by 13 children, 12 of whom
still lived in Renfrew County. His three brothers, who predeceased him, had
also stayed in the county, and it was at Edward's home that a comprehensive selection of Albert Zadow's work was exposed to the public at an auction sale, 2 June 1979, when a bachelor grandson, Driscoll, decided to retire
from farming. The farmer's mother, 86-year-old Mrs August (Anna)
Zadow, who was assisting at the sale, had a phenomenal memory for dates
and names; without hesitation she confirmed the identity of the furniture-
maker and pointed to faint initials, A.Z., with a date, '1891 Januar 14,' on
the back of the clothes cupboard. According to records in the family's Bible,
Albert Zadow was born 13 November 1854, at Steinberg, Neumark, Germany. His first marriage, to Louise Auguste Keuhl, in early 1878, took
place at Falkenwalde, Pomerania, and it was there that their first two
children were born.

Pomerania contained residents of both German and Polish origin. If
Albert Zadow learned his furniture-making skills there, then the similarity
of his pediments on cupboards to those considered typical of northern

Poland is explicable. The clothes cupboard and the kitchen cupboard made for his brother, Edward, both displayed this style, and the latter had the remains of a central fan. The clothes cupboard, with its two rows of fixed wooden pegs, ten at the back and five at the front, was in immaculate condition; the bottom drawer had no pulls but was moved by grasping the base of the drawer, underneath which a hand-hold had been excavated. The kitchen cupboard, also made of pine, had performed yeoman service, judging from its scarred surfaces, but the competence of the maker showed in the chamfered panels of the doors and the dovetails of the drawers. Much of Zadow's work was strictly functional; dough-boxes with s-shaped sides and tables with squared legs that had an outward curve at the end seem to have been made capably by many immigrants from Germany.

One of the few pieces of Zadow's work that had survived without being overpainted in white was the food cupboard that he made for his brother Edward. The single door had a couple of vertical grooves with beaded edges, the grooves having been painted light green to match the green of the simple crested pediment; this colour contrasted well with the reddish-brown paint of the rest of the cupboard, which even had chamfered corners. The cupboard had been made with considerable attention to detail considering its everyday function and its location in a basement, where its shelves were stocked with foods.

Other food cupboards made by Zadow were plainer and larger. Some have a single door, but the one he made for his oldest daughter, Emma, when she was Mrs Fred Verch and the mother of a family that grew to twelve children, was a double-doored structure of pine, with ventilation provided by two apertures protected by wire mesh. Until 1980 it stood in a stone-walled basement of a shed adjacent to the farm-house, where the dampness of an earth floor had caused damage to its bottom shelf. In his later years Albert Zadow occasionally made furniture from hardwoods such as black ash; Emma was the recipient of several pieces, including a tall clothes cupboard with an ebonized scrolled cornice and a small oblong table.

Most of the progeny of Zadow's first marriage were sons, and the father posed proudly for a studio photograph with the seven who had served in the First World War. Though some of his children had died in infancy, many lived to marry and furnish their homes with pieces made by their father. The last item that he made is believed to be a plain cupboard requested by his second wife; it had none of the carving typical of his earlier work.

Emma Verch inherited furniture from her father's home, including a kitchen cupboard with surface carvings that occupied the width of the cornice and descended the pillar between the two glazed doors. The fan symbol, common to many a trained furniture-maker, was mingled with the six-pointed star or hex sign that has been noted on German furniture in other Ontario communities. This pine cupboard, overpainted in white, emerged at an auction sale at a farm in South Algona Township, where the owner was Irish. The farm-house and its contents had changed hands twice since the building was first constructed by one of Emma's sons, to whom she had given the cupboard.

'That cupboard is from the old homestead,' said Mrs William Ristow of Hagarty Township, with complete conviction, on being shown a photograph. Mrs Ristow, née Louise Auguste Zadow, the sixteenth child of Zadow's first marriage, had never known her mother, who died on the day of her birth in 1898. She remembered her father and his skill at woodworking, however. 'He used to call the other furniture-makers *carpenters,*' she remarked with an amused smile. Shortly after she married, in 1918, she received a piece of furniture made specially for her by her father, which she treasures. Varnished brown, it is a pine chest of three drawers with glass pulls; the drawers, dovetailed back and front, run smoothly after sixty years of use. The details of its construction would suggest a mid-nineteenth-century date for this chest, but its provenance is undoubted.

Five of the seven children of Zadow's second marriage survived infancy, and they, too, had souvenirs. One descendant has a grain shovel and a rectangular bowl that was used for mixing ground meat, both made from basswood, a light-weight hardwood that was popular for food containers because of its lack of taste or odour. The cooper's adze, that was used to carve them and smooth the wood was one of the tools Zadow brought from Germany and is owned by another descendant, in another township.

Though Albert Zadow prospered mainly in agricultural dealings, his production of furniture during a long life was prolific. He may not have made it only for his immediate family. A small pine table, square-topped with fretwork edges and with four legs joined to a pedestal by a drop finial, occupies a corner in the home of one of Zadow's grandsons. A small pine table in the same style appeared in a collection of hand-made furniture from an Irish century farm, at an auction sale in Brudenell Township. Only a few miles from the rural community of Zadow (named after the most prominent family), this farm had been occupied by successive generations of Drohans since 1864. Thus Zadow's work that remains in Renfrew County may not all be in the possession of Zadow's family.

Johann Frederick Wilhelm Luloff 1859–1939

Born at Falkenwalde, Pomerania,[20] Johann Frederick Wilhelm Luloff was only eight years old when his parents decided to leave Germany with their four sons and immigrate to eastern Upper Canada in the spring of 1867. The future furniture-maker therefore did not learn his trade in the land of his birth. His parents, John Frederick and Ernestine Krüger, were among the first German couples to settle in the Golden Lake area, purchasing a farm in North Algona Township where the lake narrows into the Bonnechere River. So many branches of the Luloff family had earlier emigrated to Canada that the widowed 70-year-old Michael Luloff decided to accompany his son's family. He lived another twenty-six years on the shores of Golden Lake and may have influenced his grandson's interest in making furniture. One of the pieces known to have been fashioned by the grandfather is a two-board chair or *Bretstuhl*.

When Bill Luloff died of a stroke at the age of 80, his death was commemorated by a lengthy obituary in the *Eganville Leader* (28 April 1939), for the editor-owner, Paddy McHugh, knew him personally. The obituary was extremely detailed, if not downright fulsome, even so, it omitted to mention the furniture for which Luloff would become well known.

'As a youth he attended the government school on the Indian Reserve and later a public school when one was established in the locality. As he grew to manhood the late Mr. Luloff took a keen interest in church administration and municipal affairs. He became superintendent of the Sunday School and was a leader of the church choir. He was an unwavering supporter of the Liberal party and could discuss with knowledge and intelligence the greater problems of national life. Mr. Luloff was a frequent caller at this office and from these contacts it was discernible how his quiet humor and quaint philosophy were factors in gaining for him many enduring friendships. The late Mr. Luloff was a farm worker, maker of wagons and coffins and was not unskilled as a builder.'

The latter remark may have referred to Luloff's prowess as a builder of furniture, which he constructed in a log workshop in Golden Lake. The double doors at the front of this building betray its origin as a store, rather than a house; with its dentil cornice, corner posts, and panes of glass, the entrance resembles some of his cupboards.

'He learned the ways of making things from the older carpenters who came over from Germany,' said his niece, Teresa, who, with her sister, Sarah, lived in the homestead bought by their grandparents. She treasured especially a doll's cradle that he made for her; it has a symmetrical headboard and footboard with simple crescent-shaped rockers. It is made of black ash. Luloff also made tools in the traditional styles, such as the salt-box with a lid that moves on a wooden hinge and a dough-box with serpentine sides.

One of Luloff's best-documented cupboards was a glazed cupboard in black ash and applied basswood built in 1915 for his niece, Sarah, when she was a young child. The pediment, which includes an ornamental scroll (or cartouche) topped by symbols carved in the surface of the wood, closely resembles the distinctive style made at Rankin and in Raglan Township by August Boehme. There was a pair of cupboards bearing this style in the home of Luloff's parents, one for a kitchen, with glazed doors, two banks of drawers, and panelled doors, and the other for clothes, with two large chamfered doors above a single drawer dovetailed back and front. Whether they were made by August Boehme or someone else may never be determined, but there was certainly a skilled furniture-maker at work in the area, from whom the young Bill Luloff could learn.

In the earlier part of his life Luloff continued to live on the farm where he had been brought up. His brothers, Ferdinand and Herman, both married and left home, as did his sister, Annie, born one year after the family moved to Canada. The farm was maintained by the youngest brother, Edward, who married twice. Following a dispute between the two brothers in 1922, Bill left, taking some furniture with him, and moved into a brick house next to his workshop. In Golden Lake he made wagons, furniture, and coffins (including his own, which he kept upstairs) until his death in 1939, at his sister's farm at Augsburg. Annie inherited the contents of his home and workshop and took most of them to her home, except for the tools, such as the lathe, which were left behind.

Of a style termed the *continuous-action-mandrel-lathe* by one authority,[21] Luloff's lathe had a bed about seven feet long and could be used throughout its full length at the same time that he was pedalling it. A foot-treadle moved a big wheel, and a pulley around this wheel drove a cylinder above it; a foot-stock could be moved along the lathe bed to secure the work. A long post could be reversed so that turned detail could be fashioned at each end of the post. Cupboards made in the Golden Lake area with a couple of such posts applied to the left and right of their doors are likely to be Luloff's work.

One of the earliest pieces definitely attributed to Luloff is a candlestand, the top of which, presumably circular when first made, had shrunk to an oval shape by the time it was sold at an auction in 1977; it then measured 17¾ inches by 17⅛ inches. The top was braced by four supports mortised into the pedestal, which had been shaped by hand tools and had a drop finial. The wood was heavy but so thickly covered with paint that its identity was hidden.

Black ash was certainly used by Luloff in the chests of drawers that he made for family members. The front panels of the drawers were carefully chosen to display the grain to its best advantage, and they were surrounded by wood painted black; one of these chests had swinging posts hinged to the sides of the drawers in such a way that they could prevent them being opened. (Some of the drawers also had locks.) A hanging corner cupboard of black ash by Luloff had been in use at his sister's farm, as also was a clothes cupboard, so tall that its top was damaged when it was taken out of a bedroom and down the stairs. It had a pierced fretwork frieze at the summit, above the moulded pediment which had been painted black and decorated with gold paint. Applied pieces of basswood on the panels of black ash were similar to the style of the glazed cupboard that he built in 1915 for his niece – a style that has been described as Victorian Renaissance.

The seven craftsmen, August Boehme, Carl Gutzman, John Noack, Karl Raglan, Fred Gutzeit, Albert Zadow, and Bill Luloff, can be discussed with some confidence because examples of their work were owned by people (usually descendants) who were sure of their provenance. Apart from those, such as Gustave Michel and August Schwartz, who constructed furniture only for their own homes, there were craftsmen such as Christian Remus and Karl Timm whose furniture-making was recorded in family histories, but for whom there is no attributed work.

There were probably other skilled German furniture-makers in Renfrew County not yet identified. It was common for a furniture-maker in a rural township to list himself as 'carpenter' or 'house carpenter' on census records. In the 1871 census of Wilberforce Township, Gustave Fick, 26, and his brother, William, 22, both born in Germany and living at home with their parents, described themselves as carpenters, though no pieces of furniture have been identified as their work.

The making of furniture by individual craftsmen, who produced work on orders from customers, continued into the second and even the third generation in rural communities in Renfrew County.

Mr and Mrs Matthew Noack, who were married in 1930 and who made their home in the log farm-house in Hagarty Township built by the first Matthew Noack in 1865, ordered their furniture from the Layman brothers in Golden Lake before their wedding. 'In this way you get exactly what you want,' said Emma Noack, displaying the sliding bread-board that she had requested in her glazed flat-to-the-wall cupboard. Some of the furnishings that the Noacks had ordered had outlived their usefulness by the time they celebrated their fiftieth wedding anniversary. The dough-box, no longer used in the making of bread, served now as a container. However, the pail-bench was still in use in the summer kitchen; its style is similar to those made by the immigrants from Germany.

Four pine cupboards by August Boehme

Clothes cupboard,
Wilberforce Township

Clothes cupboard,
Wilberforce Township

Food cupboard,
Petawawa Township

Kitchen cupboard,
Wilberforce Township

August Boehme (1841–1907): portrait hanging in the house where he died

Trinket box dated 1865, made by Boehme for his wife, Mary

In the furniture-maker's home (Boehme)

Suspended pole for drying socks; two rods held rack for drying apples

Hanging bookcase pegged into beams edged with a moulding plane

Cartouche by August Boehme

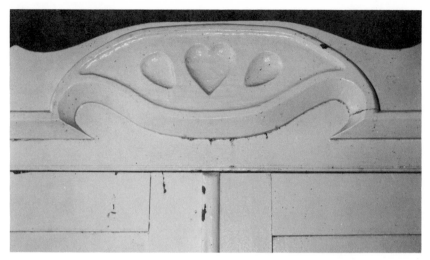

Cartouche on black ash cupboard made for his daughter, Mary, for her home in Sebastopol Township

Cartouche on black ash cupboard made for his own home at Palmer Rapid, Raglan Township

Two German furniture-makers who lived about fifty miles apart produced the same design in a kitchen stool – arched legs, aproned sides, and a cut-out hand-hold.

Made by
Carl Gutzman,
Petawawa
Township

Made by
August Boehme,
Raglan Township

Carl Gutzman (extreme left), 1906, with family, outside his log farm-house covered with concrete brick, Petawawa Township
(courtesy Mrs Evelyn Dunn, Deep River)

Two cupboards with identical squared cornices, probably by Johann Noack: *above* glazed kitchen cupboard once owned by Noack in-law Edward Radke, Highway 41; *below* cupboard from German home near Pembroke

Pine clothes cupboard with a seeming hardwood grain achieved by 'combing' the wet surface of the second colour over the first; Petawawa Township

Two cupboards by Johann Noack: *opposite* a food cupboard with shelves, owned by a grandson; *below* a clothes cupboard fitted with pegs, once owned by a Noack neighbour, Stafford Township

Crib made 1918 by Johann Noack for Biesenthal family, Alice Township

Hanging bookcase made from
pine by Karl Raglan,
Wilberforce Township

Woodworker's vise that
belonged to Karl Raglan

Matching pine cupboards by Karl Raglan, Wilberforce Township

Gutzeit's later style: two-part unpainted cupboards of black ash, South
Algona Township

OPPOSITE

top Pine cupboard made by Fred Gutzeit for his own home, South
Algona Township

bottom Pine corner cupboard, same style of cornice, Sebastopol
Township

A decorative cornice was typical of the cupboards made by German immigrants in Renfrew County, whether home handymen or skilled woodworkers, Wilberforce Township.

Cupboard used in post office (1903–40) at Budd Mills, Wilberforce Township

When Matthew Noack and Emma Okum were married in 1930, they had their furniture made to their specifications by the Layman brothers of Golden Lake. Mrs Noack requested a sliding bread board on her kitchen cupboard. Hagarty Township

left Gutzeit's pine food cupboard, of a style found frequently in the Silver Lake–Augsburg area, South Algona Township

right Pastor's cupboard, for robes and books, Lutheran Church (Missouri Synod), Augsburg, to which Fred Gutzeit belonged

Zadow family heirlooms: *above* grandson Gilbert Verch with clothes cupboard of black ash, South Algona Township; *below* Louise Ristow, Albert Zadow's sixteenth child, with pine chest of drawers, Killaloe

Four pine cupboards by Albert Zadow, South Algona Township: three made for brother, Edward; cupboard at far right for his own home

Kitchen cupboard by Bill Luloff, made 1915 for niece, Sarah, principally of black ash, with some applied pieces of basswood painted black, and hex signs at summit, North Algona Township

Black ash cupboard and chest by Luloff, sold from home of his sister Anna; some applied pieces on the cupboard are painted black and decorated with gold. North Algona Township

Joe Remus demonstrating one-man foot-powered lathe formerly used by Bill Luloff, North Algona Township

Charles Yake, German immigrant of 1892, made his clothes cupboard for a niece, Mrs George Brose, who points at a small drawer that can be locked. Buchanan Township

CHAPTER EIGHT # New horizons, painful exile

Until the Great Depression of the 1930s, small farms in Ontario remained profitable, though their fortunes fluctuated.[1] The years 1901–31 witnessed virtually no change in the population of Renfrew County (about 51–52,000) and a corresponding stability in the numbers of people of German descent (9,014 in 1901, 9,453 in 1911, 9,429 in 1921, and 10,743 in 1931).[2]

The statistics do not reveal the large number of young people, sons and daughters of immigrants, who left the area in order to seek employment in the cities or to find land elsewhere. Families were large, and the farms were small. Harvest excursions, when farm workers could travel cheaply to the western agricultural frontier of Canada for a limited period of labour, provided a chance for young men to size up opportunities in that direction, without commitment. Return rates advertised in 1902 were $28–$40 according to distance.[3]

The editor-proprietor of the weekly *Eganville Leader*, Paddy McHugh, viewed the annual foray that year with some scepticism. 'The season has arrived when the annual migration of Ontario young men for the West takes place. Hundreds are going to better their prospects in life, and many with the intention of returning when the golden fields of wheat are cut and when the whistle of the steam thresher is no longer heard on the broad prairie. Among the vast army moving westwards scores there are with but a vague knowledge of conditions existing at their objective point. It is the same old story of fortune just beyond, conditions always better further away, over beyond the horizon, just where the sky and earth seem to meet.'[4]

Since this paper had started publication just a few weeks earlier, on 2 June 1902, the owner may have been worried that some of his potential subscribers were about to leave the vicinity. The *Leader* had started in opposition to another Eganville weekly, the *Star-Enterprise*. The village was located on the Bonnechere River where it divided the townships of Wilberforce and Grattan, in the heart of countryside settled by residents of German or Irish heritage. The German people in Renfrew County had a newspaper in their own language, the *Deutsche Post*, 1901–16,[5] and this was the natural vehicle for their social news, letters to the editor, and obituaries, since German was their means of communication. The English papers, however, mirrored the contemporary scene and its economy, which affected all the rural residents in western Renfrew County.

In the spring of 1903 readers of the *Eganville Leader* were advised that the Canadian Pacific Railway was planning to run 'Colonist Special Trains' to the Canadian Northwest, every Tuesday during March and April, should sufficient business offer, leaving Carleton Junction at 9 p.m. A 'Colonist Sleeper' would be attached to each car. Advertisements proclaimed: 'The object of these special trains is to enable Colonists to travel with their effects and stock, etc., have good accommodation and make quick time. Ask any Canadian Pacific Railway Agent for a Settlers' Guide, which will tell passengers and freight rates, times of trains, of Government and railway land regulations, and how to procure A FREE FARM.'

The Canada Atlantic Railway had three westbound trains a day to North Bay and Parry Sound and also made connections at Ottawa for Montreal, Quebec, Halifax, Boston, New York, and all points east and south: 'Through Pullman Buffet Sleeping Cars between Ottawa and New York, without change, leaving Ottawa 4:25 p.m., arriving New York 7:25 a.m.'

Members of the second generation of families that had pioneered in Renfrew County could transfer to a new territory or a new country in comparative comfort. Irrespective of their origins, young men who wanted to farm went west, in search of land, and young women generally went east and south, in search of domestic jobs in the cities. Their numbers are impossible to estimate.

Moving North

In the first year that the *Eganville Leader* was published, the development of northern Ontario had received much attention from the press of the Ottawa Valley. F.R. Latchford, provincial commissioner of public works and MLA for South Renfrew, had promoted the extension of a railroad from North Bay, rather than from Mattawa, thereby encouraging a route for trade and passengers from Toronto. Editor McHugh endorsed this proposal. 'There are millions of acres of good farming land in the Temiskaming country yet unsurveyed, and there is every reason to believe that many thousands will find good homes there. The great drawback of the district is its isolation. This will be remedied by the railway to be built and operated by the Ontario government, from North Bay to Thornloe.'⁶ The lack of a railroad meant that would-be settlers could not ship their household effects and livestock to a new farm, as they had been able to do in the western provinces.

From the hundreds of obituaries of German pioneers published in the *Leader* in the 1920s and 1930s (when there was no local German newspaper), it is possible to learn where the sons and daughters of immigrants had located. Any pioneer who had lived a long life had usually made a tangible contribution to the community and was accorded a respectful obituary, lengthy and detailed; the names and addresses of surviving members of the family were listed, even if they were unable to attend the funeral.

Most of the daughters had married, and many had settled in the United States; Detroit and Chicago occur most frequently in their addresses, together with a number of smaller communities in Michigan, Ohio, and New York. Of those that had made homes in the Canadian west, there were few in British Columbia or Alberta; by far the greatest number had settled in Saskatchewan, many in small communities. In northern Ontario they were living in resource towns such as Sudbury, Kirkland Lake, or Timmins, while others had settled in the Little Clay Belt in places such as New Liskeard or Haileybury, more readily accessible after the railroad had been extended from North Bay into 'New Ontario' beginning in 1905. These areas of northern Ontario were the focus of a new wave of German settlement from Renfrew County.

'The building of the Temiskaming and Northern Ontario Railway gave ready access to the Temiskaming valley at the northern end of Lake Temiskaming, where forty-five townships of excellent land have been surveyed and are now being settled,' according to a pamphlet published in 1907 by the Ontario Ministry of Agriculture. 'The whole of the land in this section is tillable, free from stone and productive, and although heavily timbered, the timber is of comparatively small growth. This tract extends in a north-westerly direction as far as the Height of Land.'⁷

The section thus described became known at the Little Clay Belt. Northwest lies a band of Shield country that affords a soil of class 7, that is, land with no capability for crop use or pasture. But beyond that extends across the province an immense unbroken area of tillable land, 250 miles in length from east to west, with an average breadth from north to south of 100 miles, and comprising in all nearly 16 million acres. The latter area, the Great Clay Belt, was the focus of extensive advertising by the Ontario government. The agricultural capabilities of the Little Clay Belt were made known by a man who had successfully pioneered in that area.

On 29 May 1891, public lands at the head of Lake Temiskaming (a widening of the Ottawa River in northern Ontario) were made available at the price of 50 cents per acre to actual settlers, subject to certain conditions. The purchaser had to reside on the land for at least four years, have under cultivation at least ten acres for every 100 acres he owned, and build a habitable house at least sixteen by twenty feet. Twenty-five townships became available, about a half-million acres of land in one continuous block.

Settlers were arriving from the Toronto area, travelling by train via North Bay, as far as Mattawa and thence by steamboats plying on the still stretches of water beneath the rapids on the Ottawa River. It was a difficult journey and men were advised to travel without their families and livestock, to carry their own provisions, and to be prepared to be patient. The advertisements stressed the splendid soil, the lightness of the forest cover, the steady demand for farm produce from the lumbermen's shanties, and the certainty that railroads would be built from Mattawa (by the Canadian Pacific Railway) and from North Bay (by the Nipissing and James Bay Railway) to Lake Temiskaming.

One settler on the shoreline of Lake Temiskaming, C.C. Farr, who had a substantial house and twenty acres cleared by 1887, had written a pamphlet in 1894 that purported to be an accurate description of the agricultural capacity of the area.[8] It is strikingly reminiscent of the roseate claims of French's booklet on the Opeongo Road. It has the same incredible optimism, the same glibness in skirting obstacles, chief among them being the shortness of the growing season.

The building of the Temiskaming and Northern Ontario Railway, north from North Bay, made a new agricultural frontier attractive to farmers' sons in eastern Ontario. Not only did it provide facilities for the transport of possessions, but also its direct links by rail to a countryside only 200 miles away meant that those who moved would not lose touch with their families; they could visit back and forth for festive occasions and for holidays. In the years before the First World War, the *Eganville Leader* had so many subscribers in northern Ontario that regular columnists there reported on social events in places such as Haileybury, New Liskeard, Matheson, and Charlton. One rural community from which the *Leader* did not receive news was Krugerdorf, a colony of German-speaking families from Renfrew County, clustered in the township of Chamberlain, many of them sons and daughters of German immigrants who were pioneering a second area on the Canadian Shield. The leader of this adventure, which started in 1905, was a seasoned farmer, 59-year-old August Kruger,[9] who had lived in Germanicus, Wilberforce Township, for at least twenty-five years after his departure from Germany.

Only a small fraction of German people left Renfrew County to farm in the Krugerdorf area. Yet the new settlement provided once again a plain life on the land where the German language would be the means of communication and a Lutheran church would help to knit the community together. Young people who went to the cities and to farm on the prairies would be assimilated in societies heterogeneous in language and life-style. Those who moved to Krugerdorf attempted to perpetuate the type of life that they had known.

'The soil was good, but the season was short, and when you had grown anything there was no one to sell it to,' explained Ferdinand Kant, living in retirement in Iroquois Falls.[10] He estimated that Krugerdorf had at least ten fewer frost-free days than Renfrew County. Kant's father was one of three brothers who left Golden Lake by train in May 1910 to move to land in Chamberlain Township. Ferdinand Kant was only 12 years old. He remembered lumber stacked on the bottom of two box-cars and on top of this the livestock, including two teams of horses, as well as pigs, chickens, and two or three cows per family. On level well-watered land the farms were easily cleared and the settlement grew. In 1915 Zion Lutheran Church of the Missouri Synod was built by the volunteer labour of the men of the community, including 17-year-old Ferdinand. But by 1919 his family had abandoned the attempt to farm at Krugerdorf, and others followed suit.

The gradual decline of Krugerdorf as a viable place to live and work is reflected in the fortunes of the church, which had its own pastor until 1924.[11] In the years of oil-lamps and wood-fired stoves, many dwellings were destroyed by flames, including the parsonage. Not even a signpost now on nearby Highway 11 points the way to the vanishing rural community that was once so self-sufficient. Gone are the store, the post office, the school, the sawmill, and most of the original dwellings. Well-maintained gravel roads bisect the township and give access to Englehart, to highways and railroads and markets for produce, and to the amenities of civilization. It was not the settlers' fault that Krugerdorf failed to prosper – they just travelled in the wrong direction.

Petawawa

In the same year, 1905, that the Krugers were exploring a new agricultural region in northern Ontario, another community of German farmers in Renfrew County was made aware that it was going to lose its homes, church, school, in fact all the buildings and clearings that it had laboured on for twenty years or more. The Canadian government wanted its land in Petawawa Township.

Settlement there was still sparse, a fact that encouraged its choice as a military site when the Department of Militia and Defence decided that it needed a permanent camp. The alternative location, near Barry's Bay, was more heavily populated. The provincial government had offered to donate crown lands at either site, but the federal militia department had to purchase the holdings of any settlers. Both sites had the advantage of nearness to railroads and large bodies of water.

The *Eganville Leader* hoped for a military camp with 5,000 men at Barry's Bay, which would be within its circulation area. The *Pembroke Observer*, only twelve miles downstream from the Petawawa location, was in favour of the alternative. Both papers followed the negotiations eagerly. The Toronto *Globe* in March 1905 reported: 'In all, five square miles of land are required. If the South Renfrew site is selected, however, more land would have to be purchased from settlers than in the case of the Petawawa site, where most of the land is still held by the Province, and will be given free.'[12] Decision was delayed a few more months; a third site, Kazabazua, Quebec, was mooted; and the military authorities, headed by Major-General P.H. Lake, chief of the General Military Staff of Canada, performed a detailed inspection of the Barry's Bay site once again on 1 June. Travelling by train to Barry's Bay, the party embarked on a steamer for Combermere, where they were met by horse-drawn vehicles 'and at once proceeded to investigate the proposed site for Canada's Aldershot,' dogged by the press who admired the elderly general's prowess in scaling the mountains.[13]

By 3 August 1905, speculation was ended by the announcement that the artillery would be encamped at Petawawa for firing practice that summer. All twenty-four field batteries in Canada would undertake at least four days' firing, about three in camp at a time. Lieutenant-Colonel Biggar was recruiting 200 men in Pembroke to prepare the ground for the erection of buildings, though not permanent ones.[14] It was stressed, in the Eganville paper, that this was merely an experiment to test the suitability of the site. But by 13 September most of the German farmers who lived along the Ottawa River had been persuaded to sell their properties to the government.

Entry into this area had been aided by the Pembroke and Mattawan Road, started west from Pembroke and opened for forty miles in 1867. The first German settler in this community was Gustave Hampel, aged 27, who was residing on three lots on the waterfront by 1885, with a family of seven and assets that included a horse.[15] Two years later he had cleared 20 of his 341 acres and had added to his livestock 3 cattle, 4 sheep, and 2 hogs. By 1887 Jacob Juergens had located on Lots 8, Concessions 10 and 11, with a family of five and had cleared 1 acre. The following year he had cleared 3 acres and had 3 cattle, 2 sheep, 4 hogs, and 1 horse. Later widowed, Mrs Juergens kept a 300-acre farm going with the help of her children until the military department bought them out; her son, Herman, born 28 October 1886, could recall in his senior years how they would travel with a team of horses 18 miles to Pembroke, having to break a path through the snow themselves for the first 5 or 6 miles of the journey.[16]

Most of the German farmers who acquired land in this area obtained it as a free grant under the Homestead Act of 1880. Otto Greif, aged 28, and August Gust, aged 50, both appear on the assessment roll for 1888; Gustav Prange was there by 1889, as well as the Radtke brothers, Charles and John. August Behnke arrived in 1890, followed by the Woitos, the Gorrs, Carl Brumm, the Wegners, and Herman Ballsteadt.

By 1896 the settlement was sufficiently well established for twelve families to decide to build a Lutheran church (St Matthew's) of the Canada Synod. (Some farmers, such as the Blaedows and Fred Kurth, were supporters of the Evangelical church.) A school section had been created, 1895, in the Brindle Road area, Number 4, Petawawa Township. The farms now contained 100 cattle, 72 sheep, 35 hogs, and 37 horses. In 1905, when the Department of Militia and Defence required the land, the settlement extended from the Ottawa River to a depth of thirteen lots along the Brindle Road and was almost completely German. There were 211 persons living in that school section, with 618 acres cleared of the 6,401 acres occupied. The total value of property was estimated at $17,015.

By 1905 some farmers had been there twenty years, had raised their families, and had seen their sons acquire adjacent properties. Those who had left Germany because they resented military conscription must have felt it ironic that they were now being evicted by Canada's Department of Militia and Defence.

Some who lived along the shoreline, Rudolph Antler, August Wegner, Charles Brumm, Charles Gorr, Henry Gorr's widow, and Emil Antler, all sold their properties on the same day, 13 September 1905.[17] They sold to the same man, Albert Mackie, son of Thomas Mackie, former MP for North Renfrew. 'The government started to buy land in 1905,' confirmed Adolph Gust, who was born on the Brindle Road. 'Antler's was the first they bought out. They used to fire across Uncle Fred's lot, a distance of eight miles.'[18]

A press release of 19 September 1905 stated: 'The preparation of the ranges has been delayed considerably on account of the difficulty in settling with the farmers whom it was necessary to move off their places on account

of the danger and risk involved. It was at first thought that they could be in-
duced to move temporarily during the camp, but the indemnity offered was
not considered sufficient, and they refused to leave. It then became
necessary to buy them out in order to carry out the purpose of the camp.
About 17 farmers were bought out altogether, their places being nearly all
situated along the banks of the Ottawa River, some six or eight miles west
of Petawawa station.'[19]

In a letter of November 1905, Colonel L.F. Pinault, deputy minister of
militia and defence, asked the deputy minister of justice for permission to
convey to the crown certain lands at the junction of the Petawawa and Ottawa rivers, as a site for a central camp ground, enclosing with this request
a copy of an order-in-council and blue-print plans.[20] He stated, 'Negotiations have been carried on with Mr. A.J. Mackie of Pembroke, for the acquisition of certain of the properties included within the area to be purchased. These negotiations have now been completed and I enclose a list of
such properties aggregating 4872 acres, for which the purchase price
amounts to $40,340.96. As far as these properties are concerned, they may
now be conveyed to the Crown. Mr. J.G. Forgie, Barrister of Pembroke,
has been employed in connection with securing options from several
holders and searching the titles, and the Minister of Militia and Defence will
be very glad if the Minister of Justice will authorize him to act as your agent
in the matter of conveyance of these lands from Mr. Mackie to the Crown.
If there should be any objection to Mr. Forgie being employed, I shall be
much obliged if you will let me know before taking any action.'[21]

The list of properties in Petawawa Township included 16 in the Lake
Range (the shoreline) and 9 in Range A, which was parallel. This produced a
double strip of lots along the Ottawa River, where the government installed
a firing range in a west-to-east direction, with a target on the land formerly
occupied by Emil Antler. In addition 3 unpatented lots on Concessions 10,
15 and 16 in Petawawa Township and 5 properties in Buchanan Townships
were acquired.[22]

Mackie had received a reminder from the Bank of Ottawa that the interest on three loans totalling $39,750 would be $580 by 15 December,
resulting in his debt to the bank amounting to $40,340.96.[23] He was
understandably anxious to make a transfer of the properties to the crown
and be reimbursed as soon as possible, as he stated in a letter of 8 December
1905 to Colonel Pinault.

The properties of those who sold out that year ranged in size from 49 to
234 acres. Crown grants under the Homestead Act of 1880 conferred up to
200 acres to a bona fide settler, but since the shoreline was irregular the actual number of acres in each property differed. The purchase prices varied

too and depended to some extent on the number and condition of the buildings. The highest price was gained by Emil Antler, $3,500 for 234 acres; his brother, Rudolph, obtained $1,800 for 138 acres; another brother, Charles, was allowed only $600 for his 130 acres, which he had not patented.[24]

The assessment roll of 1905 reveals that some of the legal owners to land in this area had not cleared any acres or constructed any buildings and were not residents on the property. These title-holders included Pembroke barrister James Forgie, who purchased Lake Range Lot 31 on 1 September 1905 for $525 and sold it to Albert Mackie two weeks later for $1,500.[25] Thomas Murray, a Pembroke merchant and former MP, owned scattered properties, such as Lake Range Lots 23 and 25 and Range A Lot 34. Other non-residents included James Sarsfield, a clerk of Pembroke, who owned Range A Lot 33, and John Barker, assessed that year for Range A Lots 28 and 27, despite the CPR tracks that went through his land. With these exceptions, and a couple of lots in the possession of the Brindle family, the land that the government wanted was entirely in the hands of German families.

The conveyance to the crown of all the properties acquired by Mackie was officially registered as having taken place 20 December 1905, and the sale prices were remarkably uniform. Each property that had been patented by the owner who sold to Mackie was resold to the government for $26,950, regardless of clearance, acreage, or buildings. Each property not patented by a previous owner (who may have lived on the land for years and made improvements noted on the assessment rolls) was sold to the government for $14,050.[26]

Following the transactions with the farmers whose properties were required by the government, the camp was said to be extensive enough for long-range artillery and rifle fire as well as cavalry manoeuvres. But by 1906 it was obvious that the government wanted to extend the site, and some residents were balking.

According to a statement from Toronto, 14 May 1906, 'The camp in all comprises some 74,000 acres, of which 52,000 acres are still vested in the Crown. The former provincial administration offered this latter acreage free to the Dominion authorities for the purpose named. It seems, however, that a considerable part of it is yet under timber license, and the licenses have to be settled with. Some of them claim that there is still a large amount of standing timber on the lands and as the land can be held by them until cleared sufficiently for settlement purposes they are asking payment for the timber still standing ... Settlers who held patents for 22,000 acres of land sold out to the Dominion government for about $40,000.'[27] The Toronto *Star* quipped, 'The military camp at Petawawa will contain sixty thousand acres, the idea being to have a place big enough to hold the headquarters staff's opinion of itself without bulging.'[28]

On 26 July 1906, the *Pembroke Observer* carried a warning advertisement from the camp commandant at Petawawa: 'The public are hereby cautioned that Artillery Practice will take place at Petawawa between the hours of 8 a.m. to 5 p.m. daily, except Sundays, from the 17th July to about the 1st Sept. 1906.'[29] The danger zone was outlined in detail, and the public was cautioned not to touch any whole shells found on the range, but to report their whereabouts to the commandant. The sum of 60 cents was offered for each shell so reported.

In 1907 the camp superintendent had a force of men and horses clearing up a large tract of country on the Petawawa Plains to facilitate the movement of cavalry. 'By this it is not meant that he is clearing the land which is covered by a species of tough shrub about a foot high, but rather improving it so as to cover the stumps of trees which have been cut or burned down. All these stumps and fallen trees and sticks are being removed and carted away, and when the work is completed there will be at Petawawa Camp without a doubt the finest stretch of country in the world for the training of cavalry.'[30]

More land was wanted for the military camp. Otto Greif sold in 1907, August Schroeder and Gustave Prange in 1908, but others still resisted. In 1908 there was talk of action being taken against the farmers and land owners of Petawawa, who refused to give up their holdings or submit to arbitration. Many sales were made in 1909, even the school on the Brindle Road being sold to the crown for $275.[31] By the spring of that year all the members of St Matthew's Lutheran Church had disposed of their farms, except for one recalcitrant. The daily evacuations from their homes and the danger of unexploded shells must have persuaded them that further resistance was useless.

'Charles Radtke, who lived opposite us, had to take out the women and the children on his wagon from the farms on the Brindle Road,' related Adolph Gust, born in 1906. 'The women took their knitting and the kids had lots of fun. Every morning the soldiers went around the homes to see that everyone was out. One day they noticed smoke was coming out of the chimney at my grandmother's house and they found her at home baking. She refused to leave for the day, so they had to bribe her with 25 cents to leave her baking. The government bought us out in 1909. They needed more range and bought on the other side of the tracks.' Owners who sold after 1905 appear to have dealt directly with the government, without an intermediary.

August Gust, with his wife Louise and four sons, had left West Prussia in 1884. August obtained a free grant of land on the Brindle Road in 1888, and his oldest son, Albert, secured another grant beside him when he became eligible to own land at the age of 18. The father's property was transferred to his oldest son on 23 December 1908, and Albert sold 200 acres to the government on 23 January 1909, for $3,960, sufficient to buy another good farm.

Albert and his father moved to a farm in Alice Township, which he purchased from a free grant settler, James Cobourn. The Gusts took with them their household possessions and tools, including the furniture made by August and all the apparatus needed to manufacture woollen yarns and cloths – the loom, the spinning-wheel, the bobbin-winder, a bobbin-rack, and a wool-winder. In 1910 they built a new home on the property, and three generations lived in harmony under the same roof.

'It was considered a privilege to sleep downstairs with grandpa,' said his grandson, Adolph, in 1980. Adolph inherited the farm on the death of his father in 1946, and when he retired to a modern house in Petawawa years later he took with him furniture made on the plains of Petawawa. All made from pine, the pieces include kitchen cupboards and bedroom furniture, the bed having legs that must have been turned on a lathe.

The houses and barns that were evacuated would be eventually demolished. The only building rescued was St Matthew's Lutheran Church, the log church constructed by volunteer labour in 1896. On 11 March 1909, a special meeting of the congregation called by the pastor, Reverend Hamm, considered the offer of $500 made by the military board for the church. 'Inasmuch as all the members, except one, of this congregation have disposed of their property, it was moved by Albert Gust, seconded by August Schroeder, to accept the offer of the Military Board for our church property, and to present to the Evangelical Lutheran Trinity congregation of Chalk River this church with all its furniture, vestments, etc. Carried unanimously.'[32] Some members joined St John's, Petawawa; several, including Charles Budd, August Wegner, Fred Gust, moved to Chalk River; Gustav Prange went to Alice Township; some moved to Pembroke; and Herman Gust travelled as far away as California.

At the last meeting, 24 April 1909, Albert Gust received $40 to fence the cemetery. The church was abandoned, but not for long; when Trinity Evangelical Lutheran Church in Chalk River burned down, St Matthew's was dismantled and moved, on sleighs, to Chalk River in the winter of 1909–10. It served its new congregation until 1965, when the members decided to join with a Lutheran congregation in the growing town of Deep

River, four miles away. The church, which had been covered by clapboard and later by brick siding, was demolished in October of that year by thirteen volunteers, led by foremen Wilfred Gust, who were surprised to find a square-timbered structure underneath.[33]

St Matthew's cemetery remained in the territory acquired by the government, and the Brindle Road area became part of the firing range used by the military forces in a north-south direction. Restoration of the cemetery, with the co-operation of the military base, was accomplished in 1966, following appeals from members of St John's Lutheran Church of the Canada Synod, Petawawa Township, who had relatives interred there. On 11 September, a large wooden cross was dedicated, bearing a plaque engraved with the names of some of those laid to rest in the cemetery. August Behnke, aged 92, whose father had offered the land, laid a commemorative wreath.[34]

Today the base occupies 140 square miles, and the only reminder that it was begun by the evacuation of settlement of German farmers is a cairn on Highway 17. It reads: 'To honour the German Lutheran pioneers who migrated here around 1875 and who carved out of this wooded wilderness a new home and community for themselves. Spurred on by a longing for freedom and strengthened by their faith in Jesus Christ, they endured the bitter suffering and bequeathed to us OUR BELOVED PETAWAWA.'

Further upheavals

The upheaval caused by the government's acquisition of land included another settlement, on the boundary between Petawawa and Buchanan townships. Originally called the Tennant Settlement, this land was first tackled by three Irishmen and their sons,[35] followed by English and Scots settlers and by German immigrants with names such as Woermke, Prange, and Brandstead. Elsewhere, scattered farms occupied about one square mile close to the CPR tracks, east of Chalk River. Most of these farmers were displaced by 1909, some obtaining legal title to land in 1908 just in time to sell to the government. In both settlements some property owners resisted the offers of the government, which sent two different sets of valuators to appraise the farms.

The acquisition of this land, farther away from the firing ranges, proceeded in a more leisurely fashion. According to some long-time residents of Petawawa Township, such as Henry Mohns, born in 1895, the clearing of farms in the way of the military forces was accomplished speedily. 'They blew up the houses and the logs went up like sticks,'[36] he recalled. While the buildings of the German settlement on the Ottawa River were all demolished, most abandoned structures in Buchanan Township were left to the ravages of time and weather.

In 1917 the Department of Militia asked the Forestry Branch of the Department of Northern Affairs and National Resources to manage and provide fire protection for the nearly 100 square miles of forest within the Petawawa Military Reserve.[37] By 1958, when the army needed more land for training, the research activities of the Petawawa Forest Experiment Station, near Chalk River, became restricted to the northern 39 square miles of the military reserve. Within this forestry station there are still dirt roads named after the early settlers, such as Woermke. The forest cover has regenerated, and trees have grown around piles of stones that pioneers cleared from the ground that they planned to till. If a log house is left to nature the roof falls in, the chinks drop out of the interstices of the logs, and the flooring rots and buckles. If the log house is removed, the dug-out basement, lined with stone, may be the only evidence of a homestead, apart from lilac bushes at the front door.

Farmers in eastern Ontario not forced to move by the federal government or persuaded to move by the provincial government were hearing reports of more rewarding opportunities in western Canada. Apart from the propaganda of the railroad advertisements, they were receiving personal assurances from those who had already been there and returned to tell their families about it. One letter from Germanicus to the editor of the weekly *Deutsche Post*, 28 January 1913, extolled the easy life of a farmer in Saskatchewan.

Emil Antler's farm on the Ottawa River (right), Petawawa Township, acquired by Ottawa in 1905; foreground: a mobile target used in military firing practice (courtesy Norman Antler, Pembroke)

Krugers' tarpaper shack at Krugerdorf, 1908 (courtesy Mrs Alma Allsopp, Kirkland Lake)

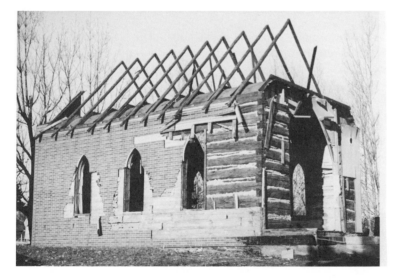

Military manoeuvres at Camp Petawawa (courtesy Champlain Trail Museum, Pembroke)

St Matthew's Lutheran Church, built 1896, was moved 1909 from campsite in Petawawa Township to Chalk River; demolition in 1965 revealed logs beneath two layers of siding.

Onetime cemetery of St Matthew's Lutheran Church, now on firing range at Petawawa military camp

Stones cleared by August Banstead in Buchanan Township are almost hidden by the forest that has grown up since 1909 acquisition by Ottawa.

CHAPTER NINE

The German heritage

The English language supplanted German only gradually in the German community of Renfrew County. In 1912 North Renfrew's public school inspector, E.T. White, complained that the education of pupils in Germanicus, in School Section 8 of Wilberforce Township, was disrupted by the absence of all seventy children, who attended German-language schools Monday through Wednesday.[1] Such truancy was an obstacle to any progress in the reading and writing of English. As late as 1928 North Renfrew's public school inspector, Norman Campbell, was expressing the same grievance in his annual report. He had found that the greatest hindrance to improvement in the rural townships was the holding of German schools during the regular sessions of the public schools.

The German schools were organized by the German churches, the Lutheran churches in particular, although other denominations such as the Baptists also arranged for the pastor to teach the German language and Bible studies to the children. They were sometimes termed *congregational* or *catechetical* schools, and early records of the rural churches show their importance.

When Reverend H.W. Schroeder travelled from the United States in 1874 to minister to the newly formed congregation of Grace Lutheran Church at Locksley in Alice Township, he preached his first sermon in Ledgerwood Public School.[2] One of his immediate tasks was to build the first Missouri Synod Lutheran church in eastern Ontario (the congregation of the Canada Synod church there having split in two because of theological differences). The thirteen founders of this new church had already gathered the necessary materials during the winter of 1873-4. The foundation and beams were to be made of cedar, and the superstructure was to be of pine logs *(Fichtenbloecken)*, covered with board.

Once the construction of the church was well on the way, the need for a
parochial school received attention. At an elders' meeting on 15 August
1874, the necessity of Christian education for the youth of the parish was
the centre of discussion. 'The parochial school is the responsibility of every
Lutheran congregation. Where there is no Christian Day School, where the
children can receive God's Word and be brought up in the nurture and ad-
monition of the Lord, there lacks also the spirit of Lutheranism.' Only six
years after the completion of the first German school at Locksley, it was
replaced by a new building equipped with new desks, benches, maps, and
slates.

Education of the young in the German language was treated with more
importance in the congregations of the Missouri Synod, which was more
conservative in doctrine than the Canada Synod. At Augsburg, Grattan
Township, a German school was built behind Zion Lutheran Church of the
Missouri Synod in 1888, and it suffered only a temporary setback in the
First World War. In 1916 it was closed and its pupils were redirected to a
public school, because the hostilities in Europe had caused uneasiness
among the adults, some of whom were not naturalized citizens.[3] The school
obviously revived, for Augsburg still had a separate German school (attached to the Lutheran Church of the Missouri Synod), as well as an English
public school, in December 1922.[4]

According to a book published in 1911 to mark the fiftieth anniversary of
the Canada Synod of the Lutheran church in Canada, this church had no
German parochial schools by that time. Nevertheless, truancy caused by
children attending German schools on weekdays was a regular problem in
the rural townships of Renfrew County until the 1930s. In his report of 1936
Inspector Campbell remarked that the number of pupils whose native
language was not English totalled 23 per cent of the children entering school
in the northern part of the county. He believed that this retarded their progress in reading and writing. Although some educated in the 1930s recall
that they learned German at Saturday classes given by the pastors, English
had gradually replaced German in the churches and in everyday communication, even for the most personal messages. In 1935 a bachelor at
Golden Lake writing to his girl-friend, who had moved to Ottawa, drafted
his proposal of marriage in English, though the formal style suggests that he
copied it.[5] He assured her that the hours spent in her company had left an
indelible impression, which was far from being a puerile fancy. 'Daily have
I had opportunities of observing the thousand acts of amiability and kind-
ness which mark the even tenor of your life until my feelings of affectionate
regard have ripened into a passion strong ardent and sincere, and I have
associated my hopes of future happiness with the idea of you as a life part-

ner.' Admiring Dorothy's charms of person and mind, the writer offered protestations of love and a modest assessment of his own character. He concluded, 'May I then implore you to consult your own heart, and should my honorable passion be crowned with your acceptance and approval, to grant me permission to refer the matter definitely to your parents.' The proposal of marriage was accepted and the letter treasured.

The maintenance of the German language in the rural areas, through three generations, was helped both indirectly and directly by the churches. Indirectly it was assisted by the parochial schools, later succeeded by Saturday classes; it was aided directly by the churches, most of which did not introduce any English services until after the First World War.

The changeover in language appears to have taken place earlier in the German communities of southern Ontario. At the annual conference of the Evangelical Association in Mildmay, Bruce County, in 1890, a petition signed by forty members requested the right to hold morning and evening services in English, with only the afternoon service in German.⁶ The petition claimed that this was the only way that the church could retain the younger generation. Though English preaching for some centres in the south of the province was arranged for the evening services, the problem was not resolved until the war years of 1914–18, when the work of this church transferred to the English language. The change occurred later in the Evangelical churches in Renfrew County; St John's Evangelical at Golden Lake continued until 1929 to maintain its church records and its meetings entirely in the German language, and even in 1939 the evening service was still conducted in the language of the immigrants.⁷

In general, the changes took place earlier in Pembroke and spread from there into the rural townships. At Zion Lutheran Church in Pembroke, the congregation decided in November 1921 to have English services in the evening on the first and third Sundays of each month; this was soon changed to include all Sunday evening services. It was felt that there was a need for the use of English for the younger generation and those 'who were not familiar with the German language.' About 6 miles south of Pembroke, at Grace Lutheran Church, Locksley, services were conducted almost exclusively in German until 1929; that year the congregation resolved to have an English service once a month, whenever an afternoon service was held. Nine miles west of Pembroke, at St John's Lutheran Church in Petawawa, the church council decided 4 April 1939 that English services would be delivered every second Sunday. About 20 miles southwest of Pembroke, at St John's Lutheran, Bonnechere, services were conducted in German from the *Kirchenbuch* until 1940. Even farther away, in the hills of Sebastopol

Township, St John's Lutheran, about 35 miles southwest of Pembroke, recorded the minutes of its parish meetings until 1949 entirely in German; in that year it began to alternate its services in English and German.[8]

Judging from the census records of Renfrew County, the thousands of German immigrants who began to arrive in 1858 did not include any clergymen. The townships in which they sought land had little population and no organized churches. Congregations were founded and encouraged by the efforts of missionaries who could preach to the newcomers in their own language – and travel through rough countryside to reach them. The border between the United States and Canada was no barrier to such missionaries, many of whom had already travelled north to found churches in southern Upper Canada; from there the pioneering work extended to the later immigration of German people in the Ottawa Valley area. By the end of the nineteenth century at least 50 churches had been built in and around Renfrew County for congregations that worshipped in the German language. The denominations included: Methodists, 4; Baptists, 6; Evangelicals, 13; Lutherans of the Canada Synod, 18; and Lutherans of the Missouri Synod, 9. (Slightly more than half the German households were Lutheran.) There were adherents of other faiths too, but not sufficiently numerous or concentrated to justify a separate church. For example, census records for 1881 show that in the five rural townships where the Germans had located in the greatest numbers, only 19 households out of 526 expressed their allegiance to the Roman Catholic church.

The pioneering missionaries were Reverend Karl Schmidt of the Methodist church and Reverend Ludwig Herman Gerndt of the Lutheran church, who both began to work in Renfrew County in 1861; Reverend Peter Alles of the Canada Conference of the Evangelical Association, who arrived in 1865; and Reverend G.A. Schultze of the North American Baptist Conference, who arrived in 1869.[9] Of these men, Gerndt, who founded almost all the Lutheran congregations (some of which split after his departure) and who lived in the area for nine years, is still widely revered.

Born in Berlin, Germany, 18 July 1821, Ludwig Herman Gerndt had studied at Bonn and Berlin universities. After ten years in India as a missionary, he was forced to return to Germany in 1857 because of the Indian mutiny. Sent to Canada, he was in charge of a parish in southern Upper Canada before he began exploring the eastern part of the province as a travelling missionary in 1861. In the next nine years he lived with his wife, Mary, and three children in a parsonage at Locksley, Alice Township. When Gerndt left eastern Ontario in 1870, there were more than 1,000 souls in his care. Continuing his career in the United States, he ended his service as a pastor in the immigration station on Ellis Island, where many immigrants landed for the first time in the New World. He died in Brooklyn, New York, 15 January, 1905. After he had left Renfrew County, and after his successor, Reverend H.W. Franke, had caused a division in many of the Lutheran churches, the fragmented congregations had difficulty in securing the services of a minister. A series of young pastors from Germany, who were not afraid to tackle the wilderness and the hardships of pioneer life, were appointed to the small and scattered German parishes.

Some plaudits for their missionary work were expressed at the 1876 annual convention of the Canada Synod. 'These brethren are laboring with self denial, travelling often on foot and through bog and forest to reach the scattered settlers in the new counties of Ontario.' When Reverend G. Brackebusch lived at Denbigh 1888–95, and served the congregation of the Lutheran church in Sebastopol Township every six weeks, he used to walk forty miles through wooded country, stopping on the way to catch and eat fish. [10]

Denbigh was the first parish served by Dr John Reble, 1909–12, later president of the Canada Synod, and his account of his early years in Canada convey the spirit of those pioneering years. [11] The director of the theological seminary at Kropp in Germany had been asked if a member of the 1909 class would be available to serve an isolated mission in Canada. One of the students, John Reble, had expressed his interest. He arrived in mid-winter 1909, via New York, and from there travelled to Hamilton, where he was examined by a five-member committee of pastors from 9 a.m. to 4 p.m. before being ordained that same evening. He reached Kaladar, at the beginning of the Addington Road, by train and was met by two of his parishioners with a horse-drawn sleigh. Paul Stein and Gustav Adam informed him that a journey of forty-three miles lay before them, a trip that took sixteen hours, and they bundled up their new minister in a fur coat and several robes to protect him from the cold.

The young pastor's schedule was arduous. 'Denbigh – a little village with a white frame church and lofty steeple lying among the hills and on the shore of a small lake, in those days had one parsonage [the Lutheran] with eight rooms plus kitchen. From here I served Raglan, 18 miles away, every second Sunday; occasionally I also conducted services at Quadeville; Maynooth, a distance of 52 miles, six times a year, and Plevna only four times a year. Imagine doing all that travelling by horse and buggy or cutter. A trip to Maynooth always required four or five days. If I wanted to serve Plevna, a distance of 25 miles, in one day, I had to rise at 5 a.m., feed the horse, leave at 6 a.m., and return at ten o'clock in the evening.'

On Sundays when the pastor was not able to be present with a congrega-

tion, the members held their own service. In the more distant congregations, one member would have a room in his house reserved for the overnight stay of the minister, a room termed the *Prophetenstube* (room of the
prophets). But not all his parishioners had such a spacious home. Some
were still living in one-room log shanties. One of Reble's earliest experiences
was an overnight stay in a one-room home with a family of seven, where he
had to undress and dress hastily to avoid embarrassment. He described the
people he served as humble, loyal, and very appreciative. Churches in
eastern Ontario were often built, furnished, and maintained by volunteers
of the congregation.

Schools and churches were not the only vehicles for the maintenance of the
language. A Lutheran pastor, Bahne Peter Christiansen, founded the
Deutsche Post newspaper in Arnprior in 1901. He believed that there were
enough people in eastern Ontario to support and read an advertising
medium in the German language.[12] The growth of the paper, with a
subscription price of $1, measured up to his expectations. It had more than
1,000 subscribers by 1905.

The offices of the newspaper moved in 1906 to Pembroke, a more popu-
lous centre. Independent in politics, the weekly was aimed at a possible
market of 10,000 readers. In 1908 it claimed to reach the best German
homes in the Ottawa Valley – this message was inscribed on the clothes
brushes given as premiums to new subscribers. The front page of 1909,
otherwise printed in German, bore the inscription, 'THE GERMAN POST is the
only newspaper in the German language in eastern and north-eastern Ontario and in Quebec.' By 1909 this weekly, published on a Thursday, was
priced at $1.50 a year if paid in advance; otherwise the cost was $2.
Reverend Christiansen died on 2 December 1908, aged 45; he was succeeded
by his son, Emil, who owned it until it ceased publication in 1916 under
suspicion of presenting German propaganda.

In 1909 each issue contained one page of news from Germany entitled
'AUS DEM ALTEN VATERLANDE' (From the old Fatherland). Under separate
heading subscribers could read news from Baden, Brunswick, Hamburg,
Hesse-Darmstadt, East Prussia, Mecklenburg, Oldenburg, West Prussia,
Brandenburg, Posen, Silesia, Pomerania, Schleswig-Holstein, Hanover, the
province of Saxony, Hesse-Nassau, Rhineland, Westphalia, the Kingdom of
Saxony, Thuringia, Württemberg, Alsace-Lorraine, Austria-Hungary,
Switzerland, and Luxembourg, all on page 5. Other pages bore Canadian
news, sandwiched between columns of advertisements from stores and
banks in Pembroke, Renfrew, Eganville, and Killaloe, most in German. The

local news on pages 7 and 12 presented detailed reports of activities (e.g. end-of-term school records) from communities such as Wilberforce, Alice, Arnprior, Northcote, and Golden Lake.

As in other Ontario German journals the paper provided a review of significant domestic and foreign events. The reporting of events from Germany, in some detail, was intended to keep readers in constant contact with their homeland, and scholars have concluded that this particular appeal explains why five German-language weekly newspapers were published in Ontario, between 1835 and 1918; the other four were published in the southern part of the province: *Berliner Journal, Ontario Glocke, Kolonist-Volksblatt,* and *Canadischer Bauernfreund*. Six weeks before the end of the First World War, German publications were prohibited in Canada. Two authors who have written on the German-language press in Ontario have been unable to find any copies of the *Deutsche Post*.[13]

The reporting of news from Germany in the *Deutsche Post* was largely responsible for the irritation in Pembroke that began to surface in late 1915. There were two English-language papers, the *Pembroke Standard* and the *Pembroke Observer*, and those who did not read German were unaware that the *Deutsche Post* might be presenting the German news in a favourable light until the *Observer* decided to enlighten them. Excerpts from an article were translated, with comments added.[14]

Predictably the *Deutsche Post* replied: 'As to the Post telling its readers all about Teutonic victories, the paper says surely the English-speaking people do not expect the paper to abuse the German people. Since the war began the official statements of both sides have been published, the German side being given a little more prominence because the reports of the Allies were published fully in all the English papers.' The *Observer* commented: 'How many German residents do not receive any English papers? And in this connection we might remark that a number of them have discontinued The Observer since the war broke out, some of whom said quite plainly that they could not continue to take the paper while we were printing such matter regarding their Teutonic friends. No paper published in Canada at this time should be giving preference to German news or news from enemy sources.' Articles such as these set the scene for the tumult that erupted in 1916 and that affected the board of education, some rural schools, and the career of a public school inspector.

At the time that the *Deutsche Post* was enjoying its greatest popularity, in the years just before the First World War, there appeared to be no antagonism toward the German language in Pembroke. The town contained the largest community of German-speaking people in Renfrew County by

1906, when the *Post* moved there from Arnprior. The efforts of German families to maintain their language appear to have been viewed dispassionately by the English-language press.

A number of German ratepayers met at the town hall in Pembroke, 29 November 1909, to discuss the advisability of approaching the board of education in order to introduce the teaching of the German language in the public schools.[15] The meeting decided on this resolution: 'That a petition be drawn up, requesting the Board of Education of the Town of Pembroke to take into consideration the introduction of the teaching of the German language in Pembroke's public schools and further that this petition be circulated among the ratepayers of the town with the view of getting signatures to it, and a committee authorized to call another meeting with results of the petition may be seen.'

The board of education considered the request 'in view of the large number of German children attending the Pembroke public schools' and appointed a special committee to investigate the matter. The committee produced a negative report. It had found that from the second to the fourth classes inclusive the German pupils numbered 40 per cent and that the German language was not dominant in the Pembroke school section as a whole. The cost of hiring an extra teacher was a serious objection, and it was thought to be difficult to secure a qualified instructor.[16]

The sober and objective manner in which this request was treated contrasts with the hysteria that prevailed during the First World War, when a public school inspector was dismissed because he was believed to be demonstrating pro-German sympathies. At a meeting of the Renfrew County council, 26 January 1916, the reeves of several townships complained that Inspector I.D. Bruels had been replacing satisfactory teachers with German girls and had refused to take action when he learned of pupils that were regularly absent two days a week to attend German parochial schools.[17] The inspector, who was responsible for schools in the northern half of Renfrew County, was summoned to appear before the county council to answer these charges the very same day.

Inspector Bruels resented the implication that he had favoured German teachers and countered stories of dismissals by stating that he could not possibly allow teachers without proper certificates to remain in schools as long as there were trained teachers available. Regarding the attendance of German pupils at German schools two days a week, he declared that there was nothing in the act to prevent this action and that parents were at liberty to send their children to private schools. As he concluded, those who suffered a penalty would be the children themselves, through the loss of time in the public schools.

In vain did Bruels protest that there was not a drop of German blood in his veins, that his remote ancestors were French and Belgian, and that his father was born in London, while his mother was of Irish descent, born in Maryland. His answers did not satisfy the county council, which placed him under suspicion while it sent a request to the minister of education for an investigation. In a letter of 16 February 1916, the deputy minister of education, A.H.U. Colquhoun, advised the county clerk, R.J. Roney, that the charges laid by the council were not supported by adequate evidence.[18] The suspension was therefore lifted and the inspector directed to resume his duties.

Even though some German immigrants had taken out naturalization papers within a few years of their arrival (e.g. Frederick Schutt, 24 December 1868), their grandsons would still meet prejudice. In Pembroke, where in 1914 one-fifth of the population was of German origin, there was openly expressed hostility, one of the leading spokesmen being Mayor J.L. Morris. In an interview in December 1915 with the *Ottawa Journal*, the mayor alleged that Pembroke was the centre of an organized spy system, the machinations of which spread to all parts of Canada.[19] The mayor stated that one resident of five in Pembroke was either German-born or of German extraction, while in the surrounding townships of Petawawa, Alice, Fraser, North and South Algona, Wilberforce, and Hagarty half the inhabitants were of Teutonic stock. Much of his suspicion stemmed from the internment of about 1,000 aliens at Camp Petawawa, housed in buildings evacuated by soldiers posted overseas. Morris believed that news about everything that happened there, as well as details of all government work undertaken in Pembroke, was carried to a German spy system in the United States. Reporters found the mayor's views echoed by the postmaster, W.A. Moffat, who stated that local Germans had been advised to take their money out of the banks, with particular reference to the post office savings department, and that there had been heavy withdrawals, both in Pembroke and in Eganville. He believed that the money was travelling to the United States by underground railway for transmission abroad. This idea too was scorned by the local papers, both English and German.

The continued publication of the German-language *Deutsche Post* was a source of much irritation and eventually violence. One evening in June 1916, a crowd of 200 or 300 began to congregate in front of the *Post* printing office, led by a half-dozen soldiers preparing to go abroad. The sign on the window was removed forcibly and the assembly was turned into a recruiting meeting.[20] The editor, Emil Christiansen, had for more than a year been defending in print his paper's publication of official German statements of war news. He had countered criticism by declaring that copies of the paper were supplied to the library of Parliament – and he had not received any objection.[21] The local MP, A.E. Dunlop, when apprised of the contents of the *Deutsche Post*, had made a statement in December 1915 that he would make it his business to see that this state of affairs was terminated. But the newspaper continued. The 10 November 1916 issue of the *Eganville Leader* announced that publication of the *Deutsche Post* had been ended.

It was a difficult period for members of the Lutheran churches in Pembroke, especially those of Zion Evangelical Lutheran Church of the Canada Synod; its pastor, Reverend P. Kleine, was on a four months' visit to Germany when war broke out.[22] After waiting for almost a year, the congregation declared the pastorate vacant; Reverend Mr Kupfer was installed 1 April 1915 and served until 1919. Throughout the war all services were conducted in German, which did nothing to allay suspicions of those who criticized the Lutheran pastors for not attending Patriotic Fund meetings, although invited. The *Deutsche Post* editor, when queried on this point by the *Toronto Daily News*, replied that the Patriotic Fund was a political movement and therefore not part of a minister's duties. Reverend Herman C. Landsky, pastor of St John's Lutheran Church of the Missouri Synod in Pembroke, readily admitted that his younger children spoke only German at home, although a son was serving in the army at the front.

Feelings ran high, judging by contemporary reports in the local newspapers. A street in Pembroke named Berlin was changed to Isabella. Some German families even changed their surnames. Yet there are German names on the war memorial in Pembroke, and there are military markers in the German churches throughout the northern and western townships.

Occasional escapes from the internment camp at Petawawa and mysterious fires that damaged munitions plants at Pembroke, Renfrew, and further afield helped to inflame the suspicions of some residents that Mayor Morris might be right. One of the most devastating blazes, in March 1916, destroyed the Renfrew Machinery Company's Shell Factory, which had been operating twenty-four hours a day. The loss was estimated at $100,000, the cause unknown.[23]

In the first three years of the war, service in the armed forces was voluntary, and recruiting had slowed down by the end of 1916. When compulsory military service was instituted 29 August 1917, all men between the ages of 20 and 45 were liable for enlistment. Though the terms for exemption were very liberal, not all farmers' sons could claim that they were needed on the

land, and some avoided conscription by hiding out in the bush. Those in
Renfrew County who succeeded in avoiding capture by the military forces
surrendered to police in Pembroke at the end of the war and were fined.
Across the 3,000 square miles of the county there was an abundance of
hiding-places and many are the legends that survive of those exploits.

One German-Canadian farmer who did not sympathize with those evad-
ing military service was Frederich Grozklags, as a Pembroke newspaper
reported in January 1918: 'Fred Grozklags ... is a constable who is
thoroughly seized of his duties and religiously performs them. This week he
has been in Pembroke on his way back from Kingston, where he delivered
three man to the military authorities who failed to report to the Military
Tribunals. This is the second batch which the Constable has landed in
Kingston, and he says there are more hidden away in the bush, but he can't
locate them until a fresh fall of snow, when he will be able to track them to
their hiding-places. He says he is determined that those who are eligible for
military duty within his bailiwick shall report for duty, or he will know the
reason why.'[24]

The newspaper account continued: 'Constable Grozklags, who is a prosperous farmer, and has plenty to do, he says, without bothering with constable work, but someone has to do it, is the father of eight sons and five
daughters, three of his sons being on active service in France, is a naturalized German, who has an intelligent idea of why his father left Germany,
and settled in this county when the constable was a little fellow. He is a
thorough Canadian, and a firm believer in British principles.'

In eastern Ontario, with its extensive areas of wooded wilderness and
thousands of people of German origin, newspapers found a fertile field for
sensational stories. One that reached the House of Commons, via an article
in the *Ottawa Citizen*, 11 March 1918, told of a band of young men, armed
and threatening, who were camping on the banks of the Petawawa River,
twenty miles from Pembroke, flying a red flag. The leaders were a couple of
Irish Protestants who had been joined by eight local Germans and four
French Canadians who were determined to avoid military service.[25]

The factions of the war left a legacy of bitterness in Pembroke. When the
town was celebrating its centennial in 1928 the special historical publications glossed over the turbulence that had existed only a decade earlier.
Former publisher of the *Pembroke Observer* D.A. Jones wrote: 'Came the
war of 1914, with all its tragic consequences. This article has to do only
with industrial matters, hence we will refer only to the part which Pembroke played in the production of shells, cartridge clips, shell boxes and
such lines.' Nevertheless he added, 'In 1914 the Pembroke Lumber Co.'s
planing mill was destroyed by fire and subsequently there were a number of

other fires all of which were, rightly or wrongly, attributed to incendiarism by alien enemies. But in 1918, within a period of one month, came two conflagrations which, combined, entailed a loss of one million dollars. There was little doubt as to their origin.'[26]

In the townships where German Canadians constituted about half the population, there was little sign of friction in the local newspapers, which were inclined to treat light-heartedly the search parties of military police and the suspicions attached to those with German names. The *Eganville Leader*'s Killaloe correspondent was quoted, 18 October 1918: 'Some people of this district have lately perceived what they thought to be a German Zeppelin in Mr. —'s field but on further discovery they found it to be only an ordinary potatoe digger.' When returned soldiers were given a reception at the Eganville town hall in March 1919, Dr M.J. Maloney, MP, an Eganville physician, made a speech in which he pleaded for the banishment of all differences of race and creed in common citizenship in Canada. Private Tiegs of Grattan, a German-Canadian soldier who had just returned, was singled out as an example of loyalty.[27]

One consequence of the First World War was the number of German Canadians who returned to Renfrew County with Scottish wives. Many who enlisted were sent to work in the Canadian Forestry Corps in Scotland, for Ottawa Valley men were renowned for their lumbering skills and in that country would find no conflicting loyalties. Travel, intermarriage, and the upheavals of war all contributed to the decline in the German language.

In the 1920s a large number of small farms in Renfrew County changed hands. Judging from the auctioneers' announcements in the weekly papers, there were several every week from March until autumn. The frequency was so great in 1927 that the editor of the *Eganville Leader*, Paddy McHugh, commented on 25 March: 'One day this week a LEADER representative [obviously McHugh himself] counted sixteen auction sale bills on display in a local hotel, all scheduled to take place in a splendid farming area and within a short space of time. Pessimists profess to see in this a decline of interest in farming but those who are inclined to look on the brighter side point to the fact that in each instance another family is moving in to take the place of the one which is moving out.' He had written in the same vein twenty-five years earlier.

Although there were movements by residents of all ethnic groups, people of Irish descent declined in numbers from 19,832 in 1901 to 15,357 in 1931. The sale of so many properties offered opportunities for farmers' sons who would not inherit the family farm to buy a property near home instead of joining the trek west, north, or south. It was a chance for German families to move from the worst farming terrain, from the heart-breaking swamps of South Algona and the rugged hills of Raglan Township, into the greener pastures of Wilberforce and Alice. They moved from the bleak upland region of the Canadian Shield into the down-faulted rift valley, the Ottawa-Bonnechere Graben, where so many German immigrants of the 1860s had found good soil. Deserted farms, derelict schools, and cemeteries without adjacent churches are mute reminders of the unrewarding toil and evacuation from the poorest townships in Renfrew County. Many long-established families of German origin did not apply for century farm plaques when the scheme was carried out in Ontario in 1967; they had farmed in Renfrew County for more than 100 years, but not on the same property.

Movement from Germany to Canada had halted in 1914. Prohibitions on German immigration to Canada were removed in 1923.[28] From 1927 to 1930, about two-thirds of German immigrants were farm labourers, most from the agrarian regions of northeastern Germany. A major factor encouraging immigration appears to have been a chain of assistance offered by the railway and shipping companies on behalf of the Canadian government. Passage, jobs, and settlement were organized for the newcomers. The Canadian government and the railway companies were aided by the close co-operation of numerous church organizations, such as the Lutheran Immigration Board and the Canadian Lutheran Immigration Aid Society. Their German denominational counterparts in Hamburg and Bremen selected the emigrants and assigned them to the appropriate Canadian agencies. Most went to the western provinces, but a small number went to Renfrew County.

Several members of the Reinert family left eastern Germany on 5 April 1927, arriving in Halifax on 27 April after an ocean journey of ten days.[29] On that Easter Sunday morning they were taken to a church where the minister was to inform them of their destinations; many were sent through to Winnipeg. August Reinert, Albert Reinert, and Edward Behnke were late getting to church and were assigned to Eganville, whence had come a demand for farm labourers. The men had been assured in Germany that they would earn $25 a month and eventually $30.

The three men travelled by train to Montreal and Ottawa, where they had to change. Since the train conductor could not speak German and the men could not speak English, a mistake was made and they boarded a CNR train instead of the CPR. Reverend Max Voss of Grace Lutheran Church, Eganville, and members of his congregation were waiting for the men at Eganville's CPR station when they learned that the men had alighted at the Admaston station on the CNR line. The minister and his son, Siegmund, went to fetch them in a car, one of only five in Eganville.

August Reinert, who had left Germany just one month before his twentieth birthday and just before he was about to be drafted into the army, was assigned to William Kumm's farm. Albert Reinert, who had completed his military service before emigrating, was sent to Otto Weckworth's farm, and Eddie Behnke went to work at Fred Griese's place. Other members of the Reinert family who had emigrated in 1929 to Canada were sent to Saskatchewan, but all made their way back to eastern Ontario, even Olga Reinert who was employed on a farm where her boss concealed letters from her relatives, in an effort to prevent her from leaving. As it was, all the Reinerts and other immigrants from Germany in the 1920s arrived just in time for the Depression.

Personal recollections of those years, in a German Lutheran household in Renfrew County, have been written by Mary Cook, née Hanniman, who spent her childhood years on a self-sufficient small farm, in an area where neighbours were all-important.[30] Her accounts of growing up in a log farmhouse, without electricity, describe how her family was poor in cash and material goods, but warm and well fed in a decade when they were envied by city cousins. The Hanniman family lived at Northcote, Admaston Township, where a small number of nineteenth-century immigrants were assimilated and intermingled with Irish and Scots. (They and their Roman Catholic neighbours took the day off from farming to celebrate the Glorious 12th of July parade in Renfrew.)

The Ontario government's $38 million Depression relief scheme was responsible for the construction of good roads in Renfrew County, beginning in 1933.[31] It was designed to provide employment and income for thousands of men and relieved the isolation of farms in townships where automobiles were a rarity and where travel was easiest in winter by horse-drawn sleigh.

The chief engineer of colonization roads, R.S. Sneath, made the announcement, 19 November 1933, in Pembroke: 'Work will commence immediately on the proposed road between Pembroke and Barry's Bay and F.W. Beatty, Pembroke, will have charge of two camps of 100 men each which will be engaged in the project.' Surveying of this section of highway had just been completed. The new road would commence at a point some 10 miles from Pembroke at the boundary between Alice and Fraser townships and proceed via Round Lake and Paugh Lake to Barry's Bay. The construction of 30 miles of roadway would reduce the distance between the two points by 17 miles, as well as improve the surface of the route to be travelled. A road to be built from Lake Dore to Golden Lake and through to Killaloe was also announced, Sneath being unable even to estimate how many men would be employed on this thoroughfare.

Pembroke's mayor, George D. Briggs, told members of his town council on 29 November that the men working on the roads would be paid 15 cents an hour and would work eight hours a day. Camps would be established along the route, and construction of the provincial highway to Barry's Bay was expected to distribute between $25,000 and $30,000 within a few months. An old school in Barry's Bay was fitted out as an office, to serve as headquarters for a program of road building that was expected to last a couple of years.

The MLA for South Renfrew was a Liberal, Thomas P. Murray, but he felt that the Conservative government's action was one of the best improvements ever made in Renfrew County. In later years, Murray recalled that 5,600 men registered for work on the roads within six months of the plan's beginning. 'It was quite a project. We had no big machines but we had picks and shovels, we had the crowbar, the wheelbarrow, the hammer and the chisel and, of course, the old gray mare. When I went to Toronto in 1929 it used to take two hours to travel from Barry's Bay to Combermere,' he said, referring to a distance of fifteen miles that can now be travelled on a good paved road in less than fifteen minutes. [32]

The extensive program of road-building included a highway south from Eganville eighteen miles to Griffith, where camps were built to accommodate 100 men. [33] In January 1934 it was reported that 700 men, in gangs of 25, recruited almost entirely from villages near Eganville were at work. They were cutting rights-of-way, brushing, straightening out the roads, 'and cutting down the numerous little hills,' as the *Eganville Leader* described their activities. They received $1.20 per day and boarded at home. The government's plan was to relieve unemployment by using as many men as possible and by prohibiting machinery. Each gang was allowed only one or two teams of horses. Tools such as picks, shovels, axes, and wheelbarrows were passed out freely, but dynamite was the only force used apart from manpower. The project had an enduring effect on the lives of those who lived in the countryside, especially when they could later afford automobiles.

The roads meant an end to most country stores and the career of many country craftsmen, such as furniture-makers. Blacksmiths were replaced by service stations. Railroad spur lines became redundant. One-room schools, only a few miles apart, would now have their enrolments merged when students could be transported by bus to larger institutions. Churches with dwindling congregations would be absorbed into other parishes, for their members could travel easily to another place of worship. The farms, no longer isolated, could be the homes of those who found employment in another type of work, and farming as a way of earning a living lost its importance in eastern Ontario.

ss 6A Brudenell and Lyndoch Townships: pupils and teacher, Mrs Alma Kauffeldt

The *Deutsche Post* brush, given as a premium to new subscribers

SS 6 South Algona Township, 1968: teacher Bill Sutherland watches 14-year-old Ross Shruder bring fuel from the woodshed.

One-room school for German pupils built 1898 for SS 6 South Algona Township, and used until 1968

Zion Evangelical Lutheran Church, near Silver Lake, South Algona Township; built 1904, demolished 1976. Only the burial ground remains. (Courtesy James Allan, Ottawa)

Epilogue

Since the 1960s the reunions organized by German families in Renfrew County have become so large, with visitors numbered in the hundreds, that halls have to be hired for meetings, campsites reserved for accommodation, and invitation lists researched for a year before the event. Such mammoth reunions serve to emphasize the loss of people from this part of eastern Ontario, which did not have the employment opportunities to hold them. Descendants of the early immigrants whose farms still support families in Renfrew County have either accumulated a large amount of land or else exercised a great deal of ingenuity.

Although Renfrew County does not have any first-class soil, the classification of land is not as meaningful as it orginally was. According to Calvin Patrick, agricultural development officer for four counties in eastern Ontario, some land in Renfrew County could be just as productive as land in southern Ontario, if treated well. In his view, thousands of acres could be improved. Productivity of land is based on drainage, heat units, type of soil, and the number of frost-free days. Little can be done about the latter, but drainage can be installed so that the soil will heat up better, and ploughing improves the quality. When pioneers settled the land, a 100-acre farm was expected to support a herd of cattle, as well as sheep and hogs, and the soil was soon depleted of nourishment by annual crops if there was no fertilizer applied. In 1983 a demonstration on soil improvement was started on privately owned land in Bromley Township. Labelled the Canadian Provincial Eastern Ontario Pasture Demonstration Farm, this experiment plot has strips of fenced land on which cattle are grazing; it will show how fertilization and drainage can make a significant improvement. In future years, the size of herds that can occupy a defined pasture will be determined.

Some farms, where the soil has been worn out and attempts at agriculture have been abandoned, have been purchased by the Ontario Ministry of Agriculture and Food and transferred to the crown – a total of 13,000 acres by 1983. This land has been planted with trees, under a reforestation program managed by the Ontario Ministry of Natural Resources.

Few German immigrants who have arrived in Renfrew County since 1950 live in the rural townships, although some have found new ways to earn a living in such a setting. A family that left East Germany in 1956 drained a swamp in South Algona Township and started a plant nursery that has been an outstanding success. Most of the newcomers have chosen to settle in Pembroke, so many that on 28 January 1955 they founded the Germania Club, a social centre with the stated objective of preserving and promoting the German language, culture, and customs. It was affiliated with the Trans-Canada Alliance of a German-Canadian Association, which embraces German ethnic groups from coast to coast. The social events held in the club's building run the gamut from choirs to cabaret, but the biggest event of the year is the annual Oktoberfest.

This harvest festival was not a common celebration in northern and eastern Germany, whence the immigrants travelled in the nineteenth century. Nevertheless, the increased interest and pride in heritage among German families in western Renfrew County has expanded to include an Oktoberfest in Eganville. The first year that advertisements for this event were published, in 1979, the invitation read, 'We are now making arrangements to seat 800 people of German descent (or those who wish they were).' It signalled a significant change in attitude. The open hostility faced by some German families in the First World War was not repeated during the Second World War, although there were some incidents of harassment. The shortening and simplifying of surnames, while not confined to any ethnic group, caused some German names in Renfrew County to resemble those of Scottish origin. A few families admit that this was done deliberately. In contrast, recent years have seen an upsurge of interest in genealogy, with members of the fourth or fifth generation eager to research their origins; they have been writing to Germany for church records of baptisms and marriages of their ancestors and have been searching shipping records in both Canada and the United States, for many immigrants arrived in the latter country en route to a new life in the Canadian wilderness. (The Mormon Archives in Salt Lake City, Utah, has proved a useful source of information on family history.)

Some German Canadians who would like to make a pilgrimage to their ancestors' village of birth have found that changes in national boundaries have made this impossible. A visa to visit the country of interest may be difficult to obtain. One retired man, who takes adventurous trips around the world on freighters, managed to make a sentimental journey in 1983 to a village now in western Poland. With the aid of a hired interpreter and a car, this grandson of Friedrich Witt travelled to the village near Stargard that used to be Sammenthin, but is now called Zamenciz. The German village had become Polish, and the Lutheran Church Roman Catholic. These transformations had occurred following the Second World War, by which time the German residents, including the pastor's family, had fled before the advance of the Russians. Subsequently the territory was transferred from Germany to Poland and the land was allocated to handicapped Polish veterans. The cemetery provided testimony of the history of the occupation of this area, but other records were not so readily available; some have literally been buried.

A 1952 study of more recent immigrants from Germany – *German Immigration into Canada*, by Wolfgang G. Friedmenn – has concluded that the immigrant of 1951 is quite different from those who came in the second half of the nineteenth century: 'In many ways he is less self-reliant. He does not expect to travel in the steerage or to build his own log cabin and make a few acres of arable land out of the wilderness of bush. The present-day immigrant expects a reasonable passage, some kind of housing and opportunities of employment provided for him direct by employers or through the good offices of the government. Many older immigrants deplore this change.'

Though the short growing season in the region has proved a handicap to agriculture, two small but thriving Mennonite farming communities have added another element of German tradition. Three families from Waterloo County bought three farms in Westmeath Township in 1980; their members immediately began to convert one of the farm homes for use as the community's church and school. The children will be educated free from pressure to conform to ways inconsistent with Mennonite philosophy. The school had thirteen students by 1982, and the community had grown to include six families. Conservative in their dress, they are liberal enough to drive cars provided that they are black and have no trimmings. The sight of women wearing lace caps and long skirts as they work in the fields is reminiscent of Mennonite communities in southern Ontario, to which German families moved in the early nineteenth century from Pennsylvania. In adjacent Hastings County, close to where some German immigrants journeyed to the end of Hastings Colonization Road in the nineteenth century, another Mennonite community began in the 1950s, east of Bancroft.

Started by Walter Braun and John and Elvin Burkholder, the congregation
had grown to seventy-five by 1983, some of it by local conversion. Here
too, the dress and life-style are modest and the children attend a private
school. The adults who head the dozen families work on the land, run a
sawmill, and operate a bakery. In both these eastern Ontario counties the
arrival of Mennonite families is a new phenomenon and unrelated to immigration from twentieth-century Germany.

Census records show that the continued influx of German newcomers to
Renfrew County has not been large enough to balance those of German descent who are leaving the area. There are some farms occupied by the third
or fourth or fifth generations of the German families that first cleared the
land, but their numbers are decreasing steadily. For the most part, the furnishings of these homes are completely modern, from the microwave oven
to the television set, but many simple objects used quite unself-consciously
in everyday living hark back to a pioneer past. These may be a bootjack
made of wood, a salt-box on the kitchen wall, blankets hand-woven on the
farm, spinning-wheels occasionally spinning, and a surprising amount of
hand-made furniture still in use after more than a century.

Some customs peculiar to German families have survived. One is the
tradition of building an archway of evergreen branches over the entrance to
the home of a girl about to be married. This is made the day before the wedding by her parents and usually taken down when the couple returns from
the honeymoon. Making sauerkraut is still an annual event, carried on by
some housewives alone in their kitchen and by some families, such as the
Schauers of Cobden, as a communal activity in which both men and women
take part. Cabbage is quartered, sliced, pounded, and salted. Those making
a large quantity use a slaw cutter, consisting of a bottomless box slid back
and forth over angled blades; the shredded cabbage is collected in a crock or
a wooden barrel and is preserved in brine. Needless to say, cabbages occupy
a prominent position in the vegetable garden on most German farms,
though they are not grown (or stored) in such vast quantities as potatoes.

Other pioneer skills practised include the tapping of maple trees in the
spring with the resulting production of maple syrup; on a few farms, which
have a dairy herd, housewives may still make butter. Neither skill is
peculiarly German, and in many cases the only identification of a German
family is the name on the mail-box. A glance through the phone directory of
the Upper Ottawa Valley shows German families scattered through every
township of Renfrew County; if there are fifty of the same surname listed in
one area the numbers in themselves are evidence of an early family. Some
surnames found in old cemeteries are not present in the phone book at all; it
may mean that no descendants have stayed in the county.

In rural areas where congregations have dwindled, the churches may have closed, the log buildings been demolished and sold for their logs, and the brick structures converted to other uses. Yet some small country churches, with very small memberships, have risen from the ashes. Often positioned out of sight of an inhabited home, the country church by its very location is vulnerable to destruction by fire. In the hamlet of Schutt, Raglan Township, Emmanuel Evangelical United Church burned down 18 May 1977, but a new church on the same site was completed in time for an opening service 30 October 1977. In just six months the seventy-five member congregation had rallied and rebuilt a structure costing $100,000, reportedly almost paid for by the date of dedication. Similarly, when St John's Lutheran Church, Bonnechere, burned down on 30 January 1981, the congregation lost no time in planning a third building to replace the second which they had just lost. Reconstruction started 28 April 1981, and the church was opened that summer, even though its congregation could have worshipped only a few miles away at Eganville or Augsburg, which are served by the same pastor. Reverend Ralph Keith, who ministered to that three-point parish, explained the enthusiasm for rebuilding. 'The rural church is the centre of the spiritual life of that community,' he said. 'With schools' consolidation, with people going to shopping centres, there's nothing left but the small churches. That's the only focal point in the rural community.'

In Renfrew County there have been no big airports built or planned, no major industrial developments or urban sprawl to change the pattern of small farms on hilly, stony, swampy, wooded land. Unlike some parts of southern Ontario with large settlements of German people, the countryside in Renfrew County has changed little, in itself an asset for growth of the tourist industry. Paved roads enable the motorist to travel easily through most of the region where the earliest German immigrants had to struggle on foot. In winter the roads carry skiers to four ski hills. The numerous lakes are an attraction in the summer, with campsites, motels, and summer cottages that encourage holiday-makers to linger and help small businesses to survive. In the fall the hunting is good.

Those who can live on the farm and find employment elsewhere can have the best of both worlds. The third generation of a German family typically holds on to the land tenaciously, whether it can yield a living or not. When the grandchildren of the immigrants have died, the fourth generation does not always feel the same loyalty – or the estate may have been left without an heir and relatives who inherit equally may wish to sell and obtain their inheritance. In this way the material evidence of German-speaking immigrants who arrived in Renfrew County in the second half of the nineteenth century is being slowly eradicated, as the log buildings are pulled down and the contents of the farms sold and moved.

Helen Sack using a bowling pin to compact shredded cabbage in brine,
Eganville

Doug (left) and Merrill Schauer slide a box of cabbage over the angled
blades of a sauerkraut cutter, Cobden. (Courtesy Marilyn Waldron,
Cobden *Sun*)

George (left) and Wilfred Bartscher, Grattan Township, believe they are the last of this surname in Renfrew County.

Zadows stuff a pig's intestine with ground, seasoned pork, South Algona Township.

The third church on this site: St John's Lutheran Church (Canada Synod), Bonnechere, Wilberforce Township, being built a second time, summer 1981

APPENDIX A

German surnames in Renfrew County cemeteries

This alphabetical list of more than 1,000 German surnames found in sixty-five cemeteries in the area of eastern Ontario where immigrants from Germany settled in the nineteenth century can be only a fragmentary record. Some pioneers were not buried in consecrated ground, and many who were have not been commemorated by a permanent grave marker. Yet this list may prove useful to families tracing their genealogy, for the discovery of even one old gravestone that bears the date of death can lead to an obituary in a local newspaper or perhaps the record of burial at the appropriate church.

Church records would reveal a more complete survey of names – if they were all available. Some early registers have been sent away to archives, especially if the church as been demolished, e.g. St Matthew's Lutheran Church, Brindle Road, Petawawa Township. Some churches admit that all or part of their records are missing, e.g. St John's Lutheran Church, Germanicus. Some pastors believe that records may not have been kept in the nineteenth century, e.g. St Patrick's Roman Catholic Church at Mount St Patrick. Those who minister to a number of scattered churches in a rural parish are very busy men; they are seldom found at home, and if they have any old record books these are written in a German script difficult to read and interpret. Most pastors, ministers, and priests simply do not have the time to respond to the growing number of inquiries they receive about long-deceased members of their congregations. One pastor took three years, despite phone calls, visits, and letters, to reply to a simple query from this author.

The idea for compiling this list began one day in the summer of 1978 on a drive around South Algona Township, which reached its peak of population about 1901, according to census records. Three burial grounds in that township have no adjacent churches; the German surnames on the tombstones there represent some of the earliest families who attempted to farm, on difficult land. Many of their children moved away, some to other parts of Renfrew County, and their surnames are recorded in other cemeteries. The recording of names on grave markers in different cemeteries became a useful index; it could be used to trace the movement of some family members away from the first home to other townships, and, conversely, to track down the original place of settlement of the earliest members of the family. The inscriptions themselves could lead to third- or fourth-generation members of the family, for in some cases where one marriage partner had died the survivor had erected a double headstone leaving the date of the survivor's death a blank. Reference to a phone book would disclose the whereabouts of the widow or widower, if he or she was still living at a private address.

Although more than 1,000 surnames have been listed separately, some are variations of the same name. The spelling was often incorrect in the nineteenth century, for the 'marble-dressing establishments' of eastern Ontario were located in the towns of Pembroke, Renfrew, Arnprior, and Almonte, and the workmen were British. The mis-spelling of names, in an age when immigrants of many nationalities were illiterate, may have had a lasting effect on the bearers of these surnames. Some were spelled phonetically, hence the name Kallies emerges as Caliss and Kaulbach as Calbeck. Succeeding generations were inclined to shorten the surnames, so that Schwandt is reduced to Swan and Kossatzmichael to Koss. The Anglicization of surnames was so deceptive in some instances, e.g. Mueller to Miller and Schmidt to Smith, that identification of the burial as that of a German person had to be founded on the Christian names or the similarity of names in the same cemetery. During and after the First World War, a few German families with monosyllabic names changed the spelling in order to resemble a Scottish surname, in order that their children would not suffer the hostility that they had known.

The purchase and transport of heavy stone markers across countryside that could be traversed only on rough wagon trails must have been a hard task in the years of early settlement. It was more expensive than the construction of a wooden cross with a scrawled inscription, and consideration of expense must have affected the choice. In the Baptist cemetery in Hagarty Township, RR 4, near Killaloe, the oldest stone decipherable commemorates the burial of Meane Kuarl (probably Keuhl) who died 16 March 1877, aged 5 years; the small marker, topped by the sculpture of a lamb, was from the workshop of D.F. Stewart of Renfrew, at least fifty miles away. There are few gravestones as early as 1877 in the western townships of Renfrew County. In contrast, when Charles Haentschel died in Pembroke, 1 September 1888, his grave was marked by an imposing headstone prepared by R. Reid of Montreal. Pembroke had railroad connections with that city. Haentschel must have been a man of substance, judging by the size of the stone which gives his birthplace as Sachsendorf, Germany. He was the founder of the Lutheran church in Pembroke, which began with services in his log house in 1883. Nevertheless his grave is located in the

Anglican cemetery in the centre of Pembroke, for the Lutheran congregation did not have a burial ground of its own at that time. It is noticeable that few gravestones were installed in the 1930s, the years of the Depression, when cash purchases had to be carefully chosen. By 1934 the government's road-building program had made travel and transport to the farthest townships of Renfrew County easy, but gravestones were not a priority when families had limited funds.

There are so few burial markers of German immigrants showing the names of their birthplaces that a sample is not statistically sound. There are more ascribed to Pomerania and West Prussia than any other part of Germany. Some simply state Born in Germany or Born in Deutschland and may carry the name of a village that cannot be found on any maps today. Not one in the sixty-five cemeteries visited had an inscription that identified a birthplace in southern Ontario or the United States.

Scrutiny of these cemeteries shows that the children of the immigrants continued to marry those of German descent. Only in areas where they were outnumbered, such as Raglan Township and Northcote in Admaston Township were there early marriages between German and non-German partners. In Northcote intermarriage and assimilation of German families have been so complete that there is no material evidence that they ever existed there; even the Lutheran church of St James has been torn down, and the members of its congregation were buried in a union cemetery at Rosebank several miles away. In townships where German people were the dominant ethnic group by the turn of the century almost all the surnames are German in some cemeteries, with marriage between members of different Protestant denominations being common.

An entry on this list means that the surname is found in a certain cemetery; it may occur only once or it may be repeated many times. It may be the woman's surname before she married. Comparison of this list of names with the surnames in appendices A, B, and D in *The Trail of the Black Walnut* by G. Elmore Reaman (Toronto 1957) shows that few are common to both areas, reinforcing the belief that the German settlement in eastern Ontario was not an offshoot of the German settlement in the southern part of the province. The list in the present book contains German surnames that do not occur now in eastern Ontario at all. In some cases the families left the area over fifty years ago, but they were part of the original immigration and struggle in the wilderness of eastern Ontario. They deserve to be mentioned. As far as possible the author has tried to exclude the names of those who came here from Germany since 1950, for they play no part in the story.

The cemeteries where German surnames were recorded were in most instances located in rural townships and villages. However, Arnprior and Pembroke were included in this study, for they were centres of employment for new arrivals anxious to earn money and, in later generations, for those who left a small farm in order to find employment elsewhere.

Abbreviations for Cemeteries

Anglican churches
A1 St John's Anglican Church, Eganville (church distant)
A2 Holy Trinity Anglican Church, Pembroke (church distant)
A3 All Saints' Anglican Church, Petawawa
A4 St Paul's Anglican Church, Combermere, Radcliffe Township

Baptist churches
B1 First Baptist Church, RR 4 Hagarty Township, and Baptist Church, Killaloe: joint cemetery near church in Hagarty Township
B2 Lyndock Baptist Church, Wolfe, Lyndoch Township
B3 Sebastopol Baptist Church, Woermke, Sebastopol Township

Evangelical churches, allied to North-West Conference
E1 Grace Evangelical Church, RR 2 Hagarty Township (church distant)
E2 Evangelical Church, Augsburg, South Algona Township (church distant)

Lutheran churches, Canada Synod
LC1   Zion Evangelical Lutheran Church, Highway 62, Pembroke
LC2   Zion Evangelical Lutheran Church, Boundary Road, Pembroke
LC3   St Peter's Lutheran Church, Alice
LC4   Grace Evangelical Lutheran Church, Greenlake, Wilberforce Township
LC5   Bethlehem Lutheran Church, Woito, Wilberforce Township
LC6   St John's Lutheran Church, Vanbrugh, Sebastopol Township
LC7   St John's Lutheran Church, Black Bay Road, Petawawa Township
LC8   St Johannes Kirche, Augsburg, South Algona Township
LC9   St Paul's Lutheran Church, Denbigh, Lennox and Addington County
LC10 Grace Lutheran Church, Eganville (cemetery at village limits)
LC11 Trinity Lutheran Church, Chalk River (church absent)
LC12 Trinity Lutheran Church, Zadow, South Algona Township (church absent)
LC13 St Matthew's Lutheran Church, Petawawa Township (church absent)
LC14 St Stephen's Lutheran Church, Schutt, Raglan Township
LC15 Christ Lutheran Church, Maynooth, Hastings County

Lutheran churches, Missouri Synod
LM1 Grace Lutheran Church, Locksley, Alice Township
LM2 St Stephen's Lutheran Church, Alice (church absent)
LM3 Zion Lutheran Church, Augsburg, Grattan Township (apart from church)
LM4 St John's Lutheran Church, Pembroke, Boundary Road

LM5   St Luke's Lutheran Church, Eganville (cemetery at village limit)
LM6   First Lutheran Church, Palmer Rapids, Raglan Township
LM7   Zion Lutheran Church, Silver Lake, South Algona Township (church absent)
LM8   Christ Lutheran Church, Airport Road, Petawawa Township

Lutheran churches of two synods sharing cemetery
LM/C   Lutheran cemetery at Germanicus, Wilberforce Township:
          St John's Lutheran Church, Canada Synod, Bonnechere,
          and St John's Lutheran Church, Missouri Synod, Germanicus

Methodist churches
M1   Alice Methodist Church, Alice Township, old highway (church absent)
M2   Emmanuel Methodist Church, Maynooth, Hastings County
M3   Greenwood Methodist Church, Westmeath Township (church absent)
M4   Combermere Methodist Church, Radcliffe Township (church absent)

Roman Catholic churches
RC1   St Columba's Cathedral, Pembroke, Highway 62, city limits
RC2   St James' Church, Eganville
RC3   St Patrick's Church, Mount St Patrick, Brougham Township
RC4   St Michael's Church, Douglas
RC5   St Andrew's Church, Killaloe
RC6   St Alexander's Church, Wylie Township (now within Deep River)
RC7   Ste Anne's Church, Cormac, Sebastopol Township

United Church of Canada churches
UC1   Salem Church, Locksley, Alice Township
UC2   St John's Church, Golden Lake (church distant)
UC3   Zion Evangelical Church, Rankin, Wilberforce Township
UC4   Calvary Church, Palmer Rapids, Raglan Township
UC5   Zion Evangelical Church, Boundary Road, Pembroke
UC6   Zions Kirche, Achray Road, Petawawa Township (church distant)
UC7   Evangelical Church, Rosenthal, Radcliffe Township
UC8   Emmanuel Church, Schutt, Raglan Township
UC9   Melville Church, Eganville (cemetery at village limit)
UC10 St Andrew's Church, Chalk River, Highway 17 (church distant)
UC11 St Luke's Church, Denbigh, Lennox and Addington County
UC12 Pentacostal Church, Quadeville, 2 cemeteries, old and new near
UC13 Evangelical Church, Letterkenny, Brudenell Township
UC14 St Andrew's Church, Westmeath

Union cemeteries (Protestant denominations of several churches)
Union 1   Dacre Union cemetery, Brougham Township
Union 2   Rosebank Union cemetery, Admaston Township
Union 3   Haley Union cemetery, Ross Township
Union 4   Arnprior
Union 5   Pembroke
Union 6   Douglas
Union 7   Cobden

Alphabetical List

This list gives surnames in cemeteries in Renfrew County and nearby communities in adjacent counties, where immigrants from Germany settled in the nineteenth century.

Abett   LC7
Adam   LC9, UC11
Adams   LC9
Antler   LC2, LC3, LC7, LC10, LC13, RC4
Ashick   LC4, LC5, LC10, LM4, UC2, UC3, Union 5
Autayo   UC2

Bahen   LC2
Bahm   M2, Union 4
Bahr   LC2, LC7
Baise   Union 4
Bakautski   LC2
Baker   LC2, Union 4
Ballstadt   LC13
Banditt   LC2, LC3
Bando   UC6
Bartelt   LC2
Bartscher   LM3
Barz   LM1
Batz   UC2
Bauman   Union 4
Bausch   RC1
Bautz   Union 4
Beaderman   LC4

Beahm   LC10
Becker   B3, LC10
Behm   LC2, LC4, LC5, LC10, LC14, LM1, LM3, LM8, Union 2
Behnke   LC7, LC10, LC14, LM4, RC1, UC8, UC10
Beier   Union 4
Beilhanz   Union 4
Berger   A1, LC2, LC7, LC9, LC4, LC11, LC14, LM6, LM/C, UC5, UC7, UC9, Union 7
Bergman   LC11
Berndt   LC9, LC10, UC2, UC5
Beskau   LC2, LC4, LC10, LM4
Berthalt   LM/C
Betz   B1, UC2, UC5
Beulow   A1
Beyer   LM/C, LM7, RC1
Biederman   LC1, LC2, LC4, LM4, Union 2
Biedermann   LC4, LM/C

Biesenthal   LM1, LM2, LM4, LM8, LM/C, RC1, Union 5
Bigelow   Union 4
Bimm   A1, LC10, LC15, LM6, UC5, UC7, Union 4
Blaedow   LC3, LM4, M1, Union 7
Blech   LC7
Blemkie   RC3
Blimkie   RC1, RC3
Block   UC7
Bloedow   B1, E1, M1, UC2, Union 4
Bloom   LC10, LC14, LC15, LM/C, UC11
Blum   LC2
Boan   LC10
Bochart   RC5
Bochert   LC10
Boehme   B3, LM6, M4, UC4, UC7
Bohart   LC2, UC2
Bohm   M4
Bohn   LC2, UC1, UC2
Boldt   LC2, LC10,

Union 5
Bolger B1
Borcharat LM2
Borchardt LM/C
Borchmann LC1
Bork B3
Born LC3, LM2, LM4
Borst LC1
Boshart LC2, LC4, LM4, UC5
Bouman LC2
Bowes UC5
Bowman LC15
Braimer UC5
Bramberger LC2
Bramburger LC2, LC4
Branisch Union 4
Brasch LM1, LM2, LM4
Brash LC3, LC10, LM1, LM4, UC6, Union 5
Branddenberg LC15
Brandenberg LC2, M2, Union 3
Brandenburg LC10
Breitkreutz LC2
Breske LM4, Union 5
Breskie LM4
Bressaeu A2
Bretzlaff Union 4
Bretzloff LC4
Brew LC7
Briese LC1, LC2
Brisca LC1
Brisk M4
Briske LC2
Brisko LM1
Brodofske LC14, LC15, UC8
Brohart UC4, UC7, UC12, UC13
Brose LC2, LC10, LC15,

LM/C, UC5, Union 3
Brown UC8
Bruggerman LC10
Brum LC1, LC2, LC3
Brumm LC2, LC7, LC13
Brunke RC3
Brussow Union 3
Bucholtz LC2, LM1, LM4, UC1, UC5
Bucholz LM2, LM4
Buchwald A1, B1, LC2, LC10
Buckwald LC10, LC12
Buckwalt Union 7
Budarick UC4, UC7
Budd E1, LC2, LC3, LC11, LM3, M1, UC2, UC5, Union 4
Budde LM/C
Buder E1, LC2, LC5, UC2, UC3, UC4, UC5, UC6, Union 4, Union 5
Buelow LC8, LC15, LM5, RC7, Union 2
Bunke UC5, UC6, Union 5
Burchart LC2
Burg RC3
Burger LC2, LC7, LM2, LM4, LM8, RC1, UC5, UC6
Burskie LM4
Buschmann RC6
Buske LC2, LM4
Butt A1, LC2, LC4, LC10, LC13

Calbeck A2, M3, Union 7
Caliss LC4
Casselman UC14
Chatsick B1, RC5

Chatson LC9
Chisan LC14, LM6, UC4
Christiansen LC1, LC9
Christink A2, LC1, LC11, LM2, Union 5
Chusroskie RC1, RC2
Cirbes UC9
Coal UC2
Colterman RC3
Consack LC14
Court LC1, LM2
Cram UC2
Crigger LC4, UC3, UC10

Daber LC2, LC3, LC7, LM4
Daechsel LC9
Dagg A2, Union 2
Dallman UC7
Dalman LC14
Damant LM4
Dament LC2, LM1, LM4, RC1, UC3, Union 5
Darrow UC5
Dayment A2, LC2
Dearing LC6
Dedman Union 5
Deiner Union 4
Deissen LC3
Delke LM1
Demant LC7, LM1, LM4
Dermann LC2
Discher LC10, LM1, Union 5
Disher LC2
Dittburner LC10, Union 2, Union 3, Union 4
Dobberman LC1
Dobring LC10, LM1, LM4

Doering LC3, LM4, M1, RC1, UC3, UC5, UC8, Union 5

Doman LC2, LC3

Dorrow UC5

Draeger LM1, UC1

Draves E2, UC5

Drefke B3, LC6, LC8, LC10, UC9

Drifke LC6

Druve UC1, UC3

Dubblestein A4, LC15

Dubblestine A4

Dublestine A4

Duchrow LC3, LM2, LM4

Dumke LC7

Eckel Union 5

Eggert E1, LC7, LC10, LM4

Egli LM4

Eichsteadt LC7

Eick LM/C

Erdmann RC1

Falk LC9, Union 4

Fein LM4

Felhaber B1, B2, B3, LC6, LC11, LM2, UC6

Felhaver Union 4

Felska LC15

Felske LC2, LC8, LC10, LM5, LM7

Felskie LM7, Union 3

Fick LC10

Fiebig A2, RC4, Union 6

Fien LM/C

Fillman Union 4

Finan Union 5

Fischer LC1, LC2, LC7, LM4, LM8, UC5, UC6, Union 5

Fisher LC1, LC2

Fiss Union 4

Fitzner LC7

Flegle E1

Fleugal E1, Union 4

Fleugel LC6, Union 7

Fleuguel E1, UC8

Florent LM5

Folber LC2, LM2, LM4, LM5, Union 5

Foss UC5, Union 3, Union 7

Franskie LC15

Frantz LC15, M2

Frederich LC7

Frederick LC7, UC5, Union 5

Freitag LC10

Frieday Union 4

Friedrich LM8

Frier RC3

Frievalt Union 4

Frisch LC8

Fritsch LC9

Frivalt UC5, Union 4, Union 5

Frobel Union 4

Furgoch LM4

Gadtke UC2

Gahr LC2, LC3, LM4, LM/C

Garskey RC3

Gebel Union 5

Geelharr LC1

Gehlert LC3

Gehrke LC7, Union 4

Geiser M2

Geissler LC10

Genow B1

Genrich LC2, Union 5

Genrick LC14

Gepperd Union 5

Getz E1, UC5, Union 5

Gienow B1

Gierman LC6, Union 1, Union 2

Giermann Union 4

Giese LC3, LC15

Giesebrecht Union 5

Gieser M2

Giesler LC2, LC5

Gieslier LC2

Gike LM4

Gilgong LC14

Glaeser LC9, UC11

Goetz E1

Gogolin UC4

Goldberg LC2, LC3, LC5, LM1, UC5

Golden M3

Goldsmith UC5, UC6

Goldt LC7, LM8

Goltz LC10

Golz LM4

Gorlitz UC9

Gorr LC1, LC2, LC7, LM4, LM5, M1, UC5, Union 5

Gould LC3

Graber LM/C

Graeber LC11, LM4, RC1, UC5

Grahl LC3, LC4, LM4

Grail LC2, UC8

Grant Union 6

Granze E2, UC7

Granzie LC10

Greer Union 3

Greif LC2, LC4,
Union 7
Griese E2, LC10, LM4,
LM5, M3, UC5, UC7,
Union 2, Union 5,
Union 7
Grife LC4
Groehl LC1, LC2, LC5,
LM4, UC5
Gromoll Union 4
Groskalas UC8
Grosklag UC8
Groskleg UC8
Grosskleg LC14, LM1,
UC5, UC8
Grozklags UC8
Gruhl LC8, LM4
Gruschwitz UC7
Guenter LM8
Guindon Union 4
Guinther UC4, UC8,
UC12
Gulick UC4, UC8
Gunter LC7, LM1, LM8,
UC14
Gurlitz UC2, Union 4,
Union 6
Gust LC7, LC11, LC13,
LM4, LM8
Gutz A1, LM5, UC7
Gutzeit E2, LC10, LM5,
LM7
Gutzheit LM3, LM5
Gutzman LC7, UC10,
Union 4

Haafe B1
Haak UC1
Haas UC1, Union 5
Haazy B2
Habecker Union 4

Hadke LC8
Haenschel A2
Haentschel A2, LC1,
LC2
Hammel LC2, LC3, M1,
Union 5
Hammell LC3
Hampel LC2, LC7
Handke E2, LC6, LC10,
LM/C
Handtke LC6
Hanneman RC1, Union
2
Hanniman RC1, RC2,
RC3
Hanusch LC1
Hartwick B1, E1, UC4,
UC5, UC13, Union 4
Hartwig B1, LM3, LM5,
LM/C
Hasel Union 4
Hass LC6, LC14, LM4,
RC1, UC4, UC12,
Union 5
Hauth LC1, LC2
Hebner LC2, LC11
Hedtke LM/C
Hehmke UC7
Hehmkie UC12
Heholke LC10
Heideman B3, LC2,
LC6, LC8, LC10, LM3,
UC1, UC6, Union 6
Heiderman B2, LC10,
UC7
Hein B2, LC2, LC8,
LC10, LM4, LM/C, RC1,
UC9, Union 5
Heins B1, LC10, Union
4, Union 7
Heintman Union 4

Heise LC2, UC5, UC6,
Union 4
Hemke UC7
Hemkie B2
Henkelmann Union 4
Hennick Union 4
Hensel Union 4
Hepting LC10
Heubner LC3
Hiderman UC5, UC11
Hiedemann LM3
Hienz M2
Hildebrand LC10
Hildebrandt E1, LC10,
LM/C, UC2, UC7
Hinze LC15, M2
Hobecker Union 4
Hoch B1, UC2
Hochberg UC7, UC12
Hoelke LC8, LC10,
LM4, Union 5
Hoeltzel LC7
Hoffman A2, LC2, LC3,
LC4, LC5, LC7, LC10,
LM1, LM4, UC3, UC6,
Union 2, Union 7
Hokum B1, E1
Hollmer LC11
Holst Union 5
Holtz UC1, UC5, Union
5
Holz UC6
Homuth Union 4
Hopp LM/C
Hout Union 5
Hubert LC3
Huebner LC1, RC1
Hugli UC2
Huhnke LC3

Jachmann LC10

Kuhen B3
Kuhl Union 4
Kuhnke Union 2
Kulke LM1
Kumm LC10, UC9, Union 4
Kunkel LM/C
Kuno LC10, LC15, LM4
Kupfer Union 4
Kurschenka RC2
Kurth LC2, UC6, Union 7
Kurtswick E1
Kurtzweg Union 4
Kuss LM8
Kutchaw RC1
Kutschke LC2, LM4, LM/C, RC1
Kutter Union 4

Laabs LC2
Labow Union 5
Lamke UC3
Lance LC1
Lang LM/C
Lange LM4
Lassman LC1
Lassmann LC1
Lau LC2
Lawrenz LM5
Layman E1, LC4, LC5, LC10, LM1, LM4, UC2, Union 5
Lebow M2
Leder LC2, LC7
Leeck Union 2, Union 7
Leeder LC2, LC7, LC11
Leek LC8, LC10
Lehman B1, LC1, LC3, LC5, LM/C, UC2
Lehmann LC1, LM3

Lehmpful UC6
Leishman Union 4, Union 5
Lembke LC2
Lemke LC4, LC10, LM5, UC1, UC5, UC6, Union 5
Lemkie LM7
Lempke LC4
Lenser LC2, LC10, LM3
Lentz LC2, LC15, LM4, LM6, Union 4
Libenthal E1
Lidkea UC5, Union 5
Lidkie LM6
Liebeck UC2, UC3, UC5
Liebenthal UC4, UC7
Liedtke LC2, LC6, LC9, LC14, LM/C, UC8
Liedtkie LM6
Lietem LC1
Linde RC1
Lindel Union 5
Lindeman LC2, LC7, UC10
Lindner LC1
Lingstrum UC14
Linkie LC15
Lipke LM/C
Lipkie UC3
Lisk A2, A4, E1, LC10, LM8, M3, UC2, UC7, UC9, Union 5
Littman B1
Loback UC1
Loock Union 4
Lorenz LM2
Lubitz LC3, LC10, LM4
Lubow LM4
Luch UC3
Ludke UC1
Lueloff LC8, LM/C

Luloff A1, A2, E1, LC2, LC8, LC10, LM2, LM4, LM5, LM7, LM/C, M3, UC2, UC7, UC13
Lusk LC7
Lydensmith Union 5
Lyndaman B3

Maahs LC3
Maass Union 2, Union 5
Maelcher LC4
Maerz LM1
Malmberg M3
Manka Union 2
Mantiefel LC14, UC4, UC8
Mantifel LC15, UC4
Mantufel LM6
Markus UC3, UC5, Union 5, Union 7
Markwardt LC14
Marquardt A4, LC9, LC10, LC14, LC15, LM3, LM5, LM7, LM/C, UC4, UC12
Martens LC7
Marwitz UC9
Masche LM4
Maschke LC15, LM6, M2, Union 4
Mau LC11, LM1, LM4
Maves A3, LC2, LM4, M1, UC5, UC6, Union 5
Meeker LM6
Meikle LM1, UC9
Meitz LM1, LM4
Melcher LC2, LC4, LC7
Mews LM2
Meyer B2, LC8, LM3, Union 3, Union 4

Petzold LC9, UC11

Pfannenhauer LC8

Pfannenhaur UC7

Pfeiffer LC9

Phanenhour UC5, UC7, UC11

Phannenhour UC4

Pietzner LC1

Pilatske E1, E2, LC2, LC15, UC2, UC5, Union 5

Pilgrim A1, LM6, UC4, UC7, UC13, Union 2

Pitzner LC7

Plath LC2, LC4, LC5, LM1

Platt LC2

Platz UC11

Pleith Union 4

Plotz UC11

Plummer A2

Pomerank LC14, UC8

Pompa M2

Popke LM3, LM4

Popkey LC10, LM3, LM4, Union 4

Popkie LC2, LC10, LC14, LM2, UC5

Popp LC2, M2, LM/C, UC5, Union 7

Porat LC8

Porath A4

Pormann LM4

Potter B3, Union 4

Prange LC3, LM1, LM4, LM/C

Prankie RC1

Preikschas LC2

Prensler Union 4

Privletz LM4

Pufahl LM4

Pumpa M2

Quackenbush UC11

Quade LC1, LC9, LC10, RC2, RC4, UC12

Quast E1, LC8, LM4, UC2, UC5, Union 2, Union 3, Union 7

Raabe LC2

Raaflaub LC2, LM4

Radatz B3

Radcke LC4

Raddatz UC5, Union 4

Radke LC2, LM1, LM4, LM/C, UC1, Union 5, Union 7

Radkey LM2

Radkie M1, UC3

Radtke LC7, LC10, LC13, LM2, UC5

Raglan LM/C

Raglin A2, LC4, LC5, LC8, LM1, LM4, UC5, Union 7

Rahm LC9, LC14

Rahn LC2, LC3, LC5

Rathfelder LC7

Rantz LC7, LM4

Rechenberg Union 2, Union 4

Rechenburg Union 4

Reckenberg Union 4

Reckzin LC10, LC11, LM4, LM/C, UC2, UC5

Reckzine LM4

Redtman Union 4

Reiche LC1, LC2, LC4, LM/C, UC5

Reinert LC10

Reinke LC2, LC10

Reise LC3, LC7, M2

Rekzin LM/C

Remus A2, B2, LC2, LC7, LM4, Union 4, Union 5, Union 7

Resmer LC2, LC4, LC8, LC10, LM3, LM5, LM7

Retzlaff LC4

Retzleff Union 5

Richter A3, LM3, M4

Rieder UC5

Ringsleben Union 3

Rinza UC12

Riske B3

Ristau B1, LM3, LM4, LM5, UC2

Risto LC1, LC2, LC10, LM1, LM4, LM5, UC2

Ristow B1, Union 4

Roda LM4

Rodberg LC9

Roeder LC2

Roesler LC2, LM4, LM8, LM/C, UC5, Union 7

Roesner E2, LC8, LM3, LM5, LM7, LM/C, Union 7

Roettger A2

Rogge LC3

Roggie B3, LC3, Union 4

Rohloff LM1, UC3, UC9, Union 4

Rohoe LM4

Romhild LM4

Rose LC6, LC10, Union 3

Rosein LC2, LC6, LC10

Rosenberger LM4

Rosenblath UC11

Roske LC3

Rosler LM4

Rossow LM8

Rucks LC3, UC6
Ruhnke LC2
Ruhs LM/C, UC2
Runge LC1
Runtz B1, B2, UC12, UC13, Union 4
Rutz LC2, LC4, LC5, LM1, LM/C

Saar LM1, LM4, LM8
Sack LC2, LM3, LM4, LM5, LM8, LM/C, UC6
Salla UC2
Salzwedel LC10
Sauer LC11, UC2
Schaber Union 4
Schade LM4
Schafer LC10
Scharfe Union 2
Schauer LM3
Schaur LM7
Schausil LC10
Schaven B3
Schaver M4
Scheel Union 4
Scheels Union 4
Scheer LC2, LC10, LM4
Scheineman Union 7
Schemmens UC7
Schettke LM1
Scheueman LC2, UC5
Scheueneman LM4
Scheuneman LC2, LC3, LC4, LC8, LC10, LM1, LM/C, UC3, Union 5
Scheunemann LC2, LC10
Scheverstine LC2
Schiemann LM5
Schilka Union 5
Schilke UC5

Schilkie UC3, UC5, Union 5
Schimmens B2, LC2, RC1, UC2, UC4, UC5
Schinfeldt UC2
Schison LM6, UC12
Schizkoske LC2
Schizoske UC5
Schizoskie LM1
Schleen B1, E1, LM/C, LM4
Schlievert Union 4
Schmidt A4, B3, LC1, LC7, LC8, LC10, LM3, LM4, LM5, Union 5
Schmitt RC7
Schneider UC5, UC6, Union 5, Union 6
Schnob Union 4
Schnub Union 4
Schoenfeldt E1, LC4, LM/C, UC2, UC5
Scholfield UC5
Scholz LC8, LC10
Schonnop E1, LM4, LM/C, UC3, UC5
Schrader UC5, UC7
Schraeder RC1, Union 5
Schreader LC8, UC5
Schrie LC2
Schroeder E1, E2, LC1 LC2, LC6, LC8, LC10, LC14, LM4, LM5, LM7, LM/C, RC1, UC2, UC5, UC7, Union 4, Union 5, Union 7
Schroter LC10
Schruder E2, LC2, LC6, LM3, LM5, RC2, RC5, UC7

Schryburt A2
Schubrink Union 4
Schuelka UC3
Schultz B1, E2, LC1, LC2, LC3, LC4, LC10, LM1, LM3, LM4, LM5, LM7, LM/C, RC1, UC3, UC5, UC6, UC14, Union 2, Union 4, Union 5
Schultze LC2, LM4
Schulz LC3, LM2, LM4
Schunke LC3
Schurman LC7
Schutt LC2, LC3, LM4, LM/C, UC2, UC4, UC7, UC8
Schutz LC14
Schwan LC3, LM2, LM8
Schwandt LC10
Schwant LC10
Schwantz LC2, LC7
Schwanz LC1
Schwartz A2, LC2, LC3, Union 5
Schweigert LC6
Schweizer UC2
Schwerdtferger Union 2
Seidlitz UC7
Seigel LM/C, UC5, Union 7
Sell LC4, LC8, LC10, LM3, LM4, LM5, LM7, UC2, Union 4
Sellars LC6
Seller RC6
Shafe UC12
Shannop UC5
Shimming LC3
Shizkoskia LM1
Shwellow LC1

Siefert   LC2, LC3, UC1
Siegel   LC2, LM4, UC1, UC3
Siegl   LC1
Sigel   UC6
Silke   LC1, LC2, UC5
Smith   RC7, UC2, UC5, UC14
Snider   UC11, Union 5
Soike   LC2, LC5
Sonder   UC2
Sperberg   LM8, LM/C
Spieker   Union 4
Splinter   UC6
Springer   LC4, LM/C, Union 2
Stagga   LC3
Stahlke   LC5
Stahlkie   LC2
Stalbe   LC7
Stark   UC11
Stashick   RC1, RC2
Stavenow   Union 4, Union 7
Stay   LC3
Staye   Union 4
Steege   LC3
Stegeman   LC1
Stein   LC9, LC14
Steinke   Union 4
Steiss   LC1
Stekenburg   Union 4
Stencell   LC2, LC7
Stencill   LC2, RC1
Stielow   Union 4
Stoneberg   M2
Storbeck   LC14
Strack   LC6
Strasman   LM2
Stresemann   LM2
Stresman   LC3, LM1, LM2, LM4, LM5, M1

Stressman   LM2
Strike   Union 4
Stuber   LM5
Suckow   LC1, LC2
Summer   LC7
Summers   LC1, RC5
Swan   LC3
Swant   LC10, LM5, Union 5
Swartz   A2, UC5
Sweigert   LC6
Switzer   LC7, RC1, UC2, Union 5

Tabbert   LC3, LC7, LM4, M1, UC5, Union 5
Tackman   B3
Tank   LC10
Tepper   Union 4
Termarsch   LC2, RC1
Teschner   LC2
Teske   LC7, LM8
Tessman   LC4
Tetzlow   RC4
Thiele   LC11
Thom   E2, Union 2
Thoms   Union 4
Thur   LC2, UC2
Tiegs   A1, LC2, LM3, LM4, Union 5
Timm   LC4, LC8, LC10, LM1, UC5, UC14
Toboldt   LC1
Tourth   UC2
Trautrim   LC2
Troutman   UC5
Tupper   Union 4

Uitricht   UC7

Vanderbeck   UC2

Verch   E2, LC1, LC2, LC8, LC10, LM3, LM5, LM7, UC5, Union 4
Vernick   B1, UC11
Vizena   RC1
Voelkner   LM5
Vogel   LC7
Vogelson   A2
Vollrath   LC11, UC10
Von Doeler   LM8
Vosbarg   LC3

Wagenblass   Union 4
Wagner   A1, B1, LC1, LC2, LC3, RC2, UC2, UC5, Union 4, Union 5
Waito   LC2, LC7, LC11, UC5
Walter   LC2, LC14, UC3, UC8
Walters   UC1, UC5, UC8, UC12, Union 4
Walther   B1, B3
Warlich   LC9, LC10, Union 4
Warlick   LC2, UC11
Wasmond   UC4
Wasmund   LC15, LM6, M2, RC1, UC2, UC4, UC5, Union 7
Webber   B1, LC2, LC7
Weber   B1, B2, LC1, LM/C, UC5, UC9, Union 4
Weckwerth   B3, LC2, LC10, LM5, LM/C, UC11
Weckworth   LC10, LM4, UC2
Weeks   UC9
Wegner   LC2, LC3, LC7, LC11, LM4

Westmeath

Eganville

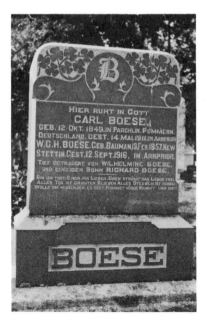

Arnprior

Petawawa

Golden Lake, North Algona Township

APPENDIX B
Wendish surnames in Renfrew County

The first observer to record that the settlement of German-speaking immigrants in Renfrew County contained some whose first language was Wendish was Reverend Ludwig H. Gerndt. As an exploring missionary sent from his southern Upper Canadian parish of Mannheim, in 1861, to the Upper Ottawa, he noticed that Wilberforce Township contained Evangelical Lutheran Germans from Pomerania, Wenden, Wuerttemberger, and Preussen-Posen. (His comments were contained in an anonymous history of Greenlake Lutheran Church, written in German for its seventieth anniversary, 31 July 1932; the document was found in August 1981 by Reverend Bernard Peatzold, pastor of the church, and donated to the church archives.)

Referring to this particular township, he wrote: 'Diese Niederlassungen liegen 450–500 engl. Meilen von hier (Mannheim, Ont. woselbst er Pfarrer war und von wo aus die Synode mit dieser Missionsarbeit ausging) im County Renfrew auf dem rechten Ufer des Ottawa-Flusses etwa 100 Meilen nordwestlich von der Stadt Ottawa. 8 Meilen von Pembroke leben etwa 50 Familien, Pommern und Wenden aus der Gegend von Cottbus Provinz Sachsen. Die Wenden verstehen nur wenig deutsch, doch sind alle evang. luth.' Translated, this reads: 'This settlement lies 450–500 English miles from here (Mannheim, Ont, where he was the pastor and whence he was sent out by the Synod on this missionary work) in the County of Renfrew on the right bank of the Ottawa River some 100 miles north-west from the city of Ottawa. Eight miles from Pembroke live some 50 families, Pomeranian and Wendish from the region of Cottbus in the province of Saxony. The Wends understand only a little German, though they are all Evangelical Lutheran.'

The homeland of the Wends is not an administrative unit with fixed political boundaries, but a vaguely defined region in southeastern Germany, approximately fifty miles southeast of Berlin. Its southern limit is defined by the boundary with Czechoslovakia along the Lusatian mountains. In recent times the Neisse and Oder rivers which separate Germany from Poland have served as the eastern boundary of Lusatia, as the Wends' homeland has been termed. The western and northern boundaries are ill-defined, but are considered to extend north to Frankfurt and west to the Schwarze and Dahme. While all Wends have come from this area, this tract of land, which includes parts of Brandenburg, Silesia, and Saxony, contains many people whose families have lived there for centuries and who are German, not Slavic. The identification of a birthplace in Lusatia, therefore, does not provide firm evidence of ethnic origin.

The Wends consituted a small Slavic group and maintained feelings of nationality in every country to which they immigrated, but they never succeeded in establishing an independent state. These people migrated in largest numbers to the United States and Australia, but smaller groups travelled to South Africa and Canada. According to Dr George R. Nielsen, an American genealogist, who has written a study on their movement from Europe, the only Wends that migrated to Canada went to Renfrew County (*In Search of a Home. The Wends [Sorbs] on the Australian and Texas Frontier*, published by the Department of Russian Language and Literature, University of Birmingham, England).

Wends who left Europe in company with German emigrants 1860–90 were probably attracted by the lure of land as advertised by the Canadian government. Estimating that the number who went to Canada might total 150, including 47 adult males, Nielsen identifies their birthplaces as Tauer, Schönhöhe, Drachhausen, Maust, Drehnow, Sachsendorf, Jänschwalde, Drewitz, Schmogrow, Heinersbrück, Preilack, Strobitz and Sielow.

While the specific geographic origin of this group of Slavs had not been determined to the satisfaction of all scholars, the lands occupied by the Wends since the sixth century have been the scene of conflict and conquest. They were under control by Prussian and German forces in the nineteenth century when the emigration took place. Although they were conscious of the ethnic distinctions, the Wends in their new Canadian home intermarried and assimilated with their German neighbours, assuming their traditions and customs. Indeed, some Wendish-German alliances had been made before the couples had left Europe, e.g. Martin Markusch, who is classified as Wendish, was married to Caroline Yandt, who is not so identified, several years before they emigrated.

During his visit to Renfrew County in 1974, Dr Nielsen compiled records of Wendish surnames from Golden Lake, Woito, Greenlake, Pembroke, Locksley, and Killaloe. Admitting that his list would be incomplete because some of the churches had not kept records, he found 43 households in which one or more ancestors had been Wendish immigrants. There were 63 surnames, some repeated in several families.

Readers of the list of surnames of German immigrants (Appendix A) will recognize some of the names here, though the spelling may have slight deviations. There are several omissions in Nielsen's list, for although he included three wives whose surname was Kilow, he did not find the descendants of Elizabeth Kilow who emigrated 'to Ammerikar' in 1867, as she wrote in the front pages of her Wendish Bible, treasured by the third- and fourth-generation descendants of her marriage to Karl Raglan. Martin Liske is included in the list, but he was one of five brothers who emigrated together from Drachhausen, so presumably the other four immigrants of that family were also Wendish; they scattered on arrival in Renfrew County. A letter of 1906 by Albert Zadow reveals that this surname is also Wendish.

Men with surnames designated as Wendish include some of the most noteworthy craftsmen within the German settlement in Renfrew County: furniture-makers August Boehme, Albert Zadow, and John Noack; the maker of vertical spinning-wheels Martin Markus (Markusch); the basket-maker Friedrich Liebeck; and carpenter Martin Schimmens, whose work ranged from bobbin-winders to smoke-houses. Also on the list are Carl Haentschel, at whose home the first Lutheran services were held in Pembroke, and Martin Krueger, who supplied land and money for the Lutheran church at Greenlake in Wilberforce Township. The minority of immigrants from Germany who were Wendish in ancestry appears to have contributed skills and effort out of all proportion to its actual numbers.

Wendish surnames

Baltzke	Guttke	Jurban	Riese*
Baschka	Haentschel	Lehmann	Rinza
Berger	Hammel	Liebech	Ruben
Boehme	Hannusch	Liske	Schergon
Bossenz	Hanschke	Loback	Schettke
Bruchartz	Hashick	Markusch	Schilka
Budarick	Huppatz	Melcher	Schmelick
Buder	Kilow	Miatke	Schneider
Coal	Klausch	Mielke	Schwitzer*
Dobring	Koina	Nagora	Suekora
Doman	Kossatz	Noack	Tadt*
Eckert	Krueger	Pasorra	Urban
Fabian	Kuester	Pletzner	Woito
Fritsch	Jonas	Regel	Wushiga
Goldberg	Jordan	Retus	Yurt*
Gollick	Junop	Richter	Zadow

* In a letter to the author, Dr Nielsen wrote that he is not positive that these four surnames are Wendish, but suspects they are.

APPENDIX C
Agricultural capability of Renfrew County soil

Soil classes (acreages)

Township	1	2	3	4	5	6	7	Organic (0)	Totals
Admaston	–	26,216	–	2,041	–	210	50,958	1,515	80,940
Algona N	–	100	1,980	2,940	2,300	920	15,220	160	23,620
Algona S	–	740	–	4,370	–	7,690	15,800	4,280	32,880
Alice and	–	5,622	7,325	8,659	964	1,437	34,821	452	59,280
Fraser	–	–	–	1,934	41	–	52,062	123	54,160
Bagot and	–	500	350	2,080	810	300	67,130	640	71,810
Blithfield	–	50	40	690	80	220	31,000	520	32,600
Bromley	–	19,600	7,600	8,030	–	4,330	9,080	2,040	50,680
Brougham	–	–	–	1,520	160	840	64,480	80	67,080
Brudenell and	–	500	1,110	780	1,690	320	50,370	720	55,490
Lyndoch	–	–	–	1,760	920	–	50,280	1,240	54,200
Grattan	–	5,440	300	10,760	7,420	2,480	45,040	1,680	73,120
Griffith and	–	–	–	120	1,280	–	44,910	840	47,150
Matawatchan	–	–	–	630	120	490	43,880	200	45,320
Hagarty and	–	300	2,260	13,940	4,420	6,520	23,210	3,280	53,930
Richards	–	–	–	9,240	1,800	–	33,920	–	44,960

Head and	–	–	–	8,640	–	–	53,480	200	62,320
Clara and	–	–	–	23,280	–	–	43,120	–	66,400
Maria	–	–	400	10,960	–	–	58,120	–	69,480
Horton	–	19,680	1,010	6,100	390	6,060	7,600	160	41,000
McNab	–	9,646	20,192	11,503	746	6,182	17,800	651	66,720
Pembroke	–	4,640	2,840	1,420	–	420	–	200	9,520
Petawawa	–	342	1,413	25,512	471	4,580	13,205	257	45,780
Radcliffe	–	–	1,224	3,398	2,430	–	34,640	548	42,240
Raglan	–	–	–	5,240	6,280	120	53,240	2,880	67,760
Rolph and	–	–	–	9,360	–	–	33,840	160	43,360
Buchanan and	–	–	–	19,160	–	–	3,560	–	22,720
Wylie and	–	–	–	11,080	160	–	39,680	120	51,040
McKay	–	–	–	920	160	40	52,000	–	53,120
Ross	–	30,450	3,520	5,730	200	9,700	7,520	320	57,440
Sebastopol	–	1,444	300	4,555	525	487	37,569	–	44,880
Sherwood and	–	–	40	4,040	5,200	–	36,590	880	46,750
Jones and	–	–	330	–	750	–	26,360	80	27,520
Burns	–	–	–	1,520	840	–	45,640	–	48,000
Stafford	–	9,900	3,520	3,370	–	4,130	120	1,360	22,400
Westmeath	–	15,860	16,960	17,740	3,300	10,540	3,740	6,680	74,820
Wilberforce	–	7,620	2,430	14,220	4,750	8,700	24,850	2,840	65,410
Indian Reserve #39	–	–	–	–	–	–	1,720	–	1,720
Unmapped	–	–	–	–	–	–	–	–	11,660
Totals	–	158,650	75,144	257,242	48,207	76,716	1,226,555	35,106	1,889,280

From Ontario Ministry of Agriculture and Food, Rural Development Branch, and Canada Department of Regional Economic Expansion *Acreages of Soil Capability Classes for Agriculture* Ontario report no 8 (Oct 1975)

NOTES

If not otherwise identified, a name (with place) signifies an interview with that person by the author.

Chapter 1: Opening up Renfrew County

1 Statistics Canada, 1860–61 census. (German immigrants were not totalled as a separate ethnic group. Residents whose nationalities were derived from Germany, Prussia, and Holland were included in one count, 405 in Renfrew County.)
2 Arthur R.M. Lower *Great Britain's Woodyard. British America and the Timber Trade, 1763–1867* (Montreal and London 1973); Charlotte Whitton *A Hundred Years A-Fellin'. 1842–1942* (Ottawa 1943); John W. Hughson and Courtney C.J. Bond *Hurling down the Pine* (Old Chelsea, Quebec, 1964)
3 Ernest Lloyd Lake *Pioneer Reminiscences of the Upper Ottawa Valley* (Ottawa 1966) 126
4 Audrey Saunders *The Algonquin Story* (Toronto 1963) 24
5 Alexander Murray *Report for the Year 1853 in Geological Survey of Canada. Report of Progress for the Years 1853–56* (Toronto 1857) 72–82
6 Keith A. Parker 'Colonization Roads and Commercial Policy' *Ontario History* LXVII 1 (March 1975) 31–8
7 J. Brian Bird *The Natural Landscapes of Canada* (Toronto 1972) 6–7, 136
8 *Bulletin of the Geological Society of America* LVIII (1942) 585–646
9 Public Archives of Canada (PAC), William Sinn *Nachweis des Fortschritts der preußischen Umsiedlung an der Ottawa* [Information on the Progress of the Prussian Settlement on the Ottawa] Imperial Blue Books on Affairs relating to Canada, XXIV, Emigration, 1851–72. (An English translation by Robbie Gorr

appeared in the journal of the Ottawa Branch of the Ontario Genealogical Society, XVI [November-December 1983] 70–1.)

10 Mrs Carl Price and Clyde C. Kennedy *Notes on the History of Renfrew County* (Pembroke 1961) 113

11 G.W. Spragge 'The Colonization Roads of Canada West' *Ontario History* (1957) XLIV 1 (1957) 1–17

12 Parker 'Colonization Roads'

13 PAC *Journals of the Legislative Assembly of the Province of Canada* XV 9 (1857) Appendix 54, Annual Report of the Minister of Agriculture for 1856

14 PAC, T.P. French *Information for Intending Settlers on the Opeongo Road and Its Vicinity* (Ottawa 1857)

15 PAC *Sessional Papers of Canada* XV 9 (1857) Appendix to the 15th Volume of the Journals of the Legislative Assembly of the Province of Canada

16 PAC *Sessional Papers of Canada* XVIII 3 (1860) Report of Bureau of Agriculture and Statistics

17 PAC *Sessional Papers of Canada* XIX 4 (1861) Report of the Minister of Agriculture of Canada

18 Sinn *Nachweis* 4–7

19 1881 census

Chapter 2: Bismarck's legacy

1 PAC *Sessional Papers of Canada* XX 21 (1862) William Wagner to P.M. VanKoughnet 11 March 1862

2 Ibid, William Wagner to P.M. VanKoughnet 31 January 1862

3 Hajo Holborn *A History of Modern Germany. 1840–1945* (New York 1969) 122–3

4 Winthrop Bell *The Foreign Protestants and the Settlement of Nova Scotia* (Toronto 1961), 120, 132

5 Hartmut Froeschle 'German Immigration into Canada. A Survey' *German-Canadian Yearbook* VI (Toronto 1981) 16–27

6 G. Elmore Reaman *The Trail of the Black Walnut* (Toronto 1957) 15–39

7 PAC *Sessional Papers of Canada* XX 4 (1862). Letters of William Wagner 27 October 1860–29 May 1862

8 Marshall Dill *Germany. A Modern History* (Ann Arbor 1961) 130–45

9 H.R. Cummings *Early Days in Haliburton* (Toronto 1963) 18–28

10 PAC RG 17, vol II, File 854, Charles James Blomfield, Secretary of Toronto Board of Canadian Land and Emigration Company Limited, Letter of 2 August 1866 to the Hon. D'Arcy McGee, Minister of Agriculture

11 Archives of Ontario (hereafter AO) RG 1 C-I-4, vol 38

12 Beatrice Verch, R.R. 2, South Algona Township
13 AO, An Act respecting Free Grants and Homesteads to Actual Settlers on Public Lands Rev. Stat. c. 23 (1868)
14 K.G. Schutt, Killaloe
15 Holborn *Modern Germany* 367
16 Walter S. Herrington *History of the County of Lennox and Addington* first published 1913 (Belleville 1972) 343
17 Mary Quayle Innis *An Economic History of Canada* (Toronto 1935) 197
18 Holborn *Modern Germany* 125
19 PAC, T.P. French *Information for Intending Settlers on the Opeongo Road and Its Vicinity* (Ottawa 1857) 10–14
20 Thomas E. Appleton *Ravenscrag. The Allan Royal Mail Line* (Toronto 1974) 121
21 PAC, Allan Brothers and Company *Practical Hints and Directions to Intending Emigrants to Canada and United States* (Liverpool) 1872) 4
22 Edwin C. Guillet *The Great Migration* (Toronto 1963) 239
23 Sketches that illustrated their journeys from German ports to the east coast of England, and then from Liverpool to Canadian ports, were portrayed in the *Canadian Illustrated News* 4 April 1874.
24 Holborn *Modern Germany* 367
25 Census, 1901
26 Gerhard P. Bassler 'German Overseas Migration to North America in the Nineteenth and Twentieth Centuries' *German-Canadian Yearbook* VII (Toronto 1983) 93–113
27 William Lemke, Green Lake, Wilberforce Township
28 James Schruder, Pembroke
29 Letter from Mrs Irene Lipke, Kitchener
30 Ferdinand Witt, Locksley, Stafford Township
31 Henry Mohns, Petawawa village
32 Oscar Michel, Black Bay Road, Petawawa Township
33 Henry Grahl, Green Lake, Wilberforce Township
34 Henry Behm, Bromley Township
35 Clem Ziebarth, Pembroke
36 Letter from Carson Kuhnke, Renfrew
37 Teresa Luloff, Golden Lake, North Algona Township
38 Letter from Mrs Ethel Michel, Ottawa
39 Obituary of Julius Popke *Eganville Leader* 30 November 1928
40 Wilfred Popkey, Lake Clear, Sebastopol Township
41 Obituary of William Michaelis *Eganville Leader* 21 August 1925
42 William Walther, Vanbrugh, Sebastopol Township
43 Allan Kosmack, Vanbrugh, Sebastopol Township

44 Mrs Eleanor Tiegs, Grattan Township
45 *Zion Lutheran Church, Augsburg, 110 Anniversary Book. 1874-1984* (1984) 7
46 George Bartscher, Grattan Township
47 Mrs. Ethel Duchrow, Alice Township
48 Mrs Esther Gorr, Alice Township; Rob Gorr, Pembroke
49 Russel E. Witt, Niagara Falls

Chapter 3: Taming the land

1 Archives, Western Pennsylvania–West Virginia Synod, Lutheran Church in America, Thiel College, Pennsylvania, Pittsburgh Synod, 19th Annual Session, May 1862, Minutes
2 Archives, West Pennsylvania–West Virginia Synod, Lutheran Church in America, Thiel College, Pennsylvania, Pittsburgh Synod, 22nd Annual Session, May 1865, Minutes
3 Lennox and Addington Centennial Society *Historical Glimpses of Lennox and Addington* (Napanee 1964) 132
4 Gene Brown and Nadine Brumell ed *The Oxen and the Axe* (Madoc, ca 1977) 29
5 AO RG A-I-7, Box 13, Letter 20 February 1980 from John Mezaks, Supervisor, Government Records Section, re files of Hastings Road agent M.P. Hayes
6 Ronald Brown 'Ontario's Hastings Road of Broken Dreams' *Canadian Geographical Journal* (August–September 1979) 44-7
7 Keith A. Parker 'Colonization Road and Commercial Policy' *Ontario History* LXVII (March 1975) 31-8
8 Mrs Carl Price and Clyde C. Kennedy *Notes on the History of Renfrew County* (Pembroke 1961) 81
9 PAC, T.P. French *Information for Intending Settlers on the Opeongo Road and Its Vicinity* (Ottawa 1857) 21
10 AO RG 1 A-I-7, Box 14, T.P. French to P.M. VanKoughnet 7 January 1860
11 Ernst Daber, Pembroke
12 *Pembroke Centennial Souvenir Book* (Pembroke 1928)
13 Champlain Trail Museum Archives, Pembroke
14 1881 census, Pembroke
15 PAC, William Sinn *Nachweis des Fortschritts der preußischen Umsiedlung an der Ottawa* [Information on the Progress of the Prussian Settlement on the Ottawa] Imperial Blue Books on Affairs relating to Canada, XXIV, Emigration, 1851-72
16 Brenda Lee-Whiting 'Edwards family "was here first" ' *Ottawa Citizen* 14 November 1977
17 Ernest Lloyd Lake *Pioneer Reminiscences of the Upper Ottawa Valley* (Ottawa 1966) 148

18 Mrs Herbert Seigel, Pembroke
19 C.R. Cronmiller *A History of the Lutheran Church in Canada* (Kitchener 1961) 152–3
20 Evangelical United Brethren Church *A Century in Canada 1864–1964* (Kitchener 1964) 14
21 County of Renfrew, Land records
22 Ferdinand Witt, Locksley, Stafford Township
23 PAC *Sessional Papers of Canada* XX 21 4 (1862) William Wagner to P.M. VanKoughnet 31 January 1862
24 AO, T.P. French to the Hon. William McDougall 2 January 1863
25 Mr and Mrs Allan Kosmack, Vanbrugh, Sebastopol Township
26 Martin Tiegs, Grattan Township
27 Sarah Luloff, Golden Lake, North Algona Township
28 Lake *Pioneer Reminiscences* 174
29 Ibid 74
30 Violet Krohn Brasch ed *Eganville and District Old Home Week* (Eganville 1948) 27
31 St John's Lutheran Church, Sebastopol Township, *Centennial Book* (1962)
32 PAC RG 17 I-1 vol 6, file 370, F. Kosmack et al to W.J. Wills, Government Emigration Agent, Ottawa, 11 August 1865
33 French *Information for Intending Settlers* 23
34 Edwin Guillet *The Pioneer Farmer and Backwoodsman* II (Toronto 1963) 211–14
35 *Tables of the Trade and Navigation of the Province of Canada for the year, 1861* (Quebec 1862) 162
36 PAC *Sessional Papers of Canada* XX 21 4 (1862) William Wagner to P.M. VanKoughnet 11 March 1862
37 Beatrice Verch, Augsburg, South Algona Township
38 Loris Russell *Everyday Life in Colonial Canada* (Batsford and London 1973) 31
39 Wilfred Bartscher, Grattan Township
40 T.J. Hunt *The Story of Cormac* (Toronto 1954) 712–2
41 Allan Kosmack, Vanbrugh, Sebastopol Township
42 French *Information for Intending Settlers* 21–2
43 Marilyn G. Miller *Straight Lines in Curved Space. Colonization Roads in Eastern Ontario* (Toronto 1978) 147
44 *Eganville Leader* 21 February 1930 '50 Years Ago' (citing a passage from the *Renfrew Mercury* of 1880)
45 Saar family records, Earl Saar's farm, Stafford Township
46 AO, RG 1 C-I-4, vol 38
47 Walter Reiche, Germanicus, Wilberforce Township
48 *Government of Ontario. The British Farmer's and Farm Labourer's Guide to Ontario* (Toronto 1880) 37–8

49 Ontario Agricultural Commission *Report of the Commissioners* (Toronto 1881)
50 AO, RG 14 B-10-2, Book 4, Allan N. MacNab, Minister of Agriculture, Report dated 27 October 1854
51 AO, RG 52 1 = A, J.W. Bridgland, Commissioner of Crown Lands, Memorandum with reference to a petition forwarded from Pembroke, 11 June 1868
52 County of Renfrew, Land records
53 Price and Kennedy *Renfrew County* 83
54 Hattie Schmidt Cramer *Good Were the Years* (Saginaw, Michigan, 1959) 15–34
55 Rev Al Rekowski 'Home Ties' Article No. 41 *This Week* Barry's Bay, Ontario, 11 July 1984
56 Sinn *Nachweis*
57 Rekowski 'Home Ties' (1982–4)
58 Eric Arthur and Dudley Witney *The Barn. A Vanishing Landmark in North America* (Toronto 1972) 178

Chapter 4: Buildings for a new life

1 Lynda Musson Nykor and Patricia D. Musson *Mennonite Furniture. The Ontario Tradition in York County* (Toronto 1977) 73
2 Amos Long jr *The Pennsylvania German Family Farm* (Breinigsville, Pennsylvania, 1972) 82–6
3 Louis Tivy *Your Loving Anna. Letters from the Ontario Frontier* (Toronto 1972) 40–1
4 Marion Macrae and Anthony Adamson *The Ancestral Roof* (Toronto 1963) 185
5 Reaman G. Elmore *The Trail of the Black Walnut* (Toronto 1957) 133
6 Eric Arthur and Dudley Witney *The Barn. A Vanishing Landmark in North America* (Toronto 1972) 88–9
7 Matthew Noack III, R.R. 2 Hagarty Township
8 Verschoyle Benson Blake and Ralph Greenhill *Rural Ontario* (Toronto 1969) 25
9 Mrs Wilhelmina Antler, Alice Township
10 Brenda Lee-Whiting 'Chored Around All Day' *The Beaver* (summer 1979) 12–16
11 John I. Rempel *Building with Wood and Other Aspects of Nineteenth Century Building in Ontario* (Toronto 1967) 40
12 Obituary of Simon Chusroskie *Eganville Leader* 17 October 1930
13 County of Renfrew Registry Office, Pembroke, Land Records

14 Emma Chusroskie a.k.a. Sister Clothilde, St Joseph's Motherhouse, Pembroke
15 *Pembroke Observer* 11 August 1965
16 *Eganville Leader* 17 January 1930
17 Reaman *Black Walnut* 133
18 Nykor and Musson *Mennonite Furniture* 77–8
19 Mrs Elsie Zadow *Zadow Family History* (Eganville 1981)
20 County of Renfrew, Land Records
21 Vera and Allan Kosmack, Vanbrugh, Sebastopol Township
22 County of Renfrew, Land Records
23 Ibid
24 Oscar Boehme, Raglan Township
25 County of Renfrew, Land Records
26 Ibid
27 St John's Lutheran Church, Germanicus, Wilberforce Township, Parish
   records
28 1881 census, Wilberforce Township (microfilm, PAC)
29 Letter from Mrs Irene Lipke, Kitchener
30 K.G. Schutt, Killaloe
31 William Lemke, Wilberforce Township
32 County of Renfrew, Land records
33 Allan Kosmack, Vanbrugh, Sebastopol Township
34 County of Renfrew, Land records
35 Arthur and Witney *The Barn* 85–106
36 Mr and Mrs Arnold Ziebell, Locksley, Alice Township
37 Mr and Mrs Walter Zadow, Zadow, South Algona Township
38 Mr and Mrs Edgar Pilatske, South Algona Township
39 Mr and Mrs Adolph Ott, Wilberforce Township
40 Mr and Mrs Herbert Sell, Rankin, Wilberforce Township
41 William Klatt, Schutt, Raglan Township
42 C.R. Cronmiller *A History of the Lutheran Church in Canada. Canada Synod*
   (Kitchener 1961) 152
43 PAC, RG 17, vol. 6, file 370, F. Kosmack et al to W.J. Wills, government
   emigration agent, Ottawa, 11 August 1865
44 St John's Lutheran Church, Sebastopol Township *Centennial Book* (1962) 3
45 Martin Tiegs, Grattan Township
46 *McCulloch's Universal Gazetteer* II (New York 1852) 657
47 *Eganville Leader* 19 April 1935
48 Annual Reports of Public School Inspectors to Renfrew County Council,
   County Council Minutes, 1871–1908, County Courthouse, Pembroke
49 County of Renfrew, Land records
50 Henry Mohns, Petawawa village

51 Carl Felske ed *School Section #6 South Algona Township Yearbook* (1968)
52 First Baptist Church, Hagarty Township *Centennial Book* 4
53 St John's, Sebastopol Township *Centennial Book* 4
54 *Eganville Leader* 21 June 1978
55 Scott T. Swank 'The Architectural Landscape' *Arts of the Pennsylvania Germans* (Winterthur 1983) 24–5
56 Nykor and Musson *Mennonite Furniture* 73–5
57 Blake and Greenhill *Rural Ontario* 46

Chapter 5: Hand-spun comfort

1 John McCallum *Unequal Beginnings. Agriculture and Economic Development in Quebec and Ontario until 1870* (Toronto 1980) 88
2 *Eganville Leader* 27 May–3 June 1932
3 McCallum *Unequal Beginnings* 11
4 *Eganville Leader* October issues 1902–16
5 PAC, T.P. French *Information for Intending Settlers on the Ottawa and Opeongo Road and Its Vicinity* (Ottawa 1857) 10, 29
6 PAC, William Sinn *Nachweis des Fortschritts der preußischen Umsiedlung an der Ottawa* [Information on the Progress of the Prussian Settlement on the Ottawa] Imperial Blue Books on Affairs relating to Canada XXIV Emigration 1851–72, 4; Mary Quayle Innis *An Economic History of Canada* (Toronto 1935) 209; *The Canada Directory. 1857–58* (Montreal 1858) 632; Violet Krohn Brasch ed *Eganville and District Old Home Week* (Eganville 1948) 39; Brenda Lee-Whiting 'Energy Crisis Ruined Osceola' *Canadian Geographical Journal* (October–November 1976) 32–7
7 Mrs Herta Ott, Wilberforce Township
8 North Lanark Historical Society *Development of the Woollen Industry in Lanark, Renfrew and Carleton Counties* (Almonte 1978) 7
9 Judy Keenleyside *Selected Canadian Spinning Wheels in Perspective* (Ottawa 1980) 139
10 Obituary of Charles Hoelke *Eganville Leader* 3 July 1936
11 Martin Lenser, Augsburg, South Algona Township
12 Dorothy K. Burnham and Harold B. Burnham *Keep Me Warm One Night* (Toronto 1972) 36
13 Solomon Kelo, Wilberforce Township
14 Mrs June Popke, Pembroke
15 Obituary of Martin Markus *Eganville Leader* 21 August 1925
16 1881 census, Wilberforce Township (detail on microfilm, PAC)
17 Emma Chusroskie a.k.a. Sister Clothilde, St Joseph's Motherhouse, Pembroke
18 Mrs Clifford Schultz, Welland

19 Edna Blackburn 'Colours from Nature' *Canadian Collector* (May–June 1978) 47–8
20 Mrs Edwin Thur, Elmira, letter to author
21 1871 census, Bromley Township (microfilm, PAC)
22 Elwood Musclow, Belleville, letter to author
23 W.E. Smallfield and Robert Campbell *The Story of Renfrew* (Renfrew 1919) 65; Violet Krohn Brasch ed *Eganville and District Old Home Week* (Eganville 1948) 39
24 Sarah Luloff, Golden Lake, North Algona Township
25 Ruth McKendry *Quilts and Other Bed-coverings in the Canadian Tradition* (Toronto 1979) 209
26 Obituary of Hannah Louise Junop Luloff *Eganville Leader* 19 May 1933
27 Mrs Helen Sack, Eganville
28 Mrs Dorothy Burnham, Toronto
29 Mrs. Betty Gutzman, Petawawa Township
30 Mrs Solomon Kelo, Wilberforce Township
31 *Eganville Leader* 7 March 1924
32 Ibid 12 September 1924
33 *Ottawa Citizen* 1 February 1982
34 Sinn *Nachweis*
35 *McCulloch's Universal Gazetteer* II (New York 1852) 659
36 *The International Cyclopedia* XII (New York 1889) 240
37 Arnold Radke, Pembroke
38 Henry Grahl, Wilberforce Township
39 Mrs William Lemke, Wilberforce Township
40 Mrs Solomon Kelo, Wilberforce Township
41 Mrs Betty Gutzman, Petawawa Township
42 'Flax in the Dominion' *Eganville Leader* 3 October 1919

Chapter 6: In the German immigrant's home

1 Arthur R.M. Lower *Great Britain's Woodyard. British America and the Timber Trade, 1763–1867* (Montreal 1973) 63–125; Charlotte Whitton *A Hundred Years A-Fellin'. 1842–1942* (Ottawa 1943) 25–60
2 *Renfrew Mercury* 'Forest Preserve Dedicated' 27 June 1979
3 Jeanne Minhinnick *Early Furniture in Upper Canada Village* (Toronto 1964) 6
4 *Canada Directory. 1857–1858* (Montreal 1858) 504, 632, 40
5 '100 Years Ago' *Renfrew Mercury* 18 October 1972
6 W.E. Smallfield and Robert Campbell *The Story of Renfrew* (Renfrew 1919) 138
7 *Pembroke Observer* March and April 1880

8 *Native Trees of Canada* Bulletin 61, Department of Northern Affairs and National Resources (Ottawa 1956) 276
9 Phillip Shackleton *The Furniture of Old Ontario* (Toronto 1973), Lynn McMurray 'Ontario-German Decorative Arts' in Donald B. Webster ed *The Book of Canadian Antiques* (Toronto 1974) 128–42; Lynda Musson Nykor and Patricia D. Musson *Mennonite Furniture. The Ontario Tradition in York County* (Toronto 1977); Howard Pain *The Heritage of Upper Canadian Furniture* (Toronto 1978); Henry Dobson and Barbara Dobson *The Early Furniture of Ontario and the Atlantic Provinces* (Toronto 1974); William Yeager ed *The Cabinet Makers of Norfolk County* (Simcoe 1975); Jean Palardy *The Early Furniture of French Canada* (Toronto 1973); Charles Foss *Cabinetmakers of the Eastern Seaboard* (Toronto 1977); Michael Bird and Terry Kobayashi *A Splendid Harvest. Germanic Folk and Decorative Arts in Canada* (Toronto 1981)
10 Henry Dobson and Barbara Dobson 'The Regency Table in Canada' *Canadian Antiques and Art Review* 1 (September 1979) 28–31
11 Pain *Upper Canadian Furniture* 313
12 Brenda Lee-Whiting 'Saga of a Nineteenth Century Sawmill' *Canadian Geographical Journal* (February 1967) 46–51
13 Detailed drawings and description for making a traditional *Bretstuhl* were given in the July–August 1981 issue (No. 29) of *Fine Woodworking*, available from The Taunton Press, P.O. Box 355, Newtown, Connecticut 06470.
14 Friedrich Lorentz, Adam Fischer, and Tadeusz Lehr-Splawinski *The Cassubian Civilization* (London 1935) 219; Bernward Deneke *Bauernmöbel. Ein Handbuch für Sammler und Liebhaber* (Munich 1969) 212–21
15 Elizabeth Ingolfsrud *All about Ontario Chairs* (Toronto 1974) 4–6
16 Elizabeth Ingolfsrud *All about Ontario Tables* (Toronto 1976) 37
17 Elizabeth Ingolfsrud *All about Ontario Beds* (Toronto 1975) 35
18 Ivor and Laurette Brown *About Antiques* (Toronto 1973) 59
19 Timm Family History Book, in possession of Mrs D'Arcy Doering, Pembroke
20 Remus Family History Book, compiled by Emilie Zeschin Remus (1964), Champlain Trail Museum, Pembroke
21 Elizabeth Ingolfsrud *All about Ontario Cupboards* (Toronto 1978) 83
22 Archives, St John's Lutheran Church, Petawawa
23 Pain *Upper Canadian Furniture* 396
24 Charles A. Armstrong *Away back in Clarendon and Miller* (Ottawa 1976) 90
25 Letter from Lizzie Gunsinger, Plevna
26 Mr and Mrs Wilfred Liebeck, Ottawa
27 Mrs Erna Hein, Pembroke
28 Letter from Mervin Quast, Guelph

29 Norman Antler, Pembroke
30 Archives, St John's Lutheran Church, Petawawa
31 William Stresman, Alice Township
32 Mrs Arnold Radke, Pembroke

Chapter 7: Furniture-makers in a new land

1 County of Renfrew, Land records
2 Brenda Lee-Whiting 'Edwards family "was here first" ' *Ottawa Citizen* 14 November 1977
3 'St John's Celebrates 110 Years' *Eganville Leader* 19 September 1979
4 'Investing in the Past' *Ottawa Citizen* 18 May 1979
5 Mrs L.E. Michel, Ottawa
6 *Pembroke Centenary and Old Home Week Souvenir Book 1828–1928* (Pembroke 1928) 27
7 Cecil J. Houston and William J. Smyth *The Sash Canada Wore* (Toronto 1980) 91–101
8 Archives, St John's Lutheran Church, Petawawa
9 Howard Pain *The Heritage of Upper Canadian Furniture* (Toronto 1978) 471
10 Mrs George Hampel *Centennial History St John's Lutheran Church, Petawawa* (Petawawa 1967) 11
11 Karl Remus, Eganville
12 Archives, Grace Lutheran Church, Locksley
13 Archives, Green Lake Lutheran Church, Wilberforce Township
14 William Lemke, Wilberforce Township
15 Archives, Zion Lutheran Church, Augsburg
16 Mr and Mrs Herbert Gutzeit, Eganville
17 Zadow Family History Book, compiled by Mrs Elsie Zadow, 1981, 1
18 'Reminiscences of Eganville and Rockingham' *Eganville Leader* 14 August 1925
19 Obituary of Albert Zadow *Eganville Leader* 10 October 1941
20 Teresa Luloff, Golden Lake, North Algona Township
21 Henry C. Mercer *Ancient Carpenters' Tools* Bucks County Historical Society (Doylestown, Pennsylvania, 1929) 221

Chapter 8: New horizons, painful exile

1 G. Elmore Reaman *A History of Agriculture in Ontario* II (Toronto 1970) 19–20
2 1901, 1911, 1921, and 1931 censuses, Statistics Canada
3 *Eganville Leader* 1902 advertisements

4 Ibid 27 August 1902
5 Herbert Kalbfleisch *The History of the German Language Press of Ontario 1835–1918* (Toronto 1969)
6 *Eganville Leader* 11 July 1902
7 Ontario Legislative Assembly *Handbook of the Province of Ontario. Products, Resources, Development* (Toronto 1907)
8 C.C. Farr *The Lake Temiscamingue District, Province of Ontario, Canada* (Toronto 1894)
9 Mrs Paul Reckzin, Golden Lake, North Algona Township
10 Ferdinand E.O. Kant, Iroquois Falls
11 *Statistical Year-Book of the Evangelical Lutheran Synod of Missouri, Ohio and Other States for the Year 1924* (PAC)
12 *Eganville Leader* 24 March 1905
13 Ibid 9 June 1905
14 Ibid 11 August 1905
15 Petawawa Township, Assessment Rolls, 1885–1905
16 James Eldon Hamilton and John Delbert Hamilton *Our Heritage* (Pembroke 1976) 64
17 County of Renfrew, Land records, Pembroke
18 Adolph Gust, Petawawa village
19 *Eganville Leader* 22 September 1905
20 PAC, RG 24, vol 6312, file HQ 67-17-1, State and Military Records
21 Ibid
22 Ibid
23 Ibid
24 County of Renfrew, Land records
25 Ibid
26 Ibid
27 *Pembroke Observer* 24 May 1906
28 *Eganville Leader* 25 May 1906
29 *Pembroke Observer* 26 July 1906
30 *Eganville Leader* 4 January 1907
31 County of Renfrew, Land records
32 Mrs George Hampel *Centennial History, St John's Lutheran Church, Petawawa* (Petawawa 1967) 24
33 Brenda Lee-Whiting 'Demolition plans reveal early area log church' *Ottawa Citizen* 27 October 1965
34 'Restore Cemetery in Joint Project' *Pembroke Observer* 10 September 1966
35 Elinor Mawson 'Some were bought out' *North Renfrew Times Township Supplement* 22 March 1967
36 Henry Mohns, Petawawa village

37 Mrs Carl Price and Clyde C. Kennedy *Notes on the History of Renfrew County* (Pembroke 1961) 150

Chapter 9: The German heritage

1 *Pembroke Standard* 6 March 1913
2 *Grace through the Years. 1873–1973* Centennial book of Grace Lutheran Church, Locksley (1973)
3 *Zion Lutheran Church. 110 Years. 1874–1984* Augsburg (1984)
4 *Eganville Leader* 8 December 1922. In the advertisement of Julius J. Schauer, who was selling his property, the proximity of the German school at Augsburg was mentioned as an advantage.
5 Mrs Marilyn Michel, Petawawa village
6 The Canada Conference of the Evangelical United Brethren Church *A Century in Canada 1864–1964* (Kitchener 1964) 14
7 'St John's Celebrates 110 Years' *Eganville Leader* 19 September 1979
8 Zion Lutheran Church *The 71st Anniversary of the Formation of the Congregation* (Pembroke 1954); *Grace through the Years; St John's Lutheran, Petawawa, Centennial Book. 1867–1967* (Petawawa 1967) 34; *One Hundred Years of Service to God and This Community. 1863–1963* St John's Lutheran, Bonnechere (1963); *St John's Lutheran, Sebastopol Township Centennial Book* (1972)
9 Letter from Louis Markus, Pembroke; C.R. Cronmiller *A History of the Lutheran Church in Canada. Canada Synod* (Kitchener 1961) 152; Canada Conference *A Century in Canada* 14; Letter from Reverend Clare English, Baptist Church, Lyndock Township
10 Archives, Western Pennsylvania–West Virginia Synod, Lutheran Church in America, Thiel College, Pennsylvania, Pittsburgh Synod, 10th Convention, 1876, Minutes; *St. John's, Sebastopol*
11 John H. Reble 'My First Parish – Then and Now' *Canada Lutheran* (February 1961) 8–9
12 Herbert Kalbfleisch *The History of the German Language Press of Ontario. 1835–1918* (Toronto 1969) 100
13 Werner A. Bausenhart 'The Ontario German Language Press and Its Suppression by Order-in-Council in 1918' *Canadian Ethnic Studies* IV (1972) 35–48. Referring to the *Deutsche Post* in his reference notes, Bausenhart remarks: 'I was unable to locate a copy of the latter.'
14 *Pembroke Observer* 9 December 1915
15 *Pembroke Standard* 1 December 1909
16 *Eganville Leader* 25 March 1910
17 *Pembroke Observer* February 1916 (cited in *Eganville Leader* 4 February 1916)

18 *Pembroke Standard* 23 Februdary 1916

19 *Pembroke Observer* 2 December 1915

20 *Eganville Leader* 23 June 1916

21 Ibid 10 December 1915

22 J.M. Zimmerman *The History of Zion Lutheran Church, Pembroke* (1954)

23 *Eganville Leader* 17 March 1916

24 Ibid 11 January 1918

25 Ibid 12 April 1918

26 *Pembroke Standard-Observer* 2 August 1928

27 *Eganville Leader* 14 March 1919

28 Gerhard P. Bassler 'Overseas Migration to North America in the Nineteenth and Twentieth Centuries' *German-Canadian Yearbook* VII (Toronto 1983) 8–21

29 Mrs Elsie Zadow, Eganville

30 Mary Cook *A Collector's Stories and Recipes* (Ottawa 1979); Mary Cook *Time to Blow out the Lamp* (Ottawa 1980); Mary Cook *One for Sorrow, Two for Joy* (Ottawa 1984)

31 *Eganville Leader* 24 November 1933

32 *This Week* 6 June 1979

33 *Eganville Leader* 12 January 1934

INDEX

Because the original spelling of German names was often anglicized and the changed spelling retained by the family, the entries in this index show the spelling that was used in Renfrew County (and different German spelling is shown in brackets if it has been used in the text). Individuals with the same surname known to belong to the same family have been grouped together. Pages with illustrations are indicated by italics.